# God's Island

## The History of Tangier

### by
### Kirk Mariner

D1478982

Miona Publications
Onancock, Virginia

ISBN  0-9648393-5-0

# Table of Contents

# Preface

It is, probably, simple curiosity that leads so many people to book passage on the tourboats that head out to the center of Chesapeake Bay, where the intriguing little town of Tangier sits on its tiny and shrinking island.

Curiosity about Tangier Island is nothing new. In the early nineteenth century, thousands of visitors descended annually upon the island for a great religious gathering that attracted not only the earnestly devout but also the merely curious. In 1916 the President of the United States, yachting on the Chesapeake, saw the island on the map and indulged his curiosity with a visit that surprised and frightened the islanders. In 1943 a vacationing couple from New England spotted it on the map, decided on the spur of the moment that they had to see it, and ended up moving there. Today's visitors, as many as 20,000 in a good season, are simply the most recent evidence of the fascination that Tangier Island continues to exert on the minds of mainlanders.

Despite centuries of curiosity about Tangier, its history has remained largely unwritten. In the late nineteenth century Thomas L. Crockett, an islander so colorful that he was known (for reasons unknown) as "Sugar Tom," published a somewhat idiosyncratic history of the place called *Facts and Fun: The Historical Outlines of Tangier Island.* Though he knew and interviewed many of the oldest islanders, Sugar Tom wrote without access to the official records on the mainland, with the result that his work preserves a good deal of island lore but not always hard, documented facts. And his book is rare and unknown today because it so scandalized the islanders that his family destroyed as many copies as they could get their hands on.

This book is the result of the curiosity of yet another mainlander — an Eastern Shoreman, to be sure, but nonetheless an outsider on Tangier. A number of islanders have helped in the writing, all of whom are named at the back of the book, some of whom deserve special mention and thanks.

Among the island residents who were especially helpful were Elizabeth B. Pruitt, who cordially granted access to her fine collection of old photographs, and Annie Kelso Parks, the island's oldest resident, who shared memories of Tangier as it used to be. Alva Crockett, Lois Crockett, Wanda Marshall, Wallace Pruitt, and Sandra Wheatley were also of great assistance in various ways.

A number of Tangier people who no longer live on the island provided information, assistance, and encouragement, among them Edward Pruitt, Robert Thorne, and Robert Cooper, all Methodist ministers; William A. Pruitt of Newport News; David Shores of Virginia Beach; and Lewis Parks of Richmond, who granted access to an extensive collection of information about the island. Dependable help and advice came, as always, from mainlander B. Miles Barnes.

Two people named Gail have had a significant impact on this book. Despite an Italian maiden name, a Polish married name, and a New York address, Gail M. Walczyk cherishes her roots in the islands of the Chesapeake, and has researched the lineages of the island people more thoroughly than any other. She has willingly shared her insights and information, and her often-surprising discoveries have given some new "twists" to the story of Tangier, for which I am grateful.

Gail Harding has once again made herself indispensable, not only with advice and encouragement, but also with long hours using her technical skills to turn a mere manuscript into a finished book. Part of my thanks to her has been the opportunity to introduce her to Tangier Island and some of its people.

Last but far from least, a priceless resource for this book was the long and crystal-clear memory of the late Ruth Wallace Clarke (1906-2004), whose hospitality and encouragement also stand behind all that is printed here. I was privileged to see the island through her eyes, and I hope that this book will preserve some of that special flavor for everyone.

To these and all others who helped I am grateful. May islanders and mainlanders, locals and visitors alike find as much enjoyment, and as much to learn, in reading these pages as I have had in researching and writing them.

Kirk Mariner

*For many years visitors to Tangier have remarked upon the number of the island's graves, and in particular the "unusual" custom of burying the family dead in the front or back yard.*

*In fact, burial in the yard will seem neither quaint nor unusual to those familiar with the Eastern Shore of Virginia and other parts of the Chesapeake region. Long before there were public cemeteries, the dead were buried in family plots located on a patch of high ground somewhere on the "estate" or farm, usually not very distant from, perhaps even in view of the main house. In this regard Tangier differs from the mainland only in being much smaller and in having much less land available for burials. The "unusual" graves in the yards are the island's miniature version of a custom that still prevails in a number of places on the mainland.*

*The pictures at the beginning of the chapters that follow depict carvings from some of Tangier's old gravestones. Although they were, most likely, not carved on the island itself, the symbols on the island's gravestones constitute a treasure too long overlooked, and a part of Tangier's heritage deserving to be admired and celebrated.*

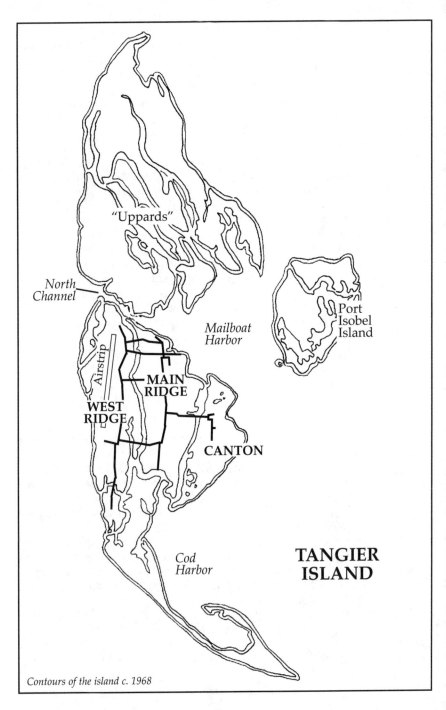

"Uppards"

North
Channel

Mailboat
Harbor

Port
Isobel
Island

Airstrip

MAIN
RIDGE

WEST
RIDGE

CANTON

Cod
Harbor

**TANGIER
ISLAND**

*Contours of the island c. 1968*

# 1
# Russel Isles

Tangier's history begins with Captain John Smith, who discovered and named the island in 1608.

That, at least, is the story told by the Virginia historical marker on the island's main street. In fact, the beginning is not quite that simple.

Jamestown was a little over a year old, and far from proving itself to be the first permanent English settlement in America, when on June 2, 1608, John Smith set out in a small open boat to explore the Chesapeake Bay. With him went a company of fourteen others: four soldiers, a blacksmith, a fishmonger, a fisherman, six gentlemen, and a "'Doctor of Physicke" named Walter Russell. They headed immediately for Cape Charles, on the "Eastern Shore" of the Bay, then traveled up the western side of that peninsula "searching every inlet and bay fit for harbours and habitations." Along the way they were welcomed at two Indian villages, by the Accomacs, who lived near the modern town of Cape Charles, and by the Occohannocks, who lived further up the peninsula on the creek of that name.

After leaving the Occohannocks, the small band continued up the Shore until, in Smith's own words, "seeing many Iles in the midst of the bay, we bore up for them." After veering towards the islands, they found themselves in the midst of one of the sudden storms for which the Chesapeake is famous, "such an extreme gust of wind, raine, thunder, and lightning happened, that with great daunger we escaped the unmercifull raging of that ocean-like water." Smith does not say how long the storm lasted, or whether they found shelter from it on one of the islands. But "the next day searching those inhabitable Iles (which we called Russels Iles) to provide fresh water," they found none, "the defect whereof forced us to follow the next Easterne channell, which brought us to the river Wighcocomoco,"[1] the river known today as the Pocomoke.

Those few sentences are all that John Smith has to say about the "Russel Iles," and not enough to guarantee that he is describing Tangier Island in particular. The island nearest the Eastern Shore mainland is not Tangier but Watts Island, which was then, like Tangier, much larger than it is today, and wooded, and undoubtedly equally as prominent upon the Bay's horizon. Did Smith and his band head for the nearest island, or pass it up for a larger one and more distant one? Was it upon Watts Island that they searched in vain for fresh water, or Tangier Island, or both? Smith's statement that they took "the next Easterne channell" into the Pocomoke suggests that it might have been Watts, for to the east of that island lies Pocomoke Sound, leading into the river of that name, while to the east of Tangier lies Tangier Sound, which leads into the Wicomico and Nanticoke Rivers in Maryland.

Regardless of this uncertainty, Captain John Smith has always been recognized as the "discoverer" of Tangier.

And, indeed, on his famous "Map of Virginia," published in London in 1612, there in the middle of the Chesapeake he depicts a cluster of islands which is undoubtedly his version of Tangier and Watts and their neighbors. And the name attached to them, more closely to Tangier than to Watts Island, is "Russels Iles."

As for Dr. Walter Russell, for whom the island was originally named, not even the combined efforts of today's best historians and Britain's Royal College of Physicians have been able to identify him.[2] After the exploration of the Bay in 1608 he vanishes from the pages of history, leaving only his name, briefly, on a small island in the middle of Chesapeake Bay.

Captain John Smith did not, of course, "discover" Tangier, nor was he the first person, or even the first European to see it.

Undoubtedly the first people to visit Tangier were native Americans many centuries before the arrival of the English, and the likelihood is that they were not the Accomacs and Occohannocks but the Nanticokes of the upper Delmarva Peninsula, whom Smith first encountered on the Pocomoke River. Though a few Indian relics of great antiquity have been found on the island, some of them dating as far back as 9000 B.C., most such finds suggest that the island was not a place where the Indians lived, but their fishing and hunting ground.

The largest evidence of native Americans on Tangier was once visible just offshore, beneath the waters within the cove at the southern end of the island. Here lay a great "shell pile" upon which islanders built first a factory in the nineteenth century, then a steamboat wharf in the twentieth. Such mounds of oyster shells, or "middens," are found throughout the Chesapeake, some of them much larger than Tangier's. The fact that such a mound once existed on Tangier's shore indicates that the Indians gathered oysters here and consumed them either in great numbers or over long periods of time, or both. The fact that the shell pile they left behind is now under water is explained by the fact that the "hook" of land at Tangier's southern end has constantly shifted over the centuries, and that the waters of the Chesapeake now cover not only parts of the sandy beach but also whatever man may have built on it.

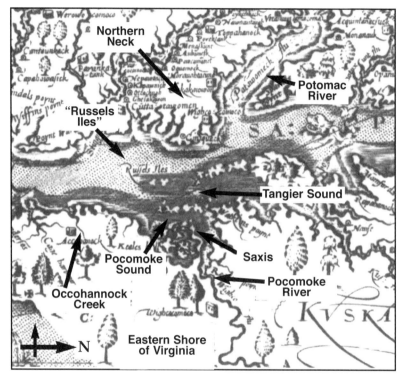

**"Russel Isles"**
on John Smith's Map, 1612

Yet though the Indians had been there before him, when Smith saw the islands they were, in his word, "inhabitable," meaning "not habitable." No English record of the 1600s suggests that Indians ever lived there, or were even encountered there.[3]

The first Europeans in the area were not British, but Spanish, to whom the Chesapeake was Bahia de Santa Maria, the "Bay of St. Mary." In 1588, Capt. Vincente Gonzales, on an expedition from Florida to investigate the extent of English settlements along the coast, probably covered the entire length of the Bay, from the Virginia capes to the Susequehanna River, and if so he undoubtedly saw Tangier Island. A Spanish scouting expedition under Capt. Francisco Fernandez de Ecija ventured up the Bay in 1609, but withdrew after encountering an English vessel "in the region of the islands."[4]

During the cold winter of 1926, nature disclosed that there was at least one other early visitor. An extraordinary combination of wind and tide in February of that year lowered the level of the waters around Tangier, beyond what had ever been witnessed in memory of the oldest islanders. As the waters receded, they briefly revealed the hulk of an old wooden vessel long submerged beneath the surface. A number of Tangier watermen observed the vessel, some sunk their oyster tongs into the depths of the hulk, and a few even walked on its slippery and decaying decks. Before the tide swept back over the wreck, the artifacts that had been retrieved from it included a heavily encrusted copper dish, several dishes "beautifully inscribed," and, most prized of all, a curiously engraved battle-ax in an excellent state of preservation.

None of these treasures remained long on Tangier. The dishes were sold to a visiting antique dealer from New York, and the battle-ax to Lorie Quinn, Sr., of Crisfield, Maryland, for the grand sum of $10. By April the weapon was at the Peabody Institute in Baltimore, where experts determined that it was manufactured from Damascus steel with an inlaid shield of brass, and they pronounced it "a remarkable specimen of the Medieval pole ax" of a type used not by the English but by the nations of the Mediterranean. From Baltimore the weapon was scheduled to be taken to New York for further examination, but it never reached that city. It vanished, mysteriously, from public view and record, and its whereabouts are unknown.

It is known that in 1611 a Spanish ship that stopped at Old Point Comfort, in today's Hampton, Virginia, to spy on the English fortifications had as its real mission to watch for another Spanish vessel that had been lost somewhere in the Chesapeake region. Was the vessel it was seeking the one that turned up in 1926? The Bay reclaimed its prize too quickly, and the mystery remains, hidden beneath the waters off Tangier.

It is not surprising that some early explorer might have run aground near Tangier, for the waters around the island are, and always have been, notoriously shallow.

In the middle portion of the Chesapeake, two island chains dangle southward from the Eastern Shore of Maryland into the waters of Virginia. On the west, descending towards the center of the Bay from Dorchester County, are the big islands: Bloodsworth, South Marsh, Smith, Tangier. On the east, closer to the peninsula itself, only slightly detached from Somerset County, lies the smaller archipelago: Great Fox, Little Fox, Watts. In each chain clumps of marsh reach out from one island towards the next, the water between them shallow, the bottom sometimes exposed at low tide.

Even today larger vessels plying this part of the Bay move necessar-

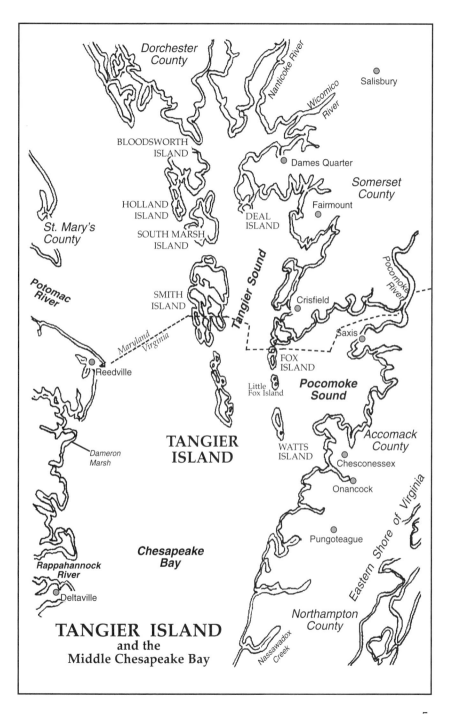

Dorchester
County

Nanticoke River

Wicomico River

Salisbury

BLOODSWORTH
ISLAND

Dames Quarter

Somerset
County

HOLLAND
ISLAND

Fairmount

DEAL
ISLAND

St. Mary's
County

SOUTH MARSH
ISLAND

Pocomoke River

Potomac
River

SMITH
ISLAND

Tangier Sound

Crisfield

Maryland
Virginia

Saxis

Reedville

FOX
ISLAND

Little
Fox Island

Pocomoke
Sound

TANGIER
ISLAND

WATTS
ISLAND

Accomack
County

Chesconessex

Dameron
Marsh

Onancock

Eastern Shore of Virginia

Pungoteague

Chesapeake
Bay

Rappahannock
River

Deltaville

Northampton
County

TANGIER ISLAND
and the
Middle Chesapeake Bay

Nassawadox
Creek

ily not east-and-west but north-and-south, either up Tangier Sound, between the two chains, into Nanticoke, Wicomico, or Manokin Rivers, or up Pocomoke Sound, between Watts Island and the mainland, into Pocomoke River. Hundreds of years ago, such north-and-south movement was even more necessary, because the islands were larger and the spaces between them smaller.

Without exception, the islands in both chains have eroded, or sunk, significantly in the centuries since Captain John Smith explored the Bay. A number of islands which were once inhabited — among them Shanks, Fox, and Queen's Ridge — are now barely above water. Some of the larger ones that once supported trees, gardens, and even farms — like Watts — are now seriously reduced. Still others — among them Little Watts, the southernmost of the eastern chain, once the location of a lighthouse — have disappeared altogether (see map page 26).

The diminishing of the islands has been going on for centuries. Zachariah "Sacker" Nelson, who lived on Great Fox Island as far back as the 1780s, observed even then that at one time he could walk from Cedar Straits, at the northern end of the smaller chain, to the southernmost end of the Fox Islands, using little more than a fence log to span the intervening waters, and that between Little Fox and Watts there then stretched another island of marsh. Smith's map seems to support the existence of such a continuous chain of islands between Fox and Watts. But within a century after Nelson, the oldtimers of the region could not remember when the space between Fox and Watts was not open, although shallow, water.[5]

Like its neighbors, Tangier has been steadily diminishing throughout its history. It was, in 1608, much larger than it is now, and covered with pine. Until well into historic times there was enough high ground to support both farms and forests. The earliest known map of the island, from 1859, shows it almost twice as wide as it is today, and half again as long, for it was then virtually connected to Goose Island on the north, from which it is now separated by more than half a mile of water. Island historian Thomas Crockett (1833-1905) observed in 1890 that the island had sunk "at least eight inches perpendicular since I was a boy." The greatest losses have occurred on the west, where the strongest winds hit; on that side the island has lost as much as 25 feet in a single year.[6]

And all the while Tangier, located at a strategic and seemingly promising spot in the Bay, has been surrounded by waters so shallow that it never developed into a large or important port. Throughout the greater part of its history, vessels of significant size and draft had to anchor offshore, and send passengers and freight ashore in smaller boats. Meanwhile generations of islanders who made their living from the Bay had no wharf or pier from which to put out into the water, but pulled their boats into "guts" or up on the beaches and marshes.

In time, two "harbors" were developed for the island. Late in the nineteenth century a wharf was built to accommodate the steamboats that then stopped at the island several times weekly. The shallow-drafted steamers could pull more closely than older large vessels into "Cod Harbor," the shallow cove sheltered from the west by the sliver of beach at the southern end of the island. But even the steamboat wharf itself was not connected to land; it stood on the shell pile out in the harbor, and served merely as an embarking point for smaller boats that would take passengers and freight ashore.

This harbor was succeeded by the present one at the northern end of Main Ridge, which was created in the 1920s when a mile-long channel was dredged to connect deep water off the eastern side of the island with the high land of the ridge. The "fill" from that dredging was used to build up more high ground at that end of the ridge, a process that has since been repeated with subsequent dredgings, with the curious result that on this steadily shrinking island a good portion of today's town sits on "artificial" land reclaimed from the sea and the marshes.

"The island was visited in 1608 by Captain John Smith," states the historical marker, "who gave it the name."

The tradition that the name "Tangier" comes from John Smith is a persistent one, despite the fact that he nowhere uses that name, and is himself the source of a different one.

The earliest known assertion that John Smith gave the island its present name comes from "Sugar Tom" Crockett, the colorful and eccentric local historian who in 1890 wrote that when Smith saw the island "it reminded him of a town that he had been to on the south side of the Straits of Gibraltar, which town was called Tangier, and he named this island the same." Crockett gives no source for this statement, and is either the inventor of the tradition or simply the reporter of what the islanders believed in his day. Later writers have not only kept the tradition alive but also embellished it, insisting that what really reminded Smith of the North African city was the similarity of the clay pots of the island's Indians to those in the ancient market of Tangier, or the similarity of the white beaches that encompassed both the island and the city.[7]

From the other Tangier itself comes another attempt to link the island to North Africa, without Captain John Smith. In 1938 an American diplomat in Tangier, in Morocco, who was considered an outstanding historian, insisted that when English forces withdrew its garrison from that city in 1684, a number of the Englishmen who had been stationed there set sail for America with their Moroccan wives. "They landed in America on an island in the Chesapeake Bay and named it Tangier Island, for the country from which they had come. However, these so-called 'Moors' remained a very short time on Tangier Island but moved to Sussex County and Kent County, Delaware." In the 1890s there were indeed people living in Sussex County who were called "moors," but they insisted that their moorish ancestor had not come up the Chesapeake Bay but had been shipwrecked near Lewes, Delaware. More recent historians consid-

# Thomas L. Crockett
## 1833-1905
### Tangier's First Historian

"Sugar Tom" Crockett learned to write on the smooth sand at the edge of Tangier, "tinkered" at grammar on his own, went to school for nine weeks off the island, and returned with "what was then called a polished education on the island." He began writing a history of Tangier at the age of 15, which became, in time, *Facts and Fun: The Historical Outlines of Tangier Island.*

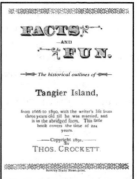

He was the great-grandson of Tangier's first Crockett, gleaned some of his accounts of the island's early years from his aged grandmother, and knew the famous Joshua Thomas. He married Margaret Spence, who bore him three children, and as a young man worked as an oysterman. In 1877 Crockett was issued a state teaching certificate, the first on the island, and three years later was serving as principal of the Tangier School. He was a Democrat — in his own words, "a South-pawed, dew-clawed, knock-kneed, double-jointed, shingle-shanked, copper-butt-boiled, double-dagger-kneed Demo-crat" — in a predominantly Republican town.

Sugar Tom's teaching career was short, for in 1884 he was visiting the mainland to promote "No. 7," a medicine of his own devising. There a mainlander labeled him a liar and a slanderer, "a patent-medicine tramp whose only claims to notoriety are the futile and vulgar attempts at humorous lecturing." In 1904 a mainland paper reported that "he knows more of the island's history than anyone else, and his reminiscences are very interesting."

*Facts and Fun* is divided into two sections. *Facts* is an important source of information about the island's history, mixed with lore and oral tradition. *Fun* is a near-bawdy reminiscence of courtship on mid-nineteenth century Tangier, full of colorful phraseology and numerous indications of how isolated and primitive Tangier was at that time. The book so scandalized the islanders that his granddaughter Nettie Pruitt destroyed every copy that she could get her hands on, with the result that it is extremely rare today.

Sugar Tom lived at 16199 Main Ridge, where he died on June 19, 1905. No one knows why he was called "Sugar Tom," and no photograph of him is known to exist.[9]

er their "moorish" connection more legend than fact. The island's part in it is even shakier, based on one man's undocumented story.[8]

In fact, the name "Tangier" simply does not appear in any known record for almost a century after John Smith's visit. "Russels Isles" continues on maps throughout the 1600s, when most maps were made in Europe by people who had never seen the Chesapeake and a lot of them were simply copies of Smith's map. A Virginia court order of 1673 refers to the island as "the Western Island," probably to distinguish it from Watts Island, but that name appears only once.

The earliest known use of the name "Tangier" is on a map published by John Thornton in London around 1682 — before the alleged arrival of the soldiers from African Tangier. Whether the name came from the locals or the Europeans is not clear, for though it was published in England, Thornton's map is an update of one drawn in America in 1673 by Augustine Herrmann of Maryland, whose map clearly shows Tangier Island but does not assign it a name.[10]

The first mention of the name Tangier in an American record is from a 1695 sale of land on the Eastern Shore, when the seller identifies himself in the deed as John Nelson, Jr., from "Tangear Island" — even though it is virtually certain that he lived on Fox Island. In 1713 the name Tangier appears again, but then it refers only to the upper part of the island; the "hook" at the end of the island was at that time called "Sandy Beach Island."[11]

It took a long time for the name "Tangier" to become attached exclusively to today's Tangier Island. In fact, for more than a century the name referred to all the islands on the western side of Tangier Sound, including Tangier, Smith and all the islands between them, and sometimes also to the islands on the eastern side of the sound, including Watts and Fox. The records of the 1700s speak more frequently of "the Tangier Islands" plural, meaning Tangier and Smith and other smaller islands, than they do of "Tangier Island" singular, meaning the one island that goes by that name today. As late as the mid-1800s references to "the Tangiers" or even "Tangiers" may mean one island or several — a fact which has misled some to assign to Tangier events that happened elsewhere.[12]

For the better part of a century after John Smith put it on the map, Russels/Western/Tangier Island was largely ignored. Jamestown survived, and became the nucleus of a colony that gradually spread across the Virginia Tidewater. The English settled permanently on the Eastern Shore of Virginia, beginning in 1620. A second colony called Maryland was established further up the Chesapeake in 1632. Yet no one looked upon Tangier as a desirable property to own, or as a place to live. Despite its visibility in the Chesapeake, the island lacked the land on which to grow and the docks from which to ship the principal crop of both colonies, tobacco. Only after most of the good land on the mainland had been taken did Virginians begin to turn their eyes at last toward the islands in the Chesapeake, and then it was not as a place to live that "the Tangier Islands" finally assumed importance, but as pasture for livestock.

In the mid-1600s Eastern Shore planters, beset by falling tobacco prices, began to diversify by planting grains and by producing beef and hides. Up until that time settlers had let their cattle run free, or fenced them into the many "necks" of land that bordered the peninsula. As herds grew larger, the low and marshy islands around the Eastern Shore of Virginia assumed new importance, for on them a plantation owner could release his livestock to forage for themselves, naturally "fenced" by the surrounding waters. In a short time virtually every island of the Eastern Shore was acquired for pasture, including not only Chincoteague and Wallops on the Seaside but also "the Tangier islands" in the Bay.[13]

Watts Island was among the first to be claimed, in 1652. In those days, the way to get title to unclaimed land was to obtain a grant, or "patent," from the colonial authorities, then to "seat" it by building on it a house at least 12 feet square, fencing in an acre for an orchard or a garden, and living there, or have someone else livē in it as a tenant, for a year. By 1685 Watts was owned by Henry Jenkins, whose overseer lived in a house located fully a mile from shore, and whose livestock was producing beef and mutton.[14]

The patenting of Smith Island began in 1665 by Robert Cager, whose name survives in "Kedges Straits" between that island and the next one to the north. Much of this island quickly came under the ownership of Henry Smith, whose name it still bears, and he "seated" it with tenants to oversee his livestock.

It was in 1668, as Smith Island was being claimed and settled, that Virginia and Maryland agreed upon the boundary separating the two colonies on the Eastern Shore mainland, and people from both colonies seem always to have acknowledged that the boundary ran also across Smith Island, dividing it into two unequal portions, the larger in Maryland, the smaller in Virginia. John Evans and John Tyler were living on Smith Island by 1686, Tyler in "Horse Hammock," in the Virginia section on the eastern side of the island. On the western side was Hog Neck, also in Virginia, which was claimed in 1703 by a number of prominent Virginians who included Rev. Francis Makemie, the Presbyterian "pioneer" in America.[15]

It was Ambrose White, a tavern-keeper in what is today the town of Accomac, who first laid claim to Tangier. White obtained his patent in 1670, then turned it over to Charles Scarburgh and John West in 1671, and their descendants still owned the island more than a century later. Neither of the first owners of Tangier ever lived on the island, and there is no record that either of them ever even visited it. John West (1638-1703) was one of the most prominent men of the Eastern Shore, affluent and well-connected, whose estate on Chesconessex Creek contained almost 7,000 acres. Charles Scarburgh (1643-1702) was, if anything, even richer. He lived on a large plantation on Pungoteague Creek, and his family was sufficiently well-heeled to have him educated in London.[16]

To such rich mainland "planters," Tangier Island was merely a small appendage to larger and more important properties, a good place to keep your livestock. Unlike Watts and Smith, there is no actual record that Tangier Island was actually "seated" and used for pasture, but it seems likely that Scarburgh and West did so. "West...went into the business of stock raising, which proved valuable," says Thomas Crockett, whose history of the island is hardly reliable for the early years, but it is possible that his statement reflects an early memory of the time when the island was inhabited largely by cattle, not people. Who, if anyone, the absentee landlords established on the island is simply not known.

In the lore that the islanders spun about their home, the beginnings of Tangier became, with the passage of time, a much more colorful story than the facts support. "It was about the year 1666," writes Sugar Tom Crockett in 1890, that "a gentleman named West came from the main land of Accomac County to Tangier Island. He told the Indians they would soon be captured and he had come to buy their Island, which he did for two overcoats, and said West became the sole owner of the Island."[17]

The purchase of the island from the Indians is pure legend. The prosaic fact is that for a century and a half after it was "discovered" by John Smith, Tangier Island was remote, inaccessible, and largely ignored, peopled if at all by a few tenants of absentee landlords who came and went leaving no trace of themselves on the island's history.

**Tangier and the "Tangier Iles"**
from the earliest marine chart of the Chesapeake, 1689

# 2
# No Man's Land

For centuries, since the time when the island was first settled, no family has been more prominent or more numerous on Tangier Island than the Crocketts. And for more than a century the lore of the island has included the story of John Crockett, who is said to have been the first of that name on the island.

According to the local tradition, John Crockett settled on the island with his family in 1686, when he bought land from John West. He was the father of four sons and four daughters, a man of limited education who taught his sons, but not his daughters, to "read a little." His sons Zachariah, John, and Thomas found brides on the Eastern Shore, brought them to Tangier, and "raised large families." Three of his daughters married men from Somerset County named Dize, Evans, and Parks, and brought those family names to the island. Only two children did not choose to remain on the island: son Joseph, who settled in York County, and a daughter who married a man named Hopkins, from which sprang the prominent family of that name near Onancock on the Eastern Shore.[1]

As with so many other details concerning the early years of Tangier, the facts do not support the tradition. No written record substantiates the existence of a John Crockett of Tangier in the 1600s. No written record substantiates the tradition that he or anybody else by the name of Crockett — or anybody at all! — lived on Tangier Island in the 1600s. While it is entirely possible that absentee landlords John West and Charles Scarburgh had employees on the island as early as 1686, none of them are known to have been named Crockett. And it is certain that none of them purchased land at that time, for no sales of land on Tangier occurred until almost a century later.[2]

Instead, more recent genealogical research identifies the first settler of Tangier, and the founder of the island line, as Joseph Crockett (1722-1806), who lived a full century later. Joseph Crockett was the son of Sampson Crockett and a native of Somerset County, where Crocketts had lived since the 1600s. Joseph was raised on Smith Island, then disappears from the records there after 1744, and by the time he turns up again is living on Tangier Island. In 1778 he purchased 450 acres of the old Scarburgh portion of the island, and became the first person to purchase land on Tangier Island, indeed, the first Crockett to own land anywhere in Accomack County. It was he and his wife Sally, not the legendary John Crockett of the 1600s, who had not eight but ten children, including sons Zachariah, John, Thomas, and Joseph (the names of the four sons of the legendary John Crockett), and daughters who (like those of John) married men named Evans, Parks, and Hopkins.[3]

In 1763, when he was probably living at South Point on Smith Island, Joseph Crockett was appointed Constable for the Tangier Islands. His appointment is one of the first indications in the written record that the officials of Accomack County even knew that the islands were there, probably because it was not until about that time that many people were there. The fact that he was appointed Constable and was able later to purchase 450 acres indicates that he was not poor. In fact, Joseph Crockett's grandfather had bequeathed him enough money to get an education and to be trained as a weaver. The founder of Tangier was a literate man who even had his own pew, paid for with his own money, at St. George's Episcopal Church in Pungoteague, where many of the gentry of Accomack County worshiped.[4]

That it was this Joseph Crockett of the 1700s who was the founder of the Tangier line, and not the legendary John Crockett of the 1600s, is proven beyond a doubt by the census of 1800. In that year the Tangier Islands had a population of 89, of whom 40 (45%) were named Crockett. One of them was Joseph, then 78 years old, and every single one of the other Crocketts was either one of his descendants or one of his daughters-in-law.[5]

By the 1770s, when Joseph Crockett became the first permanent resident of Tangier, some of the other "Tangier Islands" had been inhabited for as much as a century, for each enjoyed some natural advantage that Tangier did not possess. Smith Island was more accessible, for the deep water of the Chesapeake veered closer to it than to Tangier. Watts Island and Fox Island, though much smaller, had good wells for drinking water, and were nearer the mainland.[6] Curiously, the second largest of the islands, and the most visible to ships coming up the Bay, had remained unsettled, inaccessible behind the shallow waters that surrounded it on every side.

Joseph Crockett built on the ridge of high land known as Canton, for here, off its northeast corner, was the best juxtaposition of high land with deep water anywhere on Tangier. It was in Canton that those of Joseph's children who followed him to Tangier began to build their homes: Thomas, Zachariah, and John.[7] The first Crockett homes were undoubtedly small and simple. Though the 1700s were a time when many of the handsome homes so greatly admired today were built on the Eastern Shore mainland, no grand homes arose on Tangier, and no island architecture of that period survives.[8]

Any vessel that pulled up on Tangier's shore in those days was still some distance from the high ground where the Crocketts lived. One enterprising visitor, forced ashore during a snowstorm and in need of shelter, found cattle grazing on the marsh, and shoo-ed them inland ahead of him. When he arrived at the nearest house, Crockett asked him why he had driven his cattle up the field. "Why," replied the stranger, "I didn't know the way through the marsh, and I thought the cattle did."[9]

The islanders were "nearly all farmers" who raised corn and beans, potatoes and turnips, figs and pears, onions and peppers, and made their own bread. There were cows for milk, butter, and cheese, and hogs for pork. Meat was eaten both fresh and salted, although salt was at times a rare commodity. In addition, islanders hunted wild fowl, and from the waters that surrounded them drew fish and oysters — but not crabs, which did not become a staple of the islanders' diet until the 19th century. A day of fishing could easily yield a hundred fish, which could then be sold or bartered off the island.[10]

In some of Sugar Tom Crockett's stories, Joseph Crockett appears to be more of a rustic bumpkin than a man of stature. According to Sugar Tom, mariners who happened by Tangier spread the word that the island was inhabited by dangerous people who had hairy feet, because Crockett often wore moccasins of unfinished bullhide. When Crockett heard that his lost canoe had turned up on Nassawadox Creek, he and a friend went over to the mainland to retrieve it from a "fine gentleman's house," and Crockett greeted the gentleman while eating a hunk of boiled meat from one hand, a piece of bread from the other, with grease running down his chin. Though the gentleman's two daughters found such rustic behavior laughable, Crockett outsmarted their father and, over his objections, refloated and reclaimed his canoe.[11]

While such tales seem inconsistent with a literate man worthy to be a magistrate, they do suggest that Tangier's few residents quickly lost any veneer of refinement the founder may have possessed and in a relatively short time seemed to mainlanders to be a people both simple and unsophisticated, aggravating and amusing, primitive but clever. They were also superstitious. An islander who repeatedly failed to bring down wild fowl with his gun was apt to believe that the weapon had been put under a spell, the solution for which was to bury it in the hog pen until the swine freed it by their endless trampling over it. Sleepless nights, which might be caused by a witch, could be cured by sleeping with a chicken feather on the chest, and a real witch would bear facial scars forever if her picture was shot with gunpowder mixed with silver.[12]

Yet a number of stories testify to the hunger of the islanders for learning. Thomas Crockett (1747?-1815), Joseph's son, was sufficiently literate to know his letters, but not how "to join them into words properly, although he could record his children's ages, which he did on the flyleaves of his prayer book." In 1775, when Crockett exchanged 100 fish for a bushel of salt and a Bible, word of the existence of the book "flew over the Island," and "the public came to see it, and many wondered at some of the words that Mr. Crockett would spell and read from it." This event occurred on Smith Island before Joseph Crockett and his family moved to Tangier, but Thomas Crockett later enjoyed the respect of the other islanders of Tangier for his ability to read. Even so Sugar Tom tells of the time a friend brought to him a book with a word he could not make out, and the two struggled in vain to decipher the word "particular."[13]

When Joseph Crockett moved to Tangier Island, the American colonies were at war with England for their independence.

The cause of independence was not universally popular on the Eastern Shore of Virginia and Maryland. Among the champions of the Patriot cause were the larger landowners and planters of the mainland — the affluent "gentlemen" who had for generations looked down on unsophisticated islanders. Conversely, many of the watermen of the Chesapeake favored the British cause. In fact, the majority of the Loyalists of the Eastern Shore of Virginia came from the poorer fishermen who lived on the creeks, "guts," and necks of the Bay.

On the Chesapeake the war was, for the most part, not a conflict between the Americans and the British, but a guerrilla war waged by bands of Loyalists against the civilian populace in general and pro-American shipping in particular.[14] To the Patriots who advocated the American cause, these Loyalist bands were little more than pirates — "picaroons," they called them — and the marshes and islands of Tangier and Pocomoke Sounds provided countless hiding places for them. Raiders in a small boat outfitted with a gun could obtain provisions to sell to the British by plundering vessels or plantations, then slip into an isolated gut and lay low until the next opportunity presented itself. The Tangier Islands, by virtue of their isolated but strategic location in the Bay, were perfectly suited for such activity. Tangier Island in particular, among the largest of the islands but with a very small population, was especially so.

Whatever their opinions about the war — Joseph Crockett's views are unknown, but a number of Smith Islanders joined the American militia — the residents of the Tangier Islands lived in a virtual "no man's land." Undefended by the Americans, they were vulnerable to both the British and the picaroons. Yet when their isolated location forced them to deal with either, the Patriots suspected them of being collaborators with the enemy. Survival depended upon accommodating the force that happened to be on the scene at any given time, and the islanders quickly learned to fly whatever flag was necessary.

By mid-summer 1775, only months after the conflict began and even before Crockett moved to Tangier, the islands were already picaroon territory. Confronted with the choice of supporting the picaroons and supplying them with what they demanded, or resisting and suffering the consequences, the islanders chose compliance, though at least one islander, George Pruitt of Hog Neck, had his house burned by the picaroons, perhaps as an example to any who refused to comply. "At times," records Tom Crockett, "refugees and robbers would drift over to the Island and commit depredations, which kept these poor Island people in much trouble, being few in numbers and not able to protect themselves."[15]

The British navy also frequented the waters of the sound, adding to the dangers the islanders faced. Because the islands were completely unprotected, both crops and livestock and even the islanders themselves were vulnerable to seizure by the British. Thomas Nelson of Fox Island, a "stout boy" of draftable age, had to "skulk about to keep from being impressed by the British." Job Parks II (1758-1847) of Hog Neck on Smith Island was not so fortunate; he was forcibly conscripted and carried away on a British boat, probably to serve as a pilot around the Bay. More frequently, the British wanted crops and livestock to feed their troops. As in their dealings with the picaroons, the islanders chose to sell their goods rather than have them seized, and traded with the British throughout the war, to the continuing consternation of the Patriot authorities on the mainland.[16]

The year 1777 began with three heavily armed British warships patrolling Tangier Sound, while on the mainland the Maryland authorities were attempting to round up the Tories of Somerset and Worcester Counties. Two prominent British sympathizers, Hamilton Callallo and Thomas Moore, managed to escape the round-up, and headed for the Tangier Islands, the last stop on an underground route by which Loyalists from the peninsula eluded capture, or sought refuge on British warships. Captain James Campbell was sent after them in his vessel *Enterprise*, with instructions to hoist the British flag to lure the fugitives aboard. From the islanders Campbell learned that not just Callallo and Moore but also a number of other fugitives had come over from the mainland to take refuge in the marshes, and that the islanders were frightened, "so much afraid that I had no chance of succeeding." He sailed completely around the islands from Tangier to Hooper Straits without finding his prey, who turned up on Smith Island within two hours after he left.[17]

When it was not the picaroons or the British that the islanders had to worry about, it was the Virginia authorities. In August 1777, a large number of British ships were roaming Chesapeake Bay, and Virginia Governor Thomas Jefferson ordered that the boats of all local watermen be collected and put under guard to prevent them from being used to supply the British. Whether his order was carried out on Tangier is not known, but it is certain that new statewide regulations governing the procurement of food for the Continental army were felt on the island, for even Tangier was given a quota of cured beef and dairy products to be prepared for purchase for the army. The boat that went for the island's share of provisions carried salt for curing the meat for the next supply.[18]

Even the Maryland authorities could make life difficult for the islanders. In April 1779, the *Dolphin* and the *Plater*, two vessels of the

Maryland Navy, arrived in Tangier Sound to counter the activity of Loyalist privateers and picaroons. They established a blockade of the islands, Tangier among them, to prevent mainlanders from trading with the "villains" sequestered there.[19]

On January 13, 1780, during a bitter cold in which the Bay froze over, Job Parks, who had been seized by the British, found his way home. Having made his escape from the British in the area of Deal Island, Parks walked across the ice-bound Manokin River, headed south overland through Somerset County, and from Flat Cap Point, north of today's Crisfield, started westward across the ice toward Smith Island. There he faced the most dangerous part of his journey, the deep channel of Tangier Sound. Halfway across he saw a break in the ice ahead of him, desperately made a flying leap over it, and landed safely on the island side, falling and sliding towards home. "The people made it a thanksgiving day," records Sugar Tom Crockett.[20]

Later that year Parks and seven other Smith Island men — his brother John, Thomas Evans, the brothers Levin, William, and Jesse Evans, Spencer Tyler, and Richard Evans, who was later known as "King Richard" because he was "well off" — crossed to the mainland and joined Captain Henry Miles' company of the Somerset militia.[21] It is not known whether their enlistment in the American cause had any effect upon the prevailing mainland view that the islanders were collaborators with the enemy.

By the spring of 1780 four enemy privateers and four armed barges were operating in Tangier Sound, and by summer "enemy privateers seemed to be everywhere, raiding and robbing at will from Tangier Sound to the Patuxent River." Governor Jefferson ordered Commodore James Barron of the Virginia Navy to "strip the inhabitants of Tangier Island of their surplus food," lest they provision the enemy, but the order was never carried out. Autumn found privateers and picaroons still in control of the central Chesapeake, with several of them patrolling Tangier Sound.

By then the colorful and wily Joseph Wheland had emerged as the most visible, effective, and elusive of the picaroons. A "tall, slim gallows-looking fellow" who often wore a gold-laced jacket stolen from an Eastern Shore victim, Wheland was by trade a waterman intimately familiar with the shallow channels of Dorchester and Somerset, and is said to have "committed every type of crime in the book" in defiance of the mainland authorities. He operated out of Tangier, Smith, and the other islands of the region, moving quickly from place to place, and from his island bases proved particularly effective at disrupting the American supply lines in the central part of the Bay. In September 1780 no fewer than four Maryland vessels set out to capture him. They cornered and seized five picaroon craft off Tangier, but Wheland escaped, and continued to harass American shipping.

By October 1780 picaroon activity in the region of the islands was so bad that both Virginia and Maryland authorities set out to stop it. Virginia sent out a small flotilla under Commodore Barron to seek out picaroon vessels; Barron intercepted five schooners in the vicinity of Tangier. The Maryland legislature ordered a more radical solution: not simply the seizure of all vessels found on the islands south of Hooper Straits, but also the removal of all the islanders themselves to the mainland.

Maryland, of course, had no authority over Virginia's Tangier Island, but on November 25, 1780, Commodore James Tibbett of the Maryland Navy arrived at the islands to execute the orders of the legislature in Annapolis. Once there, he proposed to remove not the islanders themselves but all the picaroons and raiders. Once again the effort came to nothing — the weather was rough, Tibbett's four vessels were undermanned, and the picaroons were nowhere to be seen. Tibbett returned up the Bay, but it was not the last time that the mainland authorities would order the wholesale removal of the islanders themselves.[22]

The situation in the region of Tangier Island in early 1781 gave little reason to suspect that the war would end in American victory before the year was out. Two vessels loaded with corn for Washington's army were intercepted and captured by a 10-gun privateer near Tangier in January. Two months later Washington had moved his forces to Yorktown and Major General Marquis de La Fayette, the French nobleman aiding the American cause, was headed down the Bay to join him when he was diverted to Annapolis by the report of four armed ships cruising in the vicinity of Tangier and Smith Islands. La Fayette was forced to continue his journey overland. John Greenwood, sailing between Yorktown and Baltimore, found the Chesapeake in the region of Tangier to be "infested by innumerable pickaroons, barges, gallies [galleys] and small privateers," and was briefly captured by Wheland, whom he labeled "as great a villain as ever was unhung." Loyalist activity was becoming so brazen that associates of Wheland boldly stole up the Wicomico River, hauled Captain Henry Gale of the Somerset militia out of his bed, spirited him away to an island at the mouth of the Nanticoke, flogged him, and hanged him.[23]

Yet on October 19, 1781, British General Cornwallis surrendered his army to Washington at Yorktown, and the war was officially over. Washington dispatched Lt. Tench Tilghman (1744-1786), his young aide-de-camp, to carry the news of victory to the Continental Congress in Philadelphia, and Tilghman promptly set up the

**Tench Tilghman**

Chesapeake. On the evening of October 20, Tilghman's small boat ran aground on the shoals surrounding Tangier Island, and there he waited overnight for the turn of the tide, the earth-shaking news of American victory in his hand. By the time Tilghman reached Philadelphia on October 24, unofficial news of the victory had been abroad in the city for two days. There is no record that anyone from Tangier Island communicated with Tilghman, or he with them, as he waited the turn of the tide just offshore, but if they did then tiny, isolated Tangier received the news from Yorktown two days ahead of the city that was then the capital of the new nation.[24]

But the war was only officially over, and the picaroons had neither surrendered nor given up the cause. Within months British privateers and picaroons were again plundering both ashore and at sea, while the big warships of the French, allies of the Patriots, were docked helplessly at Yorktown, unable to fight the marauders because they could not operate in such shallow waters.

In April 1782, Maryland Governor Paca dispatched Commodore Thomas Grason to the islands in order to "afford security to the Bay Trade [and] Safety to the Inhabitants of the Shores" by "taking, destroying or driving off of the enemy and to depopulate the Tangier Islands within the limits of this state." Unlike the 1780 plan to remove all the islanders to the mainland, this one acknowledged that Maryland's authority did not extend over the whole of "the Tangier Islands," namely Tangier Island itself. The order to Grason was countermanded within two weeks, but even so he began patrolling the islands in the *Revenge*. In May he was south of Tilghman Island, headed for Tangier, which was still thought to be the main base of the picaroons, when he was attacked by Tories in three barges. In the battle that followed, Grason and several of his crewmen were killed, and the rest captured.[25]

With Grason's death, Captain Zedekiah Whaley was put in charge of Maryland's effort to rid the Bay of picaroons, and it was he who led both Marylanders and Virginians into the engagement that has come to be known as the last naval battle of the American Revolution. While patrolling the islands on November 27, 1782, Whaley sighted six armed British barges in Tangier Sound. The following day he divided the forces of his small flotilla to pursue a plan to capture them, and sent Captain Solomon Frazier to Tangier Island to reconnoiter for information while he himself headed south to Onancock for reinforcements.

On November 29, 1782, Frazier and forty picked men aboard the *Defence* arrived at Tangier, where not a picaroon sail was in sight. After raising the English colors, under the assumption that the islanders were Loyalists, Frazier himself went ashore, marched to the house of Joseph Crockett, and while masquerading as a Tory "cleverly made inquiry" about the American barges. Crockett professed to know nothing, except that he had seen the barges lying off Watts Island the day before, and "that 6 Barges had Left his House early that morning and stood up for

Fox Island up Tangier Sound," planning to spend the night at Kedges Straits.

This encounter between Joseph Crockett and Solomon Frazier is the only event of the American Revolution that can be said with certainty to have occurred specifically at Tangier Island, and not among "the Tangier Islands" in general. Was Crockett a supporter of the picaroons, taken in by Frazier's ruse and willing to give information about them only because he believed he was helping their allies? Or was he simply attempting to be neutral, complying with the demands of whatever armed force stood offshore? Frazier believed he had duped an unwitting Loyalist, and set out with his valuable information to join up with Whaley.[26]

Whaley, meanwhile, had been successful in his search for reinforcements, and when he and Frazier met near Watts Island, with him aboard the *Protector* were 25 members of the Virginia militia under the command of Colonel John Cropper. The following day Whaley's fleet caught up with the picaroon vessels in Kedges Straits, between South Marsh and Smith Island, and there occurred "the Battle of the Barges." It was a disaster for the Americans, "poorly planned and poorly executed." At the first sign of battle, all but one of the American vessels fled, leaving Whaley vastly outnumbered to bear the brunt of the attack alone. The *Protector*'s largest cannon had fired but twice when an ammunition chest was hit by returning enemy fire and exploded. All of Whaley's crew were either killed outright, thrown overboard, or jumped into the water with clothes ablaze. Whaley himself was killed, and Cropper put back into Onancock with 25 dead, 29 wounded, and only 11 unscathed. Whaley was buried in Onancock, and in Maryland the government launched an investigation of the cowardice of the other American commanders.

Ironically, this engagement occurred not only more than a year after the British surrender at Yorktown, but also on the very day that peace between England and the Colonies was signed in Europe.[27]

And still the Bay was not safe. Joseph Wheland and his followers spent the following winter on Smith and Tangier Islands, where they were reported to be building extensive fortifications. By February their activity had become so brazen that Governor Paca issued yet another order for the assembling of half a dozen armed barges to rout them out. But money was tight, and Paca was forced to appeal, unsuccessfully, to rich Baltimore merchants and even to George Washington. When at last the expedition was mounted it never reached its destination, because at long last, on March 29, 1783, almost a year and a half after Yorktown, peace was proclaimed.

Shortly after the proclamation of peace, the British vessels remaining in the Chesapeake were ordered to report to the larger British fleet in New York to begin the long voyage home, and with their departure the picaroon domination of the central Chesapeake collapsed. Within a short time the picaroon leaders on Tangier and Smith were captured, and a number of them hanged. Joseph Wheland, though apprehended at least four times during his career, escaped the gallows; how and where he ended his days are not known.[28]

For all its devastation, the Revolution did have one positive effect on the Chesapeake and its economy: more accurate maps and charts of the Bay, which quickly proved to be a boon to civilian as well as military vessels. By the end of the war, Chesapeake mariners could rely on charts that indicated depth soundings for Tangier and Pocomoke Sounds, the Choptank, and several rivers further north.

But the American military were not the only ones who had learned the contours of Chesapeake Bay. The British, also, now had a working knowledge of the Bay, and information about the location of sounds, shoals, and islands which might prove useful — if there were ever another war in the Chesapeake.[29]

# 3
# The Parson

On August 30, 1776, less than two months after the Declaration of Independence, a son was born to a couple who lived in Somerset County near what is today Fairmount, Maryland. The new parents were John and Martha Thomas, and they named their son Joshua.

Though he was not born on the island, and lived there only half his adult life, Joshua Thomas (1776-1853) would become in time Tangier Island's most famous figure, a man of almost legendary stature on the Chesapeake. Even today, virtually all visitors to Tangier are told about the exploits of the "Parson of the Islands," and rarely is anything written about the island's past that does not mention him.

While hardly rich, the family into which Joshua Thomas was born was probably a little better off than many in the region at that time. His paternal grandfather was fighting for American independence in a Virginia batallion, a cause not generally embraced by poor watermen; he died in the war, and never saw his grandson. Unlike many of his contemporaries, Joshua's father was a literate man, at one time a teacher, who by the time of his son's birth was in the "sea-faring" business with his brother. The Thomases were hard-working, God-fearing, and had reasonably good hopes of improving their children's worldly circumstances.

Then one day when Joshua was still quite young, John Thomas said goodbye to his family, walked barefoot towards the boat where his brother William waited for him, and was bitten by a small dog. Ignoring what appeared to be a wound of no great consequence, the brothers stopped at the islands to visit kinfolk. There his ankle began to swell, and become painful, and within a short time John Thomas was dead. His last words, borne across the sound to his wife, were: "I am going to heaven, bring the children up to fear and serve God."

Shortly thereafter the widow Thomas moved to Hog Neck on Smith Island, where her husband's kinfolk offered her "a comfortable subsistence,"[1] and her children whom their father would probably have taught to read now grew up without schooling. Three years later she married islander George Pruitt, a "clever sort of a man, standing fair in the community." But at some time around 1782, when Joshua was five or six years old, "refugees" — picaroons — burned the Pruitt house to the ground,

**Joshua Thomas**

and "destroyed nearly everything we had in the world." That loss was not only the end of any hope of worldly security for Joshua's mother, but also the beginning of his stepfather's slow decline into alcoholism. After years of "drunken frolics for weeks at a time," punctuated by "rude indignities" to his wife and her children, Pruitt met his end when he sold a prized possession — "a curious kind of flask, left by some of the British" — sailed over to the Eastern Shore, used the money to buy brandy, and drowned in a drunken stupor while attempting to return to the island. Joshua was by then old enough to go looking for his stepfather. After burying him on the mainland, he found Pruitt's unfinished bottle of brandy in his boat, carried it to the nearest house, placed it on the mantle, and urged the owner of the house to tell all his visitors where it came from, and what had happened because of it — perhaps, said he, "in that way it may do some good."[2]

Like many another poor island boy, Joshua Thomas grew to become an expert fisherman, a skillful boatman, thoroughly familiar with the waters and wetlands of the Tangier Islands, and "deplorably ignorant of letters." As he approached manhood, he apprenticed himself to David Tyler of Smith Island to learn "the vocation of a waterman." Tyler treated him well, like the father he had never known, and even bought him his first suit of clothes, purchased in Baltimore.

In 1797 Joshua Thomas married Rachel Evans (1786?-1814) of Shanks Island. After two years of making their home with Tyler, he purchased 70 acres on Tangier Island, part of the old West lands, built a house in what later became known as West Ridge, and in 1799 moved Rachel and their young son John into it. "Our entire stock of provisions consisted of three bushels of meal, and two little pigs," he later recalled. "Of furniture we

# The House of Joshua Thomas

*The House at left was Joshua Thomas Tangier Va*

This old house on West Ridge was said to have been built by the Parson of the Islands when he moved to Tangier in 1799.

Yet Joshua Thomas himself described his own house as "small," with a clay chimney. This house is large by early Tangier standards, and has brick chimneys located inside the frame structure, not attached to the outside, suggesting a later date of construction. In fact, this was probably not the home of the Parson but of one or both of his grandsons, Joshua Thomas II (1826?-1870?) or Lybrand H. Thomas (1838-1922).

The hand-printed inscription on this old photograph suggests how the mis-identification came about, for it identifies the Parson's home not as the one in the foreground, but as the old building to the left of it. That small, dilapidated house seems a much more likely candidate for the one built by the Parson. This is the only known picture of it; after its disappearance, the association of the site with Joshua Thomas remained, and became attached to the larger house.

When the older and smaller house disappeared is not known. The larger one stood until the 1980s, and was replaced by a modern house in the style of a chalet located at 4300 Joshua Thomas Lane.

had barely enough to make out with." But "when settled in my own home, I was a happy man. I used to watch the smoke curl up my clay chimney from the fire, as I lay in my bed, and it looked beautiful."[3]

When Joshua Thomas moved to Tangier, the inhabitants of the Tangier Islands were few in number — only 89 in 1800[4] — and dispersed into several communities.

On the eastern side of Tangier Sound, Watts Island had a population of 15, which consisted entirely of the family of Robert Parker and his five slaves.[5] Fox Island, also, was home to a single family, that of John Mason, whose descendants would live there for another half-century.[6] To the east of them, across Pocomoke Sound, lay Saxis Island, not one of the Tangier Islands, strictly speaking not even an island at all, for it was separated from the mainland not by water but by two miles of marsh. Yet that stretch of marshland made Saxis as remote from the mainland as Tangier or Watts, and functionally if not officially an island, more similar to its island neighbors than to the mainland to which it was attached. Like the other islands, it had been claimed in the late 1600s as pasture for livestock, and by 1800 its 35 residents consisted of only four households, three of them named Marshall.[7]

On the Virginia portion of Smith Island, Horse Hammock was still the home of the Tyler family, as it had been since the late 1600s. Hog Neck was now the home of John Parks (1756-1841?), whose house was right on the boundary, the main house in Maryland, the separate kitchen in Virginia; later Joshua Thomas would marry couples in either section of the house depending upon which state they wished to be married in.[8]

Just below Hog Neck, off the southwestern corner of Smith Island, lay Shanks Island, home since the 1770s of Richard Evans and his wife Molly, who was the daughter of Tangier's Joseph Crockett. The Evanses had nine children, who married into the other families of Tangier and Smith — Parks, Pruitt, Dise, Tyler — and then had large families of their own. Sons William and Richard II lived their entire lives on Shanks Island, where "Dicky" raised no fewer than 13 children. Daughter Rachel became the wife of Joshua Thomas. Though today little of Shanks Island remains, the large families who once lived there helped to people the surrounding islands.[9]

Even the very tiny islands of the region had owners, and sometimes inhabitants. In 1791 Richard Evans of Shanks obtained four such islands by warrant from the Governor of Virginia. When he had them surveyed, it was discovered that Queen's Ridge had 27 acres, Old Hearn Island eight acres, Rich Hammock seven acres, and Piney Island only five. Queen's Ridge was at that time virtually a part of Tangier itself, lying just off the eastern side of Goose Island, which the encroaching waters had not yet separated from Tangier. It alone of Evans' four islets had homes, and was by 1838 the home of Daniel Dise; whether it was settled as early

South Marsh
Island

Kedge's Straits

Tangier
Sound

Flat Cap Point

Annemessex River

Smith
Island

Janes
Island

Hog
Neck

Little
Annemessex River

Horse
Hammock

Shanks
Island

South
Point

Tangier
Sound

Cedar Straits

Fox
Island

Old Hearn Island

Piney Island

Pocomoke
Sound

Fishbone Island

Rich
Hammock

Goose Island

Queen's Ridge

Little
Fox Island

Black Walnut
Island

Tangier
Sound

Tangier
Island

Canton Ridge

Watts
Island

The
"TANGIER
ISLANDS"

Little
Watts Island

26

as when Joshua and Rachel Thomas moved to Tangier is not known.[10]

Black Walnut Island was the name then given to a part of Tangier, the section that would later become known as "Uppards." In 1805 it became the home of Job Parks II and his wife Rhoda, and the last four of their nine children were born there. In 1818 Parks sold the island to George Pruitt II, the respectable son of Joshua Thomas' alcoholic stepfather.[11]

On Tangier Island itself most of the few inhabitants lived on Canton Ridge. Joshua Thomas built on West Ridge, and was probably the first person to do so. Yet he was not far from his neighbors, for though his house was "quite near the water," he nonetheless had to pass the home of his uncle Levi Thomas to get to his boat. His uncle may have lived on the northern end of Main Ridge, which was the only part of the ridge with houses as late as the 1850s, when its southern end was known as "the Field."

Tangier had other patches of high ground, or "ridges," which were not yet settled in 1800 (see map page 106). A lane starting from the northwest corner of West Ridge led past Sheep Hill to Oyster Creek Ridge, which was settled by 1840. Joshua Thomas' seventy acres extended into this area, which has now been claimed by the Chesapeake.

At the northern end of Tangier, across "the Creek" which is today's main harbor, was the region known as Uppards. Here two separate but adjacent ridges would eventually support a community known as Canaan. To the east and south of Canaan was a smaller ridge later known as Rubentown. On the island that lies to the east of today's harbor would rise the small settlement known as East Point, the only Tangier "ridge" never connected to the others by bridge or road.

It is not certain when most of these other ridges were settled, and for many years to come the homes on Tangier Island would remain "comparatively few and far between." Joshua Thomas' house — small, with a chimney of clay, "inferior as to style and comfort" — was probably typical of the island homes of that day, which may have been built with wood from the island's own trees.[12]

Far from the centralized town of today, Tangier Island at the beginning of the 1800s was a series of scattered commuities whose people farmed the land and fished the waters. Islanders thought themselves to be a community without divisions or class distinctions. "When one neighbor wanted anything of another, he only had to say so and he got it, and when one lent another money there was no such thing as giving a note for it, each had confidence in the 'tother,' as they said."

Mainlanders, on the other hand, were looked upon as "rich people who thought themselves better" than others.[13] To many on the mainland the islanders must have seemed simple and rustic, as a story told about Joshua Thomas' stepfather illustrates. George Pruitt once took a basketful of fish to Onancock to sell to the prominent Col. Snead. When he was refused entry, he barged into the Colonel's dining room and sat uninvited at the breakfast table, "with his pants rolled up to his knees, and bare feet." The Colonel accused him of having "very little manners," but Pruitt replied, "Colonel, it's my opinion I have a good deal of manners, for I am sixty-two years old, and I have never used any yet. I must have a big pile somewhere." After breakfast Pruitt left, without having sold his basket of fish, but singing:

> Your shoes and stockings in your hand,
> and your bare feet on the ground,
> if you want to keep your credit up,
> why pay your money down.[14]

Already by 1800 fishing and oystering were a source of extra income, if not yet a full-blown industry, to the island farmers. Islanders also earned extra money by serving as pilots for mariners unfamiliar with the waters of the region. Joshua Thomas, at various times, engaged in both fishing and piloting. Another islander was engaged as a pilot by a captain from New England who was headed up Tangier Sound for a cargo of wood. When north of Smith Island, the captain pointed to land at what is now Little Deal Island (originally known as Little Devil's Island) and asked, "What land is that?"

"Little Devil's Island," answered the pilot.

A little further up the sound he pointed again, and asked again, "What land is that?"

"Devil's Island," answered the pilot.

Still further up the sound he pointed again, and asked, "What land is that?"

"Damned Quarter" [Dame's Quarter], answered the pilot.

"Ugh," said the captain. "Turn her around and go back, for Hell will be the next." And he headed down the Bay for Norfolk.[15]

Money was rare, and the islander who earned five or ten dollars by piloting was expected to provide a "spree" for his neighbors, complete with rum and dancing. Such merriments were probably not frequent, but it was not unknown for half a dozen islanders to sail up to Smith Island and dance all night. Young Joshua Thomas was a good dancer, and his cousin John Parks an accomplished fiddler.

Islanders who were generous with one another could also be candid to the point of bluntness: "If you stay I shall have to bake two johnny cakes, but if you go home I shall not bake but one" was the hint that it was time for a visitor to go. Doctors were unknown, and a number of women were practitioners of folk medicine: sheep tea for measles, poultice for sore throat, while for jaundice "nothing would do but to swallow seven live wood lice." And when at last an islander lay dying, his neighbors prepared the shroud and made the coffin.[16]

Though without a church, the Tangier Islanders were not without religion. In both Virginia and Maryland the Church of England was the "established" church, upheld by law and supported by taxes. Its ministers occasionally — "at long intervals" — visited the island and held services there, and islanders who found themselves on the mainland on

Sundays would occasionally attend Episcopal services at Annemessex Chapel in Somerset or at St. George's Church in Pungoteague. Joshua Thomas was raised in a God-fearing home, knew the Lord's Prayer, and often knelt in his boat to offer a prayer of thanksgiving when the fishing was especially good. He attended church at Annemessex Chapel more frequently than most other islanders. When he and Rachel were newly established in their home, he took his young son to the mainland to be baptized, where for want of an available Episcopalian he engaged a Presbyterian minister to do it. When Episcopal rector Joshua Reece agreed to come over to the island to conduct services, Joshua Thomas volunteered to ferry him from his home in Somerset County. And when on one such occasion Reece advised him to obtain a prayer book, he sent to Baltimore to purchase one, learned "by patient and painful application" to do a little reading, and began the practice of family devotions.[17]

Meanwhile over on the Eastern Shore a religious revolution was following the political revolution brought about by the War of Independence. A new faith had swept into the peninsula that would change Joshua Thomas and Tangier Island.

In 1776, when Joshua Thomas was born, there were only a few thousand Methodists anywhere in America, but the Delmarva Peninsula had already emerged as a region of Methodist strength. Strictly speaking the Methodists were not a new denomination but a lay movement within the Church of England, created by John Wesley to re-invigorate the church, but Methodism functioned more as a rival than an ally. It quickly took root throughout the peninsula, not only in communities that had been ignored by the Church of England but also in places where there were flourishing Episcopal churches. Its preachers were not properly educated gentlemen like many of the established clergy, but laymen who ventured on horseback into the furthest nooks and crannies of the countryside preaching to any who would listen. Its emphasis was not on the proper form of worship, but on each individual's personal relationship with God. Its appeal was not to the upper classes, who had traditionally attended the chapels of the established church, but to the common folk. Its theology was both simple and democratic: God's grace is free to all, and any who accept it can be changed by it into a new person. And it operated under the expectation that any who encountered and accepted God would most likely do so in a moving, perhaps spectacular inner experience.

In 1801, shortly after Joshua and Rachel Thomas moved to Tangier, a great revival broke out among the Methodists on the Delmarva Peninsula. The crowds that flocked to the small primitive meeting houses grew to number in the hundreds, even thousands, and in place after place the singing that began the services quickly turned to shouting. Worshipers fell out into dead faints, only to awaken to testify joyously and noisily to conversion. On the Eastern Shore of Virginia, where the population was fewer than 23,000, crowds at Methodist services numbered as high as 4,000, and in two years 1,090 people joined the Methodist Episcopal Church. In those same two years there were a thousand new members in Somerset County, and the Methodist preacher from Annemessex reported that "[Sinners] fall motionless, and lie for some minutes, others for hours...then they spring up with heaven in their eyes and music on their tongues."[18]

Suspicious as always of mainlanders, the islanders of Tangier "held themselves aloof" from the revival, not the least of them Joshua Thomas himself. Once when he had crossed over to the mainland to attend Annemessex Chapel, only to discover that the Reverend Reece was not preaching that day, he turned down an invitation to attend the new Methodist church in that community. "With a look of disdain...[he] seemed to say that he would not degrade himself so much as to enter the dreaded and despised place," and hurriedly headed for home "as if there was contamination in the neighborhood."[19]

Then in the summer of 1805 he found himself, somewhat by accident, at a Methodist "camp meeting" near Pungoteague. A camp meeting was a large outdoor gathering that lasted for several days, at which preaching occurred several times a day, while the people camped out for the duration. The Pungoteague camp meeting, one of three sponsored by the Methodists of the peninsula that year, was attended by over 3,000 people, and Joshua Thomas happened to be there only because he and John Crockett, youngest son of Tangier's first resident, agreed to pilot a boatload of people to the site.

Years later Joshua Thomas described what he saw at Pungoteague:

*There were a great many tents in a circle round, and seats made for people to sit on. There was a place built up with boards for the preacher to stand when he preached, and a great crowd of people moving about and talking together, while some were sitting in tents singing like the people on board the vessels.*

*Pretty soon they had preaching, and the most singular looking man I ever saw was the preacher that time. His name was Lorenzo Dow, and it was while he was preaching...[that] a woman became happy and shouted aloud, when he said 'The Lord is here! He is with that sister!' I jumped up to see him if he was there, but could not see anything extraordinary except the woman clapping her hands and saying 'Glory! Glory!' A great many people commenced crying and some fell to the ground, others were talking to them, and telling them to look to Jesus, and it was very soon a time of great confusion.*

Joshua Thomas was intrigued by such scenes, but his partner John Crockett was very uneasy, and eager to leave. "We must go," he insisted, "for if we stay here much longer there will be an earthquake, or something awful, and we shall all be destroyed."[20]

Later that summer when the Methodists held another camp meeting at Annemessex, Joshua Thomas was there, accompanied this time by islander John Parks. When Parks, who at first had been sceptical, was converted, Joshua Thomas began to pay even more serious attention. "I then began to feel very uneasy," he recalled, "and much concerned about being changed in heart."

> I felt so bad on Saturday night that I concluded I would go and kneel down with them at the mourners' seat and try it once, determined that I would not fall nor cry out as I had heard and seen others do. When praying persons came to talk with me, I would not let them, but rudely elbowed them off. I staid there some time, trying to pray secretly, until I became discouraged and concluded there was no reality in being converted, and so I arose and went away.

The next day he decided to put to the test one of the strange manifestations that seemed to accompany conversion:

> I went away into the woods again, a great way from the camp, the crowd, and noise, and...I concluded I would try what virtue there was in falling! So I looked me out a smooth place that was free from roots and sticks, that I might not hurt myself in the fall, and kept my eye a little over one shoulder to see how to fall and not hurt myself. I then came down full length on the earth. I lay about ten minutes, praying to God to convert me there; and receiving no answer, I arose completely discouraged, and very impatient besides.

But during the last sermon of the camp meeting, something happened to Joshua Thomas:

> I obtained faith that I should be converted.... I felt something drawing me right to the feet of Jesus. Immediately on the invitation being given, I went to the altar, and kneeled down and began to lift up my voice in earnest prayer.

Joshua Thomas was 29 years old when he was converted in the summer of 1805. It was an event that was to have immense and lasting effect on Tangier Island.[21]

When Joshua Thomas returned home to Tangier after his conversion, he met his wife outdoors on the path leading to the house, and no sooner had he told her the good news than he began shouting in joy, Methodist-style. "Leaping and praising God," he was soon running up and down the cornfield, and Rachel became alarmed, while a neighbor ran over to see what was the matter. The islanders were God-fearing folk, but this kind of noisy religion had never before been seen on Tangier.[22]

That first night, when things were calmer, he prayed with his family "for the first time without a [prayer] book," then began almost immediately to lay plans for prayer meetings among the the islanders. He called first upon Thomas Crockett, the island's reader, and insisted that they should call their neighbors together for worship, that Crockett should read from the Bible, and he would talk about religion and lead in prayer. Crockett was agreeable, and the next Sunday "all the people turned out — men, women, and children."

At the island's first regular worship service, Thomas Crockett read, John Parks prayed, Joshua Thomas wept, and the singing, praying, and exhortations that followed lasted six hours. On the second Sunday, they fasted before assembling. On the third Sunday, Thomas Crockett was reading as before, when "the power came, and his blind eyes were opened," and he fell to his knees and wept. Other converts followed, and the little congregation flourished.[23]

For three years the islanders met weekly without contact or help from the Methodists on the mainland, an island version of the "class meeting" which was then an important component of Methodist organization. On the mainland, Methodist ministers divided their flocks into small groups, or "classes," that met weekly to pray, share daily victories and temptations, uphold and rebuke one another, and to help each other "work out their own salvation." In the absence of the ministers, who often made the rounds between a number of congregations and could be away for weeks at a time, the responsibility for the spiritual supervision of the group fell to the "class leader," who was always a layman. The "class meeting" worked perfectly for isolated Tangier, which was not yet even on the rounds of the traveling preachers, and it was to survive on the island long after it had fallen into disuse elsewhere. Though they did not yet call themselves by that name, the members of the island congregation constituted a class, and though he was not known by that title, Joshua Thomas functioned as "class leader." Unlike his mainland counterparts, who could at times leave the responsibility for worship to the preacher, the island's class leader also conducted Sunday worship. In 1807 he managed to obtain a hymnbook, the island's first, and the singing grew even more spirited.

In the summer of 1808, two mainland ministers arrived on the island, the first contact with the Methodist churches on the Eastern Shore. William Seymour and William Lee were not ordained clergymen but "local preachers," laymen from Onancock whose field of labor was the necks and creeks, and now the islands, of the Bayside. They came to Tangier with a tent, which they set up in a grove of trees near Thomas Crockett's house, then sent out word across the islands that a "tent meeting" was about to be held. That Sunday the crowd of worshipers was larger than ever before, Seymour and Lee preached, the services lasted "both day and night," and eight or nine people were converted. "This was the most glorious day the island people had ever seen!" remembered Joshua Thomas. "Indeed, it was like a paradise below — a heaven on earth."

From the tent meeting at Tangier, revival spread northward to Smith Island. Joshua Thomas was among a number of people from Tangier who were present later that summer at a Smith Island prayer meeting when the number of worshipers was so large that many people stood outside the house, and the conversions so frightened some worshipers that they jumped out of the windows and ran away shouting that "the devil was there, and hard after them!" One of those who fled the meeting was Zachariah Crockett, who had run about two miles from the meetinghouse when he realized he had left behind his hat, and his wife. When he returned to reclaim them the meeting was still going on, his wife Polly was "down praying," and he himself fell to his knees and was converted. He later moved to Tangier, and became a pillar of the Methodist congregation there.[24]

The word of Tangier's tent meeting spread far and wide across the Chesapeake region, and the following year it was expanded into a "general camp meeting" which thereafter became an annual event. The camp meeting was a function of the circuit, with preaching by the circuit riders from the mainland, who by 1812 were holding "quarterly meeting" for all the churches at Tangier. The location was moved to the beach at the southern end of the island, where there was "a fine grove of wild cherry, cedar, and pine trees." Here the islanders built a bower for the preachers made from branches and poles, and rustic benches for the congregation. The person to whom the "chief management" of the event was entrusted was Joshua Thomas, and he became its most visible personality.

For almost half a century, from 1809 until 1857, people from all over the Chesapeake, from as far away as Baltimore and Norfolk, descended upon Tangier for the summer camp meeting, making its lonely stretch of beach one of the most beloved places in the region.[25] There was only one year during that period in which the camp meeting was not held — yet it was in that difficult year 1814 that Joshua Thomas preached the most famous sermon ever preached there, the sermon that was to make him a legend, and earn him the name of "the Parson of the Islands."

# 4
# Prisoners of War

On June 18, 1812, the United States declared war against Great Britain. Within two years Tangier Island would find itself in the center of the conflict, a player on the stage of war like no other Eastern Shore of Virginia community before or since.

On December 26, 1812, the British government issued a proclamation declaring a blockade of Chesapeake and Delaware Bays, and on February 4, 1813, the blockade began. Once again British ships roamed at will in the Chesapeake, raiding, burning, and disrupting shipping. By summer Georgetown and Fredericktown, Maryland, on the Eastern Shore, and Havre de Grace on the Western Shore had been burned. Though British attacks were turned back at St. Michaels and Norfolk, Hampton was sacked, Baltimore was threatened, and a British thrust up the Potomac River betrayed the vulnerability of the new capital at Washington.

That summer of 1813 the Methodists on the mainland decided against holding the annual Tangier camp meeting, concerned no doubt about the safety of those who would travel to and from it. Joshua Thomas was dismayed when he heard the news, and after the preachers and the Presiding Elder steadfastly refused his request to reconsider, he resolved to carry on without them, even if he had to be the principal preacher himself. He was not yet officially a preacher but an "exhorter," and the prospect of preaching filled him with fear and trepidation. But on the day the meeting was to begin, James Smith, the Presiding Elder himself, was traveling up the Bay when a dense fog forced him ashore on the island, and he was at the last minute persuaded to preach at what was almost certainly one of the smallest of the annual camp meetings.

Sometimes called the Second War of Independence, the War of 1812 was, in another context, an American extension of Europe's Napoleonic wars, and it was not until 1814, when Napoleon was nearing defeat in Europe, that England was able to step up its war effort in America. In the Chesapeake region this new, more intense phase of the war began with the occupation of Tangier Island. The choice of the island as a base was made in London by military strategists familiar since the American Revolution with its advantages: a central location in the Bay, water deep enough for large ships in Tangier Sound, and a ring of shoals and smaller islands to keep it safe from surprise attack.[1]

The British arrived at Tangier in late March 1814. "The first we knew of the British being nigh us," remembered Joshua Thomas, "was the report of their guns firing down the bay." Later that day, their ships anchored off Tangier, and a party of about fifty went ashore and marched in order towards the house of Zachariah Crockett.

"Our women and children were dreadfully scared," recalled the Parson, but he went out to meet the unwelcome visitors. "When I came near the officer, I pulled off my hat and he pulled off his, which I thought was very gentleman-like. I then approached him, and he held out his hand kindly, which I took, and we shook hands in a friendly manner."

But British manners could not obscure the gravity of the situation. The Parson was quickly and curtly informed that the islanders were prisoners of war, that Crockett's house was to be commandeered for use of the officers, and that the fleet had need of cattle, sheep, and hogs which the islanders would be required to supply. Though the Parson persuaded them not to turn Crockett and his family out of their house, the British returned to their ships the following morning with a good number of the islanders' livestock "for which they paid such price as they saw proper." The islanders watched them sail over to Watts Island, then northward out of sight, presumably to reconnoiter the other islands.[2]

Several days later, on April 5, 1814, the British returned and began to build a base not at Zachariah Crockett's house but on the beach at the southern end of the island, adjacent to the camp meeting ground. Under the supervision of an engineer named Fenwick, the troops leveled the area of its trees and built two breastworks about three hundred yards apart, mounted with eight 24-pound cannon. Between these "forts," tents were pitched in a semi-circle, and in the center was erected a building which probably served as a barracks. To make wells, they inserted open-ended wooden barrels into the ground one atop the other, and soon had an ample supply of fresh water.

All of this the islanders watched with interest, and when it appeared that the trees on the camp ground would also be leveled, Joshua Thomas determined to save them. He sailed out to the flagship *Albion*, anchored in Tangier Sound, boldly demanded to see the commander, and was shown into the presence of Rear Admiral Sir George Cockburn (1772-1853). The encounter must have been a remarkable one. Joshua Thomas was a barely literate waterman. Cockburn (pronounced "Co-burn") was a member of the British aristocracy, son of a lord, brother of a general and a duke. A portrait of him and his brothers as small boys, painted in 1773 by the renowned Sir Joshua Reynolds, hangs today in London's National Gallery. A daring "undaunted seaman," he was disdainful of Americans in general and of America's war effort in particular.

"Sir," the Parson began, "I have a request to make of you."

"*And who are you?*" the Admiral inquired. But he went with him over to the camp ground and was shown the preaching stand, the place where the worshipers pitched their tents, and the spot where mourners were prayed for.

"*Mourners,*" asked the Admiral, "how is that?" Yet despite native customs that he must have deemed strange, Cockburn acceded to the Parson's request, and ordered that not a limb be cut from the camp ground. "They all, after this, reverenced that ground," recalled the Parson, "and would not desecrate it in any way, or pitch a tent in it."[3]

By late June the British base included a hospital able to accommodate one hundred, a church, and about twenty houses "all laid out in streets" and connected by walkways. Large gardens with "vegetables of all sorts growing in perfection" flourished nearby, for the supply of the troops, and in the marshes grazed eighteen cattle commandeered but purchased from the islanders. The entire base was, in the opinion of Joshua Thomas, "a most lovely place. The fresh breeze would come in from the salt water and breathe through the grove, giving life and pleasure...while in other places the people were suffering greatly from the heat."[4]

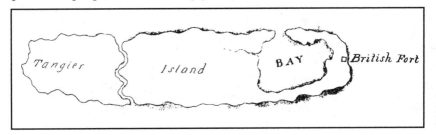

**The British Fort**
from John Wood's Map of Accomack County, 1820

On the Eastern Shore the authorities watched with both suspicion and alarm. Even while the base was being built on Tangier Beach, John G. Joynes of Onancock wrote to Lt. Col. Thomas M. Bayley, commander of the Accomack County militia (and member of Congress) to apprise him of the British ships anchored near Tangier. The largest ships included Cockburn's *Albion*, with 74 guns, an American vessel named *Chesapeake* which had recently been captured, the 50-gun *Armede, Towbridge*, and two frigates. In addition there were smaller vessels that included a brig, a sloop, a large schooner, and a number of tenders which, according to Joynes, "they have obtained from the Island people." The following day Bayley wrote to inform Governor James Barbour of the situation, and to report that he had ordered "all persons coming from the Islands to be detained" under the assumption that "men thus situated would give to the Enemy all the information they could." From the Eastern Shore the situation appeared grave, and to add insult to injury newspapers with the latest information from Washington were reaching the decks of the British ships at Tangier as much as four days before they reached the mainland!⁵

In May a British deserter brought news from Tangier that the Eastern Shore authorities found even more alarming: the British were not only encouraging slaves to escape, but also giving them refuge, and even training them for battle on Tangier.

As early as May 1813, even before Tangier was occupied, slaves of the Chesapeake region were welcoming the British invaders. In Kent Island, Maryland, and Princess Anne County, Virginia, slaves readily deserted in numbers, and many of those who fled from bondage on the Eastern Shore of Virginia proved to be useful to the British as pilots for the creeks and harbors along the coast. The loss of valuable slave property, coupled with the fear of uprising among the slave community, was a frightening prospect on the peninsula.

Now deserter David Hargraves confirmed all these fears. British boats had been gathering escapees by sailing close to the shore at night, signaling with a light, and leaving with as many as a hundred men, women, and children at a time. Many black women and children had already been sent to safety and freedom in Bermuda and Nova Scotia, and there were now no fewer than 700 black men on Tangier Island, helping to build the base and learning to use the musket.⁶

The confrontations the Eastern Shore had been dreading were not long in coming. On the afternoon of May 29, 1814, the *Albion* moved into position between Tangier and the peninsula, and that evening began to take on marines and sailors from barges that pulled up alongside from Tangier. The next morning, as the flagship lay offshore "decorated with a great number of elegant colors," eleven barges and launches entered Pungoteague Creek. The creek was guarded by two batteries, one on each bank, but the British were probably not aware that both of the defenses were small and outgunned. The battery on the south side of the creek (west of today's Harborton) had only one old cannon left over from the Revolution, while the battery on the northern bank was completely unmanned at the time.

On the morning of May 30, while the defenders on the south side of the creek watched helplessly, British barges disgorged approximately 500 men on the north bank, some of whom were highly-disciplined marines schooled in the European wars, about 30 of whom were blacks in full uniform, probably fresh from bondage. They advanced inland, the blacks in the front line, where awaiting them was a force of "about 25 old men" and a smaller number of militiamen who had rushed to the site.

The "Battle of Pungoteague" was one-sided and brief. The British opened fire, and their ships at the mouth of the creek backed them up with Congreve rockets — the latest in war technology, terrifying and deadly, though often less than accurate in aim. The Americans had only a single cannon. Though their ranks kept increasing in number, as other companies rushed to the scene, the defenders were forced to retreat. When Col. Bayley arrived with more reinforcements, the invaders were clearly in command of the field, and the single cannon had been abandoned to the enemy.

Then, surprisingly, a bugle sounded from the barges back in the creek, and the British began to fall back — their commanders had apparently seen Bayley's troops taking their place in the woods to their left and mistaken them for a larger force. By mid-morning the battle was over, and the British were headed back for Tangier. Left dead on the battlefield was one British soldier, a black man in full uniform, perhaps only recently escaped from slavery to Tangier. The Americans also found cutlasses, cartridges, and pistols abandoned by the British, and dressed beef which they had seized from a nearby house. Both sides claimed victory. Bayley reported to his superiors that the British retreated when they saw the full force of the American defenders gathering. The British records state simply: "The American surrendered."[7]

Less than a month later, British troops from Tangier tried another landing on the Eastern Shore, further up the peninsula on Chesconessex Creek. There the defenses consisted of 32 men with one cannon commanded by Capt. Thomas J. Joynes, and once again the invading force numbered 500 or more, and included black soldiers. With the British approaching from two directions, Joynes ordered a retreat, and abandoned breastworks, food, barracks, and cannon. The British burned the site, including the adjacent home of a farmer, before returning to their boats. The cannon lost here probably suffered the same fate as the one lost by the Americans at Pungoteague, which was taken to Tangier and mounted on the fort there.[8]

The residents of the Eastern Shore called them "battles," but such encounters were undoubtedly not so much military maneuvers as attempts to replenish the provisions for the British fleet and the base on Tangier. The British had larger plans and more important targets than the landings of the Eastern Shore. They were waiting for reinforcements from England before mounting an attack on Washington, the capital, and on Baltimore, one of the country's largest cities and the source of the privateers that preyed so successfully upon British shipping in the Atlantic.

The waiting grew difficult for the British troops. On June 20, a lieutenant and six crewmen were dispatched from the *Albion* to Watts Island, and once there the crewmen abandoned the officer, deserted, and headed for Chesconessex. They brought news of deteriorating conditions among the British on Tangier. The water in the wells on the beach had turned brackish, and many of the crews were sick. The crew of the flagship had only recently been paid, after being on short allowance for two months. The fort on Tangier Beach was not yet complete. Admiral Cockburn was said to be waiting to be relieved of his duty.

The islanders, meanwhile, had evolved a routine of peaceful, if not altogether comfortable co-existence with the occupying forces. Joshua Thomas was a frequent visitor and a familiar figure on the British flagship. The ship's doctor, having heard that his wife was ill, sent medicines which did her "a great deal of good," though Rachel Thomas died shortly thereafter. Among the troops were a number of enlisted men who were Methodists, products of the Wesleyan revival in England, and they enjoyed friendly relations with the islanders. The troops, for their part, did nothing to upset the islanders. When their own wells proved unusable and they had to walk to and from the wells of the islanders, they were always polite, and careful not to stray into fields and gardens.

Yet Cockburn had ordered that every man on the island be registered and all boats numbered, and he permitted no one to leave the island without a "passport." Even the Parson had to obtain the admiral's permission to attend a Methodist service on Smith Island. The islanders could do little but obey when the British ordered them to corral their cattle, then selected the ones they wanted for their own use. At such times they would pay "a fair price," and even an extra two or three dollars to the owner's wife if the butchering were done swiftly, but "it took a great deal of grace to love these enemies." On at least one occasion Cockburn attempted to engage Joshua Thomas in a debate about the war. Replied the Parson: "How should I know about things done in Washington or England, seeing I live on this little island so far from those places; and how can I know about the king's business, or [President] Madison's business?"[9]

To the mainland authorities the islanders' accommodation with the British bordered on treason. Having received reliable information that the islanders were supplying the British with seafood, and "that it is a voluntary act on their part," Col. Bayley "refuse[d] permission to the islanders from coming to the main[land], and hope[d] thereby to cut off all intercourse." He further ordered that "all of the canoes and boats within the limits of my Regiment on the sea and bay shores...be taken from their owners and secured." Though he recognized that this order was "very severe upon the poor who supply their families by fishing," he deemed it necessary to keep slaves from fleeing to the enemy, and the enemy from obtaining provisions from the locals. In June he arrested Middleton Mason of Fox Island and James and Josiah Parker of Watts Island when they crossed over to the mainland. Two were promptly released, having been determined to be "ignorant of orders," but Josiah Parker was detained. "I have no doubt of his improper intercourse with the enemy," Bayley reported to the Governor, adding, "It now appears that my suppositions against...the inhabitants of Tangier are well founded."[10]

The wait ended in August, when Vice Admiral Sir Alexander Cochrane (1758-1832) arrived in the Chesapeake with an even larger fleet bringing an even larger corps of soldiers. Cochrane, though now the overseer of the entire war effort in America, was less a military man than a career administrator, at one time a member of Parliament. He despised Americans, had already issued orders to British vessels blockading the

American coast to "destroy and lay waste such towns and districts...as you may find available," and was convinced that the Chesapeake region "might be restored to the dominion of Great Britain, if under the command of enterprising generals." His flagship *Tonnant* brought over 4,000 soldiers, and he rendezvoused with Cockburn on August 14, 1814.

The situation now appeared even more grim to the Eastern Shore. Bayley's informant on Tangier (an "old gentleman" who has never been identified) reported that the force at the fort had risen to 1,500 blacks and 500 marines. Three brigs and twelve schooners lay near Tangier, in addition to the larger ships of Cochrane and Cockburn and their attendants. Clearly something was up, and Bayley informed the Governor of his opinion that "the object of the Enemy was to burn Onancock Town."[11]

But on the very day that Bayley was writing to the Virginia governor, an express rider galloped into Washington, D.C., with the news that the huge British fleet had entered the Patuxent River and was headed for the capital. Six days later, having vanquished the American defenses that hastily formed to stop them, four thousand British soldiers under General Robert Ross entered Washington from the east. Within hours President James Madison had fled, and the Capitol, Arsenal, Treasury, War Office, and White House were in flames.[12]

After the capture and burning of Washington, the British returned to Tangier and began preparing to strike their next target.

"Towards the close of summer, in the year 1814," recalled Joshua Thomas, "we were made aware of some important movement among the forces encamped on the island. Preparations began both on shore and through the fleet in the harbor. Signals were exchanged, orders were given, and all became bustle and activity."

When he learned from some of the officers that they were headed for Baltimore, the Parson tried to dissuade them. "I told them they had better let it alone; they might be mistaken in their calculations, for the Baltimoreans would resist them, and would fight hard for their city and their homes." Furthermore, "God would fight for the good people in that city, and aid them in defeating their enemies."

Despite his vocal opposition to the upcoming expedition, Joshua Thomas soon received word from the British leaders that their troops would assemble on the camp ground on the Sunday before departure, and that he was to hold a worship service and address them. Surprised, and at first unwilling, he decided after much prayer to accept the "invitation," reasoning that "some of these men might be killed in battle, and never have another opportunity of worship."

On Sunday, September 11, 1814, the southern end of Tangier Island buzzed with activity. Offshore lay the British fleet in full regalia, and from some of the ships wafted the music of their bands playing for the occasion. On the shore flags waved in the breeze as islanders gathered on the camp meeting ground — it was about two weeks later than the camp meeting would have convened, had it been held that year — while British troops filed in to a drum beat from the adjacent base. Once assembled, the crowd numbered in the thousands — 12,000 according to Joshua Thomas, though Cochrane's soldiers, Cockburn's marines, and the newly trained black troops probably totaled only about half that number. The sandy spit of land, larger then than it is today, had probably never held so large a crowd, though the attendance at some future camp meetings would rival it in size.

At the appointed hour, Parson Thomas mounted a small platform at the end of the camp nearest the shore, and faced row upon row of soldiers standing in formation, "all the men facing me with their hats off, and held by the right hand under the left arm." An English officer stood on either side, and sentries a little to the rear of the platform.

"As I looked around on my congregation," he remembered later, "I never had such feelings in my life; but I felt determined to give them a faithful warning, even if those officers with their keen glittering swords would cut me in pieces for speaking the truth." But after prayer and a little singing, Joshua Thomas warmed to his task and spoke "as freely as ever I did" to any ordinary group of Methodists.

He began by telling them what causes war, "what made this once

**Joshua Thomas Preaching to the British Army**
September 11, 1814

41

good, happy world so full of evil and misery as it is now...*Sin*, I said, done all this." He went on to tell them how he had once been a sinner, and urged them to turn from their sins. He repeated the commandment "Thou shalt not kill," and exhorted them to embrace salvation, lest death be waiting for them in battle. And then "I told them it was given me from the Almighty that they *could not* take Baltimore, and *would not succeed in their expedition*."

Unlike most of the rest of his exhortation, that prediction was not standard Methodist fare. Nor was it a safe prediction to make, since the British had already taken Washington and must have appeared invincible. But he said it not once but several times — *"You cannot take it!"* — and confessed later that he had not planned to say it, that it just "came to him." If the British considered such talk subversive or demoralizing for their troops, they let it pass; no officer stepped forward to cut him in pieces with a keen glittering sword.

When the sermon wound to a close, and people came up to him to talk to him about it, he was still saying it: *"You cannot take it!"* Some of the troops expressed the hope that he would be proved wrong, but "he shook his head, and said he felt that many that day had received their last call."[13]

Soon afterward the fleet weighed anchor and "with pennants streaming and decks bristling with the machinery of war" headed up the Bay for Baltimore. There on September 12 through 14, 1814, British land and naval forces launched an attack upon the city. On the first day of the battle, General Robert Ross, commander of the British land forces, was killed. On the second day, Francis Scott Key, detained aboard a British vessel in the harbor, watched anxiously while bombs rained down on Fort McHenry, then finally "in the twilight's last gleaming" glimpsed the American flag flying over the fort. On the third day, as he penned the words to "The Star-Spangled Banner," the British withdrew, and Baltimore stood unbowed.[14]

Back on Tangier, people waited with "sleepless eagerness" for news of the struggle, and when the fleet returned to the island Joshua Thomas was among the first to meet them. "We have had a bloody battle," reported the officers, "and all the time we were fighting we thought of you, and what you told us. You seemed to be standing right before us, still warning us against our attempt to take Baltimore."[15]

Hardly were they back at Tangier before most of the British forces left the Chesapeake. By mid-October over one hundred ships were far out in the Atlantic headed for home. The small force left behind on Tangier was still able to make its presence felt and feared. Captain Robert Barrie, aboard the *Dragon*, led a squadron north to the narrowest part of the Bay, between the Choptank and Patuxent Rivers, and there established a blockade. On October 19 the British made a brief landing in Dorchester County, Maryland, where a few weeks later the local militia managed to seize another British ship after it had run aground. By late November the squadron was back at Tangier, still in control of the Bay and still able to

# Elizabeth Kelly

### 1796-1910
### Eyewitness to the Parson's Famous Sermon

Elizabeth Kelly was there when Joshua Thomas preached to the British in 1814 — and was still telling people about it almost a century later.

The daughter of "Young Dicky" and Rachel Evans, Elizabeth Evans was born on Smith Island in 1796 and was 18 in the year the British occupied Tangier. She claimed to have prepared bird pie, a local delicacy, for some of their officers, and was present on the day the Parson preached to their troops.

Hers is the only account of that day that does not come from the reminiscences of Joshua Thomas himself, and it contains one embellishment that even the Parson did not claim. According to her, he not only told the British that "You cannot take Baltimore, the Almighty God has told me so!" but also "If you attack that city, as I understand you are going to do, you will not only suffer defeat, you will lose your best general!" Not even the Parson claimed to have predicted the death of General Ross.

Eleven years later, when she was by the standard of that day a "spinster," she married Elijah Spence, a man of ill-temper who one day went off to Baltimore and never came back. In 1855 she married widower Daniel John Kelly, and moved with him to the mainland, where they lived near Wachapreague.

In the early 1900s she recounted the story of the sermon to Sidney R. Spence (1897-1975), and in 1960 he submitted it, with her photograph, to *Together* magazine, a Methodist publication.

She died in 1910 at the age of 114, having lived in three centuries, and was buried in an unmarked grave on North Street just outside of Onancock.[16]

harass the mainland.

The War of 1812 came officially to an end with the signing of a treaty of peace in Ghent, Belgium, on December 24, 1814. The news of peace took weeks to cross the Atlantic, and did not arrive in New York City until February 11, 1815. By then Tangier Island already knew it, for the island was one of the first places in the nation to learn of peace.

"In the month of January, 1815," according to Joshua Thomas, "we perceived a mighty stir in the [British] camp one day, and witnessed signals flying and great commotion on ships and shore. We could not tell what it meant for some time. By and by, one of the officers came riding up to my house as hard as he could gallop, crying out, 'Oh! Parson Thomas! Parson Thomas! *There's peace!* THERE'S PEACE!!' I inquired, 'How do you know?' 'Oh!' said he, 'yonder is the ship,' pointing down the bay to where a large vessel was seen coming up, 'and she has a white flag at her mast head. That signal means peace, and now we know the war is over!'"

Congress ratified the Treaty of Ghent on February 12, and later that month the British left Tangier. According to Joshua Thomas, the scene was more like the parting of friends than the ending of war:

"As the ponderous men-of-war piped to weigh anchor for the last time, we all were gathered on the beach to return their waving farewell.... Many tears were shed between us as we took the parting hand[shake], for though in general they were enemies to our beloved country, we found many of them [to be] friends...."[17]

When in late summer of 1815 the Methodists gathered once again at the camp meeting ground, the British base adjacent to it was a major attraction. Cannon, including two captured on the Eastern Shore of Virginia, had been stripped and carried away, and none of the wooden buildings remained, but the embankments which had housed the two forts were still very much in evidence, and there were a number of graves "along the shore to the south, where many of their dead had been buried." The crowds who gathered "wonderingly listened while Brother Thomas recounted the history of the past few years on that remarkable spot."

It was during the previous summer of 1814, when the camp meeting could not be held because the British were putting the finishing touches on the base, that Col. Bayley on the mainland was already proposing that Tangier might someday be strategic to the American military. "In case of peace and the Enemy should abandon Tangier and not destroy his camp, it will be valuable," he wrote to Virginia Governor Barbour. "I expect he will give it to the Islanders. Shall it be taken possession of for the State of Virginia, or the U.S., and by whom?"

Late in 1815 the U.S. Senate passed a resolution urging the Navy to examine several places around Chesapeake Bay as a potential site for a naval base. Tangier was among the places to be considered, the British fortifications there to be surveyed for whether they could be used to advantage. The surveying party that later came to Tangier was not impressed with its possibilities. The fort's embankments were still in place, but equally as prominent were the British graves ("monuments of death") at the site. The Navy advised against locating the proposed base at Tangier, and it was constructed instead at Norfolk.

The "British fort" on Tangier Island shows clearly on a map of Accomack County published by a man named John Wood in 1820, but that is its last known appearance.[18] The following year a tremendous hurricane swept over Tangier Island, and by mid-century the site lay completely under water.

By then, the Parson of the Islands and his sermon with its remarkable prediction were virtually legend up and down the Chesapeake. The story, if not the site, survives.

# Place of Pilgrimage

The vessel that put into Norfolk on May 24, 1815, was small compared to the British warships that sailed from the Chesapeake only three months before. Though little more than a barge, its open deck sheltered by a canopy, the *Washington* made a big impression in Hampton Roads, where local newspapers called it "beautiful" and "elegant," and citizens were "highly gratified" to see what it could do.

The *Washington* was a steamboat, the first ever seen at Norfolk. It was bound for Washington, where it was to ply the Potomac, but Norfolk's own steamer, the *Eagle*, arrived the following month, and on June 19 inaugurated regular passenger service between that city and Baltimore. The *Eagle*, also, had an open deck, and the papers pronounced it, also, "spacious and elegant."[1]

It was only eight years since Robert Fulton had demonstrated the viability of the steamboat. The age of sail was far from dead, but the steamboat was about to revolutionize travel on the Chesapeake. Though the early steamers were often primitive affairs, prone to mishap and far from their attractive and comfortable counterparts of the latter part of the century, they were not dependent upon winds, and could maintain a fixed schedule when sailing vessels could not. Within a few years all the major cities of the Chesapeake, and many of the smaller points on the Western Shore, had regular freight and passenger service by steamboat.

Not until 1838 did regular steamboat service find its way to the rural and more isolated Eastern Shore of Virginia, and not until after the Civil War to the even more isolated and rural Tangier Island. But the earliest known reference to any steamboat at any Eastern Shore of Virginia port is from 1820, and that port was Tangier.

It was the camp meeting that first brought the steamboats to Tangier. By 1820 those attending the annual Methodist event were coming from as far away as Norfolk, and in that year a city newspaper advertised that "The Steam Boat *Powhatan* proposes to accommodate those who may be disposed to attend." The steamer plied between Norfolk and Tangier every day during the camp meeting, left at 6:00 a.m. each morning, and on the way stopped at Old Point Comfort to pick up additional passengers. A round-trip ticket cost $2, and meals 50¢ and 75¢.

**Camp Meeting on the Chesapeake**
No picture of the Tangier Camp Meeting is known, but it probably looked much like the Deal Island Camp Meeting, pictured here.

The next summer the steamboat *Virginia* offered the same excursion for the same price. The *Virginia*, 158 feet long, 26 feet wide, burned wood for fuel, and had three masts for sails, in case the fuel gave out; she was later the first steamboat to be in regular service to the Eastern Shore of Virginia.[2]

The Tangier camp meeting grew rapidly in renown in the years following the War of 1812. The first record of attendance at the event is from 1821, when a Norfolk newspaper reported that there were over 400 boats docked in the harbor, over 264 tents pitched on the camp ground, and between 5,000 and 6,000 people present.[3] As its fame increased, what had begun as a religious service became increasingly a festive social event. The meeting had always attracted not simply the devout but also the merely curious, and the Methodists had always tolerated a certain amount of commercialism, such as the sale of food for those participating in the services. As the years passed, attending the camp meeting became, for many, less a religious pilgrimage than a vacation opportunity, and many people would "charter a vessel, provide themselves with fishing apparatus, and take an excursion for pleasure and health, timing their trip to the week of the camp." "Hucksters" from the larger towns and cities descended on the island for the event, and the annual array of goods for sale around the edge of the camp grew to include not simply food but also pots and pans, hardware, wood, dry goods, and clothes.

One year the booths and stalls of the hucksters attracted so much business that attendance at the preaching services fell off, and the preachers began to complain about it in their sermons. Joshua Thomas resolved to take care of the "shore folk," as he called them, and when the next preaching service started, he remained outside the camp, mounted a vacant table in the midst of the traders, blew "a sharp blast on a tin horn," and announced that those who wanted to hear a "fine discourse" should take their seats in the camp, for he was going to preach to any that remained outside. If his intent was to scare them into the camp he failed, for a crowd gathered around him, and he ended up conducting his own meeting outside, at which three were converted. As a result of his efforts, that year's tradesmen agreed that they would close their booths when the preaching services began.

Far more distressing to the Methodists was the appearance of the "abomination of liquor," which "despite the utmost vigilance" on their part was inevitably available for purchase on the fringes of the camp ground. On a number of occasions someone under the influence of liquor would start a fight at the edge of the camp, or even interrupt the preaching services. The Methodists maintained their own makeshift "jail" for such miscreants. One such troublemaker, the son of an influential family, was ushered out of the meeting by the "managers," and hours later an angry group of his friends, swearing and "all ready for fight," appeared upon the scene to rescue him. They found him not in the jail, but in Parson Thomas' tent, sleeping it off on the Parson's own cot, while Mrs. Thomas (Charlotte "Lottie" Bradshaw Thomas, the Parson's second wife, whom he married less than a year after Rachel's death) sat there fanning him in the summer heat. In 1828, when the Methodists advertised the camp meeting in the Norfolk papers, they included the warning that "All persons are forbid the carrying of spirituous liquors for sale, as such trade will be put a stop to if possible." Eighteen years later the annual announcement declared that "All huxtering and traffick are forbidden," but it is doubtful that either decree had much effect, and likely that the Methodists never succeeded in ridding the event of commercialism.[4]

In 1828 a young Eastern Shore lawyer

**Henry A. Wise**

on his way to Baltimore happened by Tangier during the camp meeting. Henry A. Wise (1806-1876) would later have a distinguished career as

Congressman, U.S. Minister to Brazil, Confederate General, and the only Governor ever to hail from the Eastern Shore of Virginia. A sophisticated Episcopalian not given to noisy forms of worship, Wise was nonetheless fascinated by the "variety of strange scenes" he witnessed at Tangier: quiet meditation next to "a loud-mouth braying of hymns," powerful preaching followed by "*chasséing* shouters, cutting in and out...in a mazy dance of praise," the quiet of the sleeping camp at night while around its fringes "drinking, fiddling, dancing and...shameful frolic" held sway until dawn. Even while services were going on, hucksters peddled "chicken pies, and barbecued, broiled, fried, and boiled fish, and peaches and melons and cantaloupes, cider, crabs, and ginger-cakes, June apples, lemonade, and ice-cream." And, warned Wise, "If you cannot find religion, you may — and if not on guard, you will — lose your purse, for camp meeting time is always a time for...picking and stealing in the midst of the crowded camp...."[5]

Small wonder that the camp meeting was nothing less than a "jubilee" to the islanders themselves, who looked forward to it with eager anticipation and talked about it enthusiastically long after it was over. For all its popularity during that one week each summer, Tangier Island itself was still a small and isolated community. In 1821, when thousands gathered on the beach for preaching, the island's population totaled only 74. Even Wise was impressed by the evening worship sessions, when campfires and torches reflected off the waters, and hymns "came softly stealing by moonlight o'er the mirrored bay." The islanders, also, found the worship services moving and memorable.[6] Though there is no record that the locals patronized the hucksters to purchase some of their goods, the likelihood is that many of the wares peddled on the beach each August were appealing to an isolated community so small that it did not yet have a general store. In all, the worship services, the goings-on around the edge of the camp, and the annual influx of visitors from far away must have been, for the islanders of Tangier, the high point of every year.

On September 3, 1821, only two weeks after the camp meeting crowds had dispersed for that year, Tangier Island was struck by the worst hurricane in its history.

The "Great September Gust," as it came to be known, passed over the Bahamas on or about the first day of September, and raced inland upon the continental United States near Cape Hatteras at daybreak on September 3. At 11:30 a.m. it swept over Norfolk, wreaking extensive damage that totaled over $200,000. As it moved up the coast, the eye of the storm passed straight up the Eastern Shore of Virginia. On the Seaside, storm tides surged over the Barrier Islands, while on the Bayside even large sections of the mainland lay completely under water.

Sugar Tom Crockett was not yet born when the storm hit, but he undoubtedly heard many an account of it and described it in his history of the island: "The wind blew a storm from the east and the southeast" until shortly after midnight of September 3, when "suddenly the wind changed to northwest, and blew a perfect hurricane...." With the winds came a tide that has not been equaled since: "The hurricane brought the salt water from the Chesapeake Bay over the Island until it covered the Island. Even the highest land had three feet of water over it" for a period of three hours.

"This deluge of salt water on the land made the poor Islanders feel sad at heart, thinking their land was ruined, and supposing they would not be able to raise any more wheat, corn or potatoes, as they had been doing every year before. But Joshua [Thomas] soon came to their rescue. He called the people together and told them they should not fear for, said he, 'The Lord knoweth what things ye need, and His Word says the right-eous shall never be forsaken, nor their seed beg bread.' And the people took courage, and they went to work covering their land with drift and sea ordure and everything of the manure kind, and the next spring, 1822, they ploughed and planted their lands, and cultivated all summer, as they had done years before, and the result was they raised the best crop they had ever raised in all their lives...."[7]

The Parson who rallied the islanders in 1821 was gone by 1825. In that year, for reasons that no writer of that period bothers to explain, he took up residence on Deal Island in Maryland. He was, by then, a Deacon in the Methodist Episcopal Church, having been ordained at some point before 1823, and it was probably to function more fully in that capacity that he made the move. Once there he became "a worthy successor" to the late Reverend David Wallace of that place, and "began to extend his labors and visits far into the interior of the country." Eventually he acquired a sturdy canoe, which he re-christened *The Methodist*, and with it he "navigated the winding rivers [to be] present at every quarterly or camp meeting within a wide circle," and made himself a fixture of an even wider landscape than Tangier. [8]

The Methodist congregation he left behind was quite small: 18 peo-ple in 1825. Because there was not yet a church building, Sunday services, both morning and evening, and Thursday night prayer meetings rotated among the homes of the believers. To this small group fell the annual duty of preparing the ground for the camp meeting, a three-day task that included laying out the "streets" that separated the seating areas, repair-ing the benches, and making the bower that sheltered the preaching stand. Though Joshua Thomas was long remembered as the foremost fig-ure of the Tangier camp meeting, it was only in 1821 and 1823 that he was officially designated by the mainland Methodists to oversee it, and though after 1825 he was often present, it was not as superintendent but as visitor.[9]

After the Parson's departure, the leadership of the Methodist band fell to Zachariah Crockett (1760?-1844), a "godly and zealous man" who was licensed as an exhorter in 1823. A second generation of leaders was

# Zachariah Crockett
## 1760?-1844
### Head of the Church

When Joshua Thomas moved from Tangier, his mantle as "head of the church" — class leader — fell upon the "impetuous" Zachariah Crockett.

Eighth of the ten children of Joseph, Zachariah Crockett was born on Smith Island before his father became the first settler of Tangier. He was living there still in 1808 when he and his wife were converted under the preaching of David Wallace at a prayer meeting at the home of his father-in-law "King" Richard Evans.

Exactly when Zachariah and Polly moved to Tangier is uncertain, but it was prior to 1814, for their house in Canton narrowly escaped being commandeered as the British headquarters. He was licensed as an Exhorter in the Methodist Episcopal Church in 1823, and two years later he and his wife were listed among the eighteen members of the Tangier congregation. It was in that year that Joshua Thomas moved away, and Crockett assumed the leadership.

Crockett was "a godly and zealous man...of great earnestness, who commanded the respect and love of all about him." "How well I remember," wrote Sugar Tom Crockett, "seeing old Mr. Zachariah Crockett coming over the marsh on Sunday morning with his Bible and hymnbook tied up in a handkerchief." On such days "a curious death-like stillness would prevail" when all were assembled for worship, until Zachariah broke it by "lining out" the hymn that preceded his exhortation.

Crockett's "ardent, impulsive temperament" is illustrated by an incident that occurred when Joshua Thomas lay sick and requested him and his brother John to anoint him with oil, as in Biblical days. Since no oil was available, the Parson proposed that they use goose grease instead. John Crockett was aghast at this suggestion, but Zachariah readily anointed the Parson with "an unctuous application of the goose grease," knelt in prayer, and began to shout, whereupon "Brother T....leaped from his weary bed, cured in body and filled with the Holy Ghost."

Crockett was the father of eight, and a farmer. He died in late 1843 or early 1844, and at his death the mantle of leadership fell upon the Parson's son John Thomas.[10]

also stepping forward. George Pruitt II, the son of Joshua Thomas' step-father, joined the congregation in 1827 and "though he could not read a word proved to be a very useful man." Pruitt was said to have prayed more often than any other person who had ever lived on the island. John Thomas (1799-1865), oldest son of the Parson, joined the band in 1829. He often had new hymns to teach the congregation, learned on the frequent visits he made to Baltimore to sell seafood, for he was one of a growing number of islanders who made his living on the water.[11]

Had the Great September Gust spoiled the fertility of Tangier's soil, it would have been a major catastrophe for islanders who still raised much of their own food. Yet by 1820 agriculture was no longer the predominant occupation on Tangier, for the census of that year reveals that already it had been surpassed by "commerce." Though the word "commerce" is undefined in the census, on Tangier Island it undoubtedly included fishing, for in the early nineteenth century the islanders began to see the bounty of the waters around them not simply as food for their own tables but also as a product for export and a source of income.[12]

The beginnings of the oyster industry on the Chesapeake reach back to the period between the two wars with England. As Baltimore's population grew rapidly after the Revolution, and hungry for seafood, Tangier Sound emerged as its principal source of oysters. But oysters were harvested by the slow and laborious process of tonging, and for the most part the watermen of the region tonged for oysters only when they felt like it.

Meanwhile the oyster beds of New York and New England had become unproductive, and in 1811 vessels from that region entered the Chesapeake in search of greener pastures. They brought with them the very device that had depleted their own oyster beds, the "dredge," which scraped from the bottom masses of oysters that were beyond the reach of the tonger. Virginia passed the nation's first conservation law in that year, outlawing the use of the oyster dredge, but the legislation proved to be of little avail. The dredge was quickly adopted, and with not only Baltimore but also New York, Philadelphia, and New England calling for oysters, what had begun as a casual, part-time source of income for watermen became a profitable full-time profession. By the 1830s the Chesapeake was experiencing "a general migration of New England seafood brokers," and within 30 years the Bay was producing nearly half the world's oysters.[13]

With the increase of such traffic on the Bay came the region's first lighthouses. The first on the Tangier Islands was built in 1827 at Fog Point, on the northwest corner of Smith Island, well into Maryland. The second was erected east of Tangier, at the point where Tangier Sound and Pocomoke Sound converged. In 1832 Josiah Parker of Watts Island sold to the Federal government the seven acres known as Little Watts Island, and here in 1833 John Donohoo erected a 48-foot masonry lighthouse and an adjacent home for the lighthouse keeper. The Watts Island lighthouse cost $4,735, but was described as "neglected and filthy" only seven years later by the captain of the lighthouse service supply boat.[14] Yet it was an important aid to navigation, and for more than a century a landmark to Tangier watermen and residents alike, who could see its beam from their island home.

Tangier Island shared in the new prosperity. "I have seen fourteen New York and New Haven vessels at anchor on the Oak Hammock Rock at once," observed Sugar Tom Crockett, "all with flags flying at the same time, which was telling the people, as plain as if words had been spoken, that their captains wanted to buy oysters." Islanders who worked the water for oysters could now earn more money in three days than they could previously have earned in a month, and the islanders often agreed among themselves that being surrounded by oysters was like having "a 'smoke house' and 'corn stack' before their doors."

One result of the new business of seafood was a steady increase in the population of the island, as outsiders moved in to participate in the boom, and young Tangiermen found themselves better able to start families earlier. In 1820 Tangier's 74 residents consisted of ten families named Crockett, two named Parks, plus one household each of Pruitt, Paul, Shores, and Thomas. By 1850 the island had 178 residents, and by 1860 it had 411, an increase of more than 500% in four decades. As outsiders began to move in, often because they had married into island families, new names appeared: Dise (as early as 1825), Powell (1825), Spence (1860), Charnock (1860). One new family line was established by Joseph L. Cooper (1839-1917), who was born in England and probably came to the island as early as 1857. Family tradition insists that he was the only educated man on the island, and the son of one of the British naval officers who had occupied the island in 1814. Another person known to have come to Tangier in the 1850s was Catherine Cutler Sturgis (1811-1865), a widow. By 1860 there were 39 island residents who were born outside of Virginia, 36 of them in Maryland, one in England. The population in that year also included six black residents.[15]

The new prosperity also manifested itself in the building of the island's first church. "Islanders had begun to go to the cities and elsewhere," reports Tom Crockett, "and they learned more of the world and how other people were doing, some of them had made some money, and they began to think of having a church built, which was a wonderful undertaking, as they thought, for they were poor." The congregation decided to build in 1835, and by the fall of 1838 the new church was complete. It was a frame building 18 feet square, made inside and out of lumber full of knot-holes (which later fell out, leaving holes in the walls). There was a single door, two windows, and no floor, only sandy ground. The pulpit was "box shape," the pews "rude constructed benches" without backs, and eight feet from the ground on the wall next to the pulpit was a row of pegs "to hang your hat on." Even so, wrote Crockett, "I doubt whether the completion of Solomon's Temple was looked forward to with more anxiety than was the completion of that little rough house." The new church was proudly named "Lee's Bethel," in honor of William Lee, one of the ministers who had conducted the first camp meeting. It stood twenty yards east of John C. Crockett's house, a site which cannot be determined with certainty, though a granite marker on the edge of the burial ground in Canton marks the probable site.[16]

Two years later another landmark appeared when John Thomas opened the first store on the island. Built in 1840, the store stood in Oyster Creek, on lands which Thomas had bought from his father when the Parson moved away. Thereafter John Thomas listed himself as merchant, the island's first, and enjoyed prominence in both church and community.[17]

Slowly, not always surely, the first evidences of a town emerged as the islanders, isolated and poor by many standards, enjoyed a prosperity and a contact with the outside world they had never known before. The first, though unsuccessful, attempt at public education was a Sunday school which the Methodists opened in 1845. Its curriculum included used spelling books, for if islanders were going to learn to read the Bible, they had first to learn to read. Though the effort began promisingly with 17 scholars and four teachers, it was apparently short-lived, "on account of the teachers having to go off by water." In 1847 the island's first public school opened after a new state law allowed localities to create school districts and John Thomas was appointed to a district for the island. This too proved to be short-lived, and there is no record of it beyond that first year. Thomas Crockett, who was 14 in that year, had to "learn to write on the smooth sand along the bayshore of Tangier Island with my finger." Another attempt at a Sunday school was made in 1856 by Catherine Sturgis, assisted by several others including Lewis Crockett (1811?-1882?), grandson of Joseph. This effort was successful, and created the only education available on the island until the establishment of the public school system in the 1870s.

Up until 1850 any islander who chose to vote had to travel to Onancock to do so, but in 1853 Tangier was made a voting precinct. Mainlander Henry A. Wise was probably politicking when he returned to Tangier in the late 1840s — he had by then served in Congress and in Brazil — and it is testimony to the island's contact with the outside world that he was sufficiently well-known to be recognized by sight by Tom Crockett's mother, who was sufficiently mannered in his presence to eat her chicken with knife and fork and not with fingers.[18]

Yet always the center of the island's life, its most visible symbol of progress and change, was the church. Lee's Bethel was improved by the addition of a wood stove in 1840, given by a Negro captain named Scott from the Pocomoke River who often stopped by the island and visited the church. "The church was then made so comfortable that it would be full in winter," remembered Sugar Tom Crockett. Scott was not the only outsider who assisted the church, for "some of the captains of those [northern] vessels were very good Christians, and they would come to the church on Sabbath and render excellent service by singing and prayer." Particularly remembered was a Captain Willett, who was "a powerful exhorter." Such visitors frequently helped the church financially, and spread word of the Tangier camp meeting as far as New York and other cities of the North.

Preaching by the itinerants from the mainland circuit was still irregular, and their arrival was announced by running a flag up a pole in front of the church. In 1840 a mainland preacher named Cosney spoke to a full house, and the following year a revival repeatedly drew crowds larger than the building could accommodate. In the spring of 1842 the congregation decided to build again. Severn Crockett (1811-1875) was dispatched to the Potomac River to purchase the lumber, and upon his return the islanders met him in their canoes to bring it ashore. The materials were carried by hand to the site where Elias D. Joynes, a carpenter from the mainland, erected the second Lee's Bethel. The new church measured 22 by 26 feet. It stood on the northern end of Main Ridge, where the present church stands, and when it was built the land south of it was known as "The Field" for the corn that grew there. When the new building was finished, George Pruitt purchased the old building in Canton.[19]

The second church, also, was outgrown in a few years. A revival in 1849 brought so many people that many were left standing outside the door. Not until 1860 was an additional eight feet added to the length of the building.[20]

By 1860 there was on Tangier "hardly a point from which some twenty or more dwellings may not be seen, each freshly painted white, with fancy colors to set off the contrast." The ridges were becoming separate little communities, for "as the children grow up and marry, a part of the paternal acres is set off for the new family." Thus by degrees the island was "assuming the appearance

**The Second "Lee's Bethel"**
from *The Parson of the Islands*

of a scattered village."

"A great change has come over the islands," wrote a Methodist minister in that year. "Fishing and catching or killing wild fowl is still necessarily a branch of business...but there are so many new ways and means to make a living, and such facilities of trade have sprung up, that wealth has been realized as the reward of industry, and luxury, in many an instance, may be found where it [once] took all a man's thrift and economy to procure the commonest necessaries of life."

Behind the change was the seafood industry. "The oyster business is their main dependence." Oysters that were "formerly almost all (except those consumed by the islanders themselves) conveyed to the Baltimore market" were by 1860 being exported by "numerous Philadelphia, New York, and New England vessels." The islanders, meanwhile, released from the occasional job of piloting, "do a very remunerative trade in 'dredging.'"[21]

So observed Adam Wallace (1825-1903), Irish-born Methodist minister in late 1860 as he penned *The Parson of the Islands*, a biography of Joshua Thomas. His book proved to be an Eastern Shore classic, and did much to keep the legend of the Tangier parson alive.

Joshua Thomas last visited Tangier Island in the summer of 1846, to attend the camp meeting that opened on July 31st of that year.

He was then just short of 70 years old, "greatly afflicted with the rheumatism," unable either to stand or to walk, but still able to shout "Amen" and "Glory!" during the sermons of a younger generation of preachers.

He himself arranged the little ceremony of his own departure from the camp meeting, for he judged it would be his last visit to the island. "I want Brother [James] Brindle to give out a certain hymn, and sing," he ordered, "after which I want Brother [John] Laws to pray. I will then give an exhortation to the people, and you will have me carried by two of the largest men you have on the ground to my canoe, when I will pronounce the benediction." They carried out his request in every detail, and one of the men who helped him down to *The Methodist* was his own son John. "There were many tears shed that morning, at parting with this dear old Father in Israel," reports his biographer Wallace, "and hopes exchanged that we might all meet to part no more at last."[22]

The Tangier camp meeting was then in its 37th year, and it too had changed with the passage of time. It was no longer as urgently needed for the conversion of sinners, for Methodism was closing in on the evangelization of the Chesapeake region. As a result, sermons on the beach were as likely to be heard by church-goers as by the unconverted, and to be followed by "fresh evidence of God's love" as by conversion. Preachers were now remembered as much for "genial wit" as for piety, and preaching might now include an appeal for foreign missions, followed by an offering for that cause — Joshua Thomas himself led one such meeting in

# Adam Wallace
**1825-1903**
**Biographer of Joshua Thomas**

Though Adam Wallace is known to have visited Tangier Island only two times, his contribution to its history and renown is immense, for he became the biographer of Joshua Thomas.

After immigrating from his native Ireland at the age of 18, Wallace lived in Philadelphia, where he joined the Methodist Episcopal Church and shortly thereafter became one of its ministers. He served most of his career on the Delmarva Peninsula, including the Northampton Circuit in Virginia (1854-55).

Wallace was serving in Somerset County when he met Joshua Thomas in the early 1850s, and the Parson was nearing the end of his life. He was appointed to Somerset a second time at the end of that decade, and it was then that he undertook to complete an unfinished memoir of the Parson begun years earlier by the Reverend Levin M. Prettyman.

He began the task in "the dismal days of December 1860," and published *The Parson of the Islands* the following year. The book is the chief source of information about Tangier's most famous character, and was republished a number of times over the next century.

Wallace visited the Tangier camp meeting the first time in 1849, when he "took passage down the Sound" from Somerset County. His second visit was in 1854, when he was serving in Virginia and set out from Onancock on "a pleasant voyage across the Sound." His description of the camp meeting in *The Parson of the Islands* seems to have conflated these two visits, for the events he dates to 1849 more likely occurred there in 1854.

Wallace's remarkable career, based on his own memoir, is described in *My Business Was to Fight the Devil*, by Joseph F. DiPaolo.[23]

1840. Announcements of the camp meeting, and results of such appeals, appeared with regularity in *Christian Advocate*, the Methodist newspaper published in New York City. Despite the "hum of the ubiquitous mosquito," camp meeting now had more comforts that in earlier days. Preachers were afforded "a comfortable lodging place," and their wives and children a separate one, "for most of the women had their little flocks in charge." Some even brought chairs from home for the preaching services, though most of the crowd still sat on benches, or even the sandy beach itself.

In 1844 after wrestling for years with an issue that little concerned Tangier Islanders — slavery — the Methodist Episcopal Church divided into northern and southern denominations. On the Eastern Shore the division was a painful one, accompanied by outright violence, as ministers of the northern church were bodily expelled from their pulpits by proponents of the southern church, and worshipers determined to protect their ministers went to worship with weapons strapped to their sides. The mainland difficulties reached the camp meeting in 1847, when a small pro-southern group landed after midnight and set about vandalizing the site. "This most promising meeting had to be brought to a close in great haste," reported the *Christian Advocate*, before those in attendance were "assailed in person." Tangier's congregation, and its camp meeting, retained its affiliation with the northern Philadelphia Conference, but most of the Virginia churches withdrew to the southern Virginia Conference, and with the schism interest in the camp meeting waned considerably.[24]

One of the last descriptions of the Tangier camp meeting is from the pen of John Hersey (1786-1862), a Methodist minister who attended the event in August 1853. A dour and cheerless man who was said never to have cracked a smile, Hersey was unimpressed with the site of the camp meeting, its leaders, and its participants. The Tangier beach he termed "a desolate looking place," while some of the sermons were so long and uninteresting that "many went to sleep, others walked away." The hundreds of people who arrived by boat from Baltimore on August 7, 1853, were, in his opinion, "no advantage to the meeting and no credit to themselves."

Hersey's own sermon on that day was long remembered by those who heard it, and illustrates how much Methodism, and the camp meeting with it, had changed over the

**John Hersey**

years. He was by then nearing the end of his career, and was thought by most to be a colorful oddity, a hold-over from the more austere days of early Methodism. He even dressed the part, favoring the style of dress of the earlier ministers, including "a straw hat which sold for twelve and one-half cents." When Hersey preached that Sunday, he waxed eloquent on the sin of pride, and one younger preacher on the stand behind him had the misfortune to be wearing a fine satin vest. In the midst of his sermon, Hersey turned suddenly and pointed at him with a long, crooked finger: "Pride has its roots right here in this pulpit," he shouted. Dashing from the pulpit to the side of the thunderstruck preacher, he ran his long, bony hand over the vest, stroking it in derision. His well-dressed colleague was soon bathed in his own tears, to the immense emotion of the crowd.[25]

Four years later, in 1857, the forty-ninth camp meeting — it would have been the fiftieth if the British occupation had not prevented its being held in 1814 — turned out to be the last one. The annual gathering had outlived its patriarch, for Joshua Thomas died peacefully at home on Deal Island on October 8, 1853. It had outlived its usefulness in ferreting out sinners, for Methodism was maturing into a more sedate and settled institution, the predominant faith of the region. But in the process it had helped to change Tangier, for never again would the island be quite so remote, simply because so many people had flocked to its shore every summer for almost half a century.

# 6
# War and Pestilence

It is impossible to know, but not hard to guess, what the people of Tangier Island thought of the issues and events that led the nation to war in 1861.

Slavery was all but unknown on Tangier. The only slave on record was the young girl owned by Priscilla Crockett in 1820. The 411 residents of the island in 1860 included six blacks who were undoubtedly "free Negroes." The islanders associated slavery with the rich landowners of the Eastern Shore, of whom they traditionally disapproved, and were generally tolerant of the few blacks who found their way to Tangier, where no one was rich and everyone had to work to make a living.[1]

No surviving record tells us how the islanders voted in the Presidential election of November 1860, when Lincoln was elected, nor of their votes on May 23, 1861, when Virginia's Ordinance of Secession was put before its citizens. The Eastern Shore of Virginia overwhelmingly approved Secession, and willingly followed the rest of the state out of the Union — with two exceptions. The first exception was Chincoteague Island, which by a vote of 134 to 2 chose not to secede.[2] The second exception was Tangier Island. The result of the vote there is not known, but it was almost certainly against Secession, because for the entire Civil War, Tangier remained functionally a part of the Union.

As in previous wars, the Chesapeake was blockaded, this time by the Union navy, which was under orders to seize any vessels attempting to enter or leave ports of the Confederacy, and to confiscate their cargoes. As in previous wars, the creeks and marshes of the Tangier Islands became convenient hiding places, this time for smugglers who carried on a thriving illegal commerce with rebel Virginia.

The smuggling, and the Union attempts to stop it, had begun as early as June 1861. Vessels leaving Baltimore bound legally for points on Maryland's Eastern Shore stopped instead at the islands and waited for the opportunity to cross to the Western Shore of Virginia. The harbor at the southern end of Tangier was a good place to wait before making a dash for the Rappahannock or York Rivers. The Union patrolled the Bay with gunboats, but the Chesapeake was large, the smugglers knowledgeable of its many nooks and crannies, and the profits enticing.[3] Even with its superior manpower, the Union was not fully successful in ending the illegal commerce.

With the Union in control of the Bay, the lighthouses of the region became an important target for Confederate sympathizers, for Union shipping and communications suffered whenever these aids to navigation were shut down. The Watts Island lighthouse was one of several that the rebels succeeded in extinguishing, at least temporarily, early in the war. A bay without lighthouses was also preferred by those who attempted to "run the blockade," hoping either to supply the rebels on the Western Shore or to join their ranks. George Douglas Watson and George Scarburgh were only teenagers when in late 1861 or early 1862 they set out from the Eastern Shore to join the Confederate army. Crossing the Chesapeake while evading the Union patrols was "a perilous journey, as the boat was small and could carry no lights for fear of discovery." After almost succumbing to the cold, they managed to reach Watts Island, where they spent two days before resuming their journey. They arrived safely in Urbanna, and from there Watson found his way to General Henry A. Wise, under whom he served as a volunteer for most of the war.[4]

The Union steamboat *Penguin* was in pursuit of a smuggler when, on July 3, 1861, Commander J. W. Livingston spotted an American flag flying at Tangier, and stopped at the island. The *Penguin* was too large to dock at still wharf-less Tangier, so three island men came out to board her, and reported to Livingston the state of events on Tangier: There was only one man on the island who favored secession, he had a plan to raise a rebel flag on July 4, and the islanders feared that that flag would be a signal for secessionists from the Eastern Shore to invade them. They requested that the *Penguin* remain in port for a day, and Livingston agreed to do so. When the Fourth of July dawned, no rebels from the Eastern Shore appeared, but the smuggler did, only to turn tail and run when the steamboat was seen in the harbor "dressed...in honor of the day."[5]

The following month the *Fanny* was patrolling the region, and on August 8 visited Tangier and delivered supplies to the lighthouse keeper on Little Watts Island. The next day was spent further up the Sound, and pursuing a vessel in the Pocomoke Sound, but on August 10-11 the *Fanny* anchored again at Tangier, and Lt. Pierce Crosby, its captain, later reported to the Union authorities that:

"...I had all the men on the island called together, some thirty-five of them, and administered the Oath of Allegiance to them. I was informed that a number were absent on their business, fishing.... I warned them not to hold any communication with the shores of Virginia under a penalty of imprisonment and a confiscation of their vessels."[6]

Even had the residents of Tangier been reluctant to take the Oath of Allegiance to the United States, they had a strong economic incentive for doing so. Without it, they could not be licensed to fish, catch oysters, ship produce, or even operate a boat on the Bay. Yet taking the Oath did not automatically guarantee them the necessary papers. "They have some eight or ten small schooners there which they are anxious to use," reported Crosby to the military authorities at Hampton Roads, "but as their license comes from Accomac[k] County they are prohibited from engaging in trade, and earnestly request that some provision be made for them." The loyalty of the islanders of Tangier was not an issue for Crosby. "I found the people on the island to be loyal citizens and ready to give all information in their power that would be of benefit to our Government. They also express serious apprehension that they will be attacked from the Eastern Shore. The lighthouse keeper on Watts Island is likewise anxious for protection."

Crosby's request that the islanders be issued papers for work and travel was sent on to the Secretary of the Treasury. It is not known when the licenses were issued, but it is known that the islanders spent the war years profitably harvesting and marketing their seafood.[7]

In fact, Tangier Island seems to have been remarkably disengaged from the conflict, and content to be in the Union while the war raged elsewhere. There is no record that any islander served on either side during the war. "Be it said...to the credit of this people, that a Secession banner never waved over it," wrote the island's pastor decades later. "It never would consent to go out of the Union. No Confederate soldiers ever went from it, and no Union soldiers, as to that." The conflict never ventured far enough up the Chesapeake to involve Tangier. As for the smuggling, there is no record that the people of Tangier were directly involved in it. One of the most prominent smugglers was a man named William Pruitt; he lived near Mobjack Bay on the Western Shore, and whether he had relatives among the many Pruitts of Tangier has not been determined.[8]

The war years eventually proved to be prosperous for Tangier. "The islanders had free trade," observed Tom Crockett, "and as oysters were plenty and the prices good, they accumulated more money than they ever had before." The only military presence was the patrolling Union gunboats, the "passes" necessary to travel that part of the Chesapeake were easily obtained, and the trade in seafood not only continued but flourished. "It is the verdict of the people," wrote a later pastor, "that more money was made here during the years of the war than at any other time."[9]

In November 1861 the Union army entered the Eastern Shore of Virginia and secured it for the North. Thereafter the peninsula, and Tangier with it, was governed not from Richmond but from Wheeling by the "loyal" Virginia government that convened there until 1863, when that city became part of the new state of West Virginia. The parts of Virginia under Union control were widely scattered and disconnected, and the General Assembly, meeting in Wheeling, designated March 15, 1862, as the date for a referendum on the Eastern Shore, to give its citizens the opportunity to decide whether or not to become a part of

Maryland. To oversee the referendum on Tangier six local men were appointed — Commissioners Lewis Crockett, Peter Crockett, Severn Crockett, Thomas A. Lewis, and John P. Thomas, with Lybrand H. Thomas as Officer — but no record of the vote survives, if, indeed, it was ever taken.[10] Tangier and the Eastern Shore remained, of course, a part of Virginia.

In many ways the routines of life on Tangier continued largely undisturbed by the war.

The war interrupted the availability of preachers from the Eastern Shore. In the winter of 1861-62 a number of islanders engaged William H. C. Long of Somerset County to preach on Sunday and to teach their children during the week, for $50 a month. The arrangement lasted less than a year, leaving the Sunday school the only education on the island and the congregation dependent upon local leadership. The pillars of the church now included Peter and Severn Crockett, exhorters, and Joshua Thomas II, "the best singer on the island, and a very popular man in the church." The mantle of "head of the church" rested on John Thomas, the Parson's son, until his death in 1865, when he was succeeded by Severn Crockett.

The island's first hotel was built in the year the war began. On January 15, 1861, the title to "Tangier Cod," the spit of land at the southern end of the island that included the old camp meeting ground, was conveyed by the state to Edmund J. Poulson, who lived near Onancock. Poulson erected there a 35-room "boarding house" which he called the Chesapeake Pleasure House. The local Methodists were doubly displeased, for not only did the hotel occupy the very site of the old camp meeting, it also permitted drinking, fiddling, and dancing — or so they believed, despite the fact that one minister of that time described it as "well conducted on temperance principles." The venture quickly failed. Poulson was offering it for sale by June 1862, but did not succeed in unloading it until after the war, and then only as a gift to his nephews.[11]

There is an island tradition that this small oasis of peace in a nation at war attracted a number of new residents who were eager to escape the war. Islander William Henry Harrison Crockett (1846-1896) is credited with bringing a number of people to the island who didn't agree with the war, or who were uprooted by it. One such person was said to have come from near one of the battlefields around Fredericksburg, and to have settled her family on Main Ridge while her husband was away fighting for the Confederacy. Henry Frazier, a black man, is also said to have come to the island during the early years of the war; tradition credits him with building the southernmost "dike" that connects Main Ridge and West Ridge, over which Factory Road passes today.[12]

In 1864 the military authorities on the Eastern Shore fanned out across the peninsula to administer the Oath of Allegiance to everyone over 16 years of age, and Edward L. East, a member of the Accomack

County Court, was engaged to visit the islands of Chesapeake Bay for that purpose. Only an incomplete list of those who took the oath survives, but it includes the women of the islands: one on Fox Island, one on Watts Island, nine on the Virginia portion of Smith Island, and 61 on Tangier Island. There were 25 Crockett women who took the oath on Tangier, and they with nine others named Evans, six named Dise, four Parkses, three Pruitts, and two Thomases comprised over three-quarters of the total. The other last names of the island women in that year were Charnock, Eskridge, Fawbaugh, Gaskins, Gibbons, Johnson, Laird, Moore, Shores, and Sturgis.[13]

Meanwhile Watts Island, according to tradition, fared less well than Tangier during the war. It was the home of three families in 1861, but as the war progressed "nearly all the trees on the wooded bluffs of the island were cut and used for firewood by soldiers on passing war ships, or by Chesapeake boatmen." Soon afterward a storm washed a swath through the southern end, "cut[ting] its way into the soul of the little island."[14]

Towards the end of the war Union gunboats were again back in the region to track down not smugglers but occasional rumors that Confederate sympathizers from the Western Shore were planning raids upon Tangier and Smith Islands.

According to one such report in August 1864, three hundred "rebels" from the Northern Neck were about to raid Smith Island. The steamboat *Fuchsia* was dispatched to patrol the islands, and her captain found the inhabitants of both Smith and Tangier "expecting a raid." Not only the Union navy but also the army took precautions. General Henry H. Lockwood toured the area, and "took measures for the security of the islands of the Chesapeake" but recorded his opinion that the reports had exaggerated the danger — correctly, as it turned out, for no such raid materialized.[15]

A second alarm, sounded on February 22, 1865, warned that rebels had already set out in several boats from the Northern Neck headed for Tangier Sound, where they hoped to plunder Union supplies, rescue "refugees and deserters" who had escaped from Virginia to Smith Island, and if possible capture a steamboat with which to disrupt Union shipping in the Bay. The Chesapeake came alive with alarms, messages, and orders which were for days telegraphed back and forth between anxious Union officials. On February 28 the steamboat *Anacostia* was ordered to Tangier Sound to search out the rebels. Not until the next day did the Federals finally pin down the location of their prey: they were already back home on the Northern Neck, having quickly abandoned the raid after losing the element of surprise.[16] The scare had long outlived the aborted plan that caused it — but it was about as close as Tangier got to any real involvement in the Civil War.

The Civil War passed lightly over Tangier, but the year following the close of hostilities proved far more deadly. In 1866 the island, like many other places in the country, was struck by an epidemic of cholera.

Cholera is caused by a microscopic bacterium that attaches to the walls of the small intestine, then releases toxins that cause massive discharges of water. These discharges, often as much as five gallons a day, drain the body of water and salts, leaving the victim dehydrated, fatigued, and malnourished. When the toxins reach the stomach, severe vomiting occurs, followed by declining blood pressure, muscle cramps, fever, intense perspiration, coma, and — for about fifty percent of its victims — death. Cholera can be treated today with fluids and salts, but the nature of the disease was unknown in the mid-nineteenth century, and most treatments were useless, or even harmful. It was widely believed that the sickness spread from passengers arriving on ships from Europe, but one of the chief avenues of its spread is unsanitary drinking water, which made not only thousands of city-dwellers but also mid-nineteenth century Tangier Islanders vulnerable.[17]

Baltimore reported its first case of cholera on September 27, and by mid-October as many as 26 people were dying there each week. Because one victim had arrived by steamboat from Savannah and another had recently returned from Philadelphia, the newspapers, ignoring the unsanitary conditions in which it flourished, theorized that the disease was imported from other places, or, alternatively, entered the body through bad food or drink. "Nearly every case of cholera reported during the week has been traced to carelessness in diet," reported *The Sun* on October 13, and at least two men had died after eating what seemed to be a major culprit, raw oysters.[18]

Within weeks there were reports of cholera in Annapolis, and in Talbot County on the Eastern Shore of Maryland. By October 24, when it was raging on Tilghman Island and Poplar Island,[19] the disease had also found its way to Tangier.

The deaths on Tangier began on October 10, 1866, when seamstress Hetty Evans succumbed. On October 12 four-month-old Thomas Evans died; on October 13 Malinda Lord, age 22; and on October 14 no fewer than four people — William and Lucy Ann Crockett, and Stephen and Polly Dies. Between October 19 and 26 there were five deaths, including two children. "The fall of 1866 was the most distressing of all we had ever witnessed," writes Tom Crockett. "The cholera set in and the people began to die very fast. We did not know what it was until the physicians told us, and as many as six adults would die in twenty four hours. I could hear the voice of weeping all night." The dead were buried hastily, but deaths occurred so quickly that burials could not keep up with them.

At least twelve people are known to have died during the epidemic, but the total number of deaths is unknown. The island traditions that state that hundreds died are undoubtedly exaggerated, for Crockett states that only "several of our citizens [went] to the grave." A number

**Cholera Victim, Fall 1866**
Old Cemetery, Main Ridge

survived the deadly disease — the usual statistic was 50 percent — and it is said that some of those who did bore facial pocks for the rest of their lives as a result.[20] If there were twelve known deaths, and they constituted 50 percent of those who contracted the disease, then by the most conservative estimate 24 people — approximately one of every 17 islanders alive on the island in 1860 — were victims of cholera. It is, of course, altogether possible that the twelve known deaths are only a portion of the victims, and that far more than one in 17 were stricken.

The epidemic was over by December, perhaps as early as November, and swift on its heels came a religious revival, "with much excited repenting and men praying in the cornfields when people started to die." "On Tangier Island," reported the *Christian Advocate* in December 1866, "where the cholera raged most fearfully about the 1st of November, some sixty have been converted, and united with the M.E. Church." That the dying had ceased and the revival begun by December 1 at the latest is suggested by the *Advocate*'s report that "the first Sabbath night of this month fifteen were at the altar."

Yet, writes Tom Crockett, "the contagion appeared to increase until nearly all the people left the island."[21]

Sugar Tom was an eye-witness to the epidemic, so some credence must be given to this tantalizingly ambiguous statement that people left the island because of cholera. An island tradition handed down through the family of Joseph Cooper, another eye-witness, goes even further: "It is said that every inhabitant of the island was evacuated to the mainland," and that many of them never came back but settled permanently in the Crisfield region. [22]

There is most likely a grain of truth in these conflicting facts and traditions. That the epidemic was over and the church active by December 1866 seems certain from the *Christian Advocate*. That some people left the island, as Crockett states, is arguably consistent with the *Advocate's* report, for he does not allege that they were gone a long time. That the entire island was abandoned is undoubtedly an overstatement, but it is possible that some of the more distant ridges may have been completely abandoned, and the tradition may reflect the experiences of islanders who lived in those parts of the island. That some Tangier Islanders may have relocated to the mainland near Crisfield as a result of the epidemic seems only reasonable.

Unless new documents of that period are discovered, the full story of the epidemic will probably never be known, but the island's population figures suggest how devastating the epidemic must have been. The island had 411 residents in 1860, and 412 in 1870, a gain of only one. Yet the island's population had grown steadily with each decade since 1820, and Tom Crockett observed that "the population increased rapidly" during the Civil War,[23] which means that by the mid-1860s the number of islanders must have been a good deal more than 411. Yet Tangier entered the 1870s with fewer residents than in the mid-1860s because of the terrifying disease that had killed some of its people and scattered others, though how many of each is simply not known.

# 7
# High Gear

The years following the Civil War found most of Virginia devastated, while Tangier Island shared in the booming post-war economy that swept across the North.

It was at war's end that the problem of how to ship oysters over great distances was solved by the development of a reliable steam-canning process.

Though before the war Chesapeake oysters were a rare delicacy only a few hundred miles from the coast, after the war the new technology made it possible for them to be a staple of diet as far away as California.

It was at war's end that a prosperous economy brought disposable wealth to greater numbers of people, especially in the North, and made it possible for them to indulge their palates in fashionable delicacies — like the oyster.

And it was on November 4, 1866, just as the island was recovering from the cholera epidemic, that the first train pulled into a new terminus at water's edge in Somerset County, only 12 miles up the Sound from Tangier.

The convergence of these developments threw the oyster industry of Tangier Sound into high gear. The markets of Philadelphia and New York, hungrier than ever for oysters, were now hours, not days away. The railroad was not only faster but also bigger than even the largest schooners, able to transport much more seafood much more often. Now that the oysters could be sent anywhere without fear of spoilage, the marketplace was vastly expanded. Soon Tangier Sound oysters were being shipped not only to Baltimore, Philadelphia, New York, and New England, but also to Europe and even Australia.[1]

Where the railroad met the Bay, near a small community known previously as Somer's Cove, the new town of Crisfield sprang up almost overnight, built literally on mounds of oyster shells discarded when the bivalves were "shucked" for canning. Oysters delivered by local watermen to Crisfield's docks could be purchased, while still in the shell, for 10¢ to 25¢ a bushel. A bushel, when shucked, yielded a gallon, at an additional cost of 15¢ a gallon for processing. Yet when that gallon reached the markets of the cities, it sold for $1 or more, a gain of over 100 percent.

With such profits at stake, Crisfield danced to a get-rich-quick tune, and with its influx of merchants, immigrants, gamblers, bootleggers, and prostitutes resembled more a mining town of the western frontier than the nearby communities of old Chesapeake Bay. By the mid-1870s the oysters funneling through Crisfield numbered in the millions of bushels each year, and twenty to thirty railroad cars full of oysters left for market every day except Sunday. By 1900 the number of seafood processing plants in the Crisfield area totalled over 150. By 1910 the Customs House at Crisfield had the largest registry of sailing vessels of any port in the United States.[2]

With oysters so valuable, the scramble for them turned old rivalries into outright enmities. Tongers quarreled with dredgers, who frequently poached upon oyster beds designated for tonging only, and numerous angry encounters between them erupted into violence. In 1867 the Maryland legislature created the Maryland State Fishery Force — the "Oyster Navy" — to enforce the laws designed to keep tongers and dredgers in their separate parts of the Bay.

Virginia was slower to create its fisheries police force, prompting some locals to take action on their own. In 1883 Ambrose Taylor, a justice of the peace on the Eastern Shore, raised a posse of armed men, secured the use of two vessels, and "with the skill and judgment worthy a Norse

**Packing and Canning Oysters**
Crisfield, Maryland
from *Harper's Weekly*, March 16, 1872

Viking" ran several "oyster pirates" out of Pocomoke Sound. Later that year George W. Hinman of Accomack was appointed oyster inspector. In December 1883 his police boat found three vessels dredging just south of Pocomoke Sound; one of them managed to elude him, but two were captured: a schooner from Baltimore, and the pungy *Thos. B. Hamilton* of Tangier. Hinman had successfully cleared Pocomoke Sound of dredge boats by March 1884, when the Virginia legislature approved the creation of its own "Oyster Navy." In both states the "Oyster Wars" raged for years against those who illegally dredged on oyster beds set aside for tongers, oyster culture, or recovery from over-dredging.[3]

Meanwhile Virginians and Marylanders quarreled over the location of the boundary between the two states. Exactly where the line crossed Smith Island was traditionally a matter of some debate, but far thornier was the question of where the boundary crossed the waters of the Bay itself. At stake was over 150 square miles of open water containing some of the finest oyster seed beds in the world, and the issue of which state's watermen could harvest them according to which state's laws. Former Governor Henry A. Wise was appointed one of three Virginia commissioners to resolve the issue with their Maryland counterparts. He entered the negotiations with the observation that though Maryland's portion of the Chesapeake was less than half as large as Virginia's, "if Maryland acquires the seed beds of Tangier and Pocomoke Sounds, her lesser

**The Oyster War on the Chesapeake**
from *Harper's Weekly*, January 9, 1885

domain will be as valuable as the greater owned by Virginia."

After a number of delays, claims, and counter-claims, commissioners from the two states began meeting to resolve the boundary issue in 1872. They held sessions in Annapolis, Crisfield, Baltimore, and Richmond, visited Smith Island, took numerous depositions, and proved unable to reach an agreement. The issue was then submitted to arbitration by a board of three Congressmen, who in 1877 announced the decision that established the boundary that zig-zags across the Chesapeake today. Maryland retained sovereignty over the valuable "Great Rocks," but Virginia got the larger share of the contested waters in both sounds.[4]

In 1867, the year after the railroad reached Crisfield, a group of shipbuilders from Wilmington, Delaware, organized the Eastern Shore Steamboat Company, and the golden age of the steamboat came to Tangier Sound.

The new company was hardly the only one operating on the Chesapeake, for by the late 1800s the Bay was crisscrossed by steamers that weaved a network of connections between virtually every port, large and small, from Norfolk to Baltimore. The first of the company's steamers to connect Crisfield with Baltimore, and with smaller ports along the way, was *Sue*, which plied the route until 1874. By then *Maggie* (1869) and *Helen* (1871) were also in service, and the next few years would bring

**The Steamboat *Helen***

*Tangier* (1875), *Eastern Shore* (1883), and *Pocomoke* (1891).

Regular steamboat service to Tangier began in August 1884, and the first steamer to service the island was *Helen*. The steamer pulled into the cove formed by "the hook" at the southern end of the island, which became known as Steamboat Harbor, but not for a number of years is there mention of a wharf. The likelihood is that in the earliest years the steamers, like all the other larger vessels that had preceded them to Tangier, anchored in the harbor, where they were surrounded by small local boats which ferried passengers and freight to Banty's Wharf, at the southern end of Main Ridge. The island was on the Pocomoke River Line, one of several routes operated by the company, and was serviced at various times by *Helen*, *Maggie* and *Pocomoke*. There is, ironically, no record that the steamboat *Tangier* stopped at the island from which it took its name [5]

Now, for the first time in its history, Tangier Island had a regular and on-going means of contact with the outside world. By 1890 the island was visited by the steamers four times a week. The *Maggie* called on Tuesday mornings as she headed down the Bay from Baltimore and Crisfield, and on Wednesday afternoons on the return trip. The *Pocomoke*, headed up the river for Pocomoke City and Snow Hill, stopped on Wednesday mornings, and on Thursday afternoons as she headed back towards Crisfield and Baltimore. An islander taking passage to Baltimore had two opportunities to do so, by boarding the *Maggie* at 4:30 p.m. on Wednesday or the *Pocomoke* at 4:00 p.m. on Thursday. Both ships deposited passengers in the city early the next morning, where they had until 5:00 or 6:00 p.m. to attend to affairs before setting out again for Crisfield and points south.[6]

Steamboat travel to Baltimore must have seemed unbelievably luxurious to the islanders of Tangier. "Meals were fit for a king, scenery was beyond comparison, and the passenger was lulled to sleep by the swishing of the paddle wheels and gentle rocking of the boat. Upon awakening at sunrise, the passenger discovered he was in Baltimore. After a day of leisure shopping, visiting, performing business tasks, or going to the theatre, one would board the same boat at the close of the day and make the return trip home...."[7]

The steamboats carried freight as well as passengers. Though seafood was still shipped in more traditional working vessels, the steamboats could accommodate as many as 3,500 barrels of produce, and passengers often had to share the voyage with not only seafood but also crates and barrels of potatoes, onions, and strawberries.[8] The same steamboats that shipped materials from the island also brought produce and merchandise to it. The island's general stores depended upon merchandise shipped by steamboat. John Wallace, owner of the big general store on Wallace Road at West Ridge, had not only to meet the steamboats early in the morning when they arrived from Baltimore, but then also to wait for the right tides before he could barge his merchandise under the "Hoisting Bridge" and up the "Big Gut" to his store. In addition to supplying merchants with merchandise, the steamboats brought to the island traveling salesmen — "drummers" — who were eager to peddle their wares to stores and individuals alike.

Buoyed by flush times in the seafood industry, in contact with the outside world as never before, Tangier Island entered a period of unprecedented prosperity and progress which transformed the very looks of the island. The town as we know it began to take shape in the years when oyster was king.

The first of many new buildings was yet another church built in 1870 by the Methodists, now 110 members strong. The new church cost $2,400, and for its dedication not one but two Methodist bishops visited the island. "Mariner's Bethel," as it was called, stood at 16152 Main Ridge Road, where the Methodist educational building stands today.[9]

Virginia's public school system was born in that year, and in 1871 Tangier Island gained a school at last. A list of islanders so long as to be "too tedious to mention" donated a lot, and a small building was erected near the present school building. By 1880 the school was "graded" — divided into classes, one of the first on the Eastern Shore of Virginia to be so. There were 63 students, and the principal was none other than the historian Thomas Crockett, one of "scarcely a score of inhabitants that could read or write" when a lasting school finally became a reality on the island.[10]

John Thomas, the island's first merchant, was deceased, and his storebuilding in Oyster Creek used as a polling place, but Tangier now had several general stores — seven by 1890. The largest was J. E. Wallace & Co. on West Ridge. Established by John Wallace (1855-1926), a native of Gloucester who came to Tangier in the 1870s, it sold groceries, general merchandise, and coffins, for Wallace also worked as an undertaker, and the smaller building next to his store was known as "the Coffinhouse." The store of Crockett & Wallace, jointly operated by Travis Crockett and John Wallace in 1896, stood on West Ridge opposite the store still standing at the eastern end of Factory Road. John Chambers' general store stood at 4417 Chambers Lane, a site known as Chambers Wharf. On July 6, 1881, Chambers became the first postmaster of Tangier, and the new post office was located in his store. By 1890 there were three mails a week, brought in by steamboat.[11]

The houses of the islanders also reflected the new prosperity. The typical island home — one-and-a-half stories with a smaller one-story kitchen attached at the back — proliferated as the population more than doubled between 1870 and 1900. The ridges, Main Ridge in particular, filled in with housing. Many houses were large and up-to-date by mainland standards. The home of Capt. Peter Williams at 16116 Main Ridge Road sported Victorian "gingerbread" on porch and eaves (it has since been removed). The Joshua Pruitt house at 16216 Main Ridge still displays its gingerbread, and was large enough to serve as a boarding house,

# George W. Nock

## 1843-1922
## Teacher of Islanders and Indians

A number of people who lived on Tangier in the late nineteenth century came as teachers for the new public school, taught briefly, and moved on. Few of them had as varied a career as George Nock.

A native of Accomack County, Nock eluded the Union blockade of Chesapeake Bay to join the Confederate forces during the Civil War. During guard duty at Libby Prison in Richmond, he  fired at a Yankee prisoner and shot off his ear, an incident later covered in *Century Magazine*. After the war, he farmed, ran a store near Keller, and married a local girl who agreed, despite her misgivings, to follow him to Arizona after he suddenly accepted a position at the Colorado River Agency.

The Nocks arrived in Parker, near Yuma, Arizona, in September 1887, and for two years he was principal of the government school for the children of the Mojave Indians. His wife Mary was also on the faculty. Their sons Walter and Henry studied at the school, and became fluent in the language of the Mojaves.

After returning to the Eastern Shore, Nock became principal of the Tangier Graded School in 1893, and was teacher at the one-room school on Canaan Ridge in 1894. During both of those years his wife taught at the school on Main Ridge. He later taught at Mappsburg, Chancetown, and Melfa, and retired in 1905.

Nock wrote a short historical sketch of the island during the winter of 1894-95, when the frozen Chesapeake had Tangier locked in ice. "While I write these lines," he penned, "we have been shut in for two weeks and no sign for early communication with the outer world.... I look out upon the snow-clad earth and our rugged, ice-bound coast and hear the shrill whistle of the bleak west wind as it sweeps across a dreary waste of ice...."

After the heat of the desert and the cold of Tangier, the Nocks moved back to his old family homestead near Keller. She died in 1918, he in 1922, and both are buried in the family burial ground.[12]

**J. E. Wallace & Co. Store**
"The Coffinhouse" stands at the right of the store

though the nearby Stephen Pruitt house at 16186 Main Ridge was even larger.

Three of the prominent homes of this period are used today as inns, the latest in a line of island homes to serve as "hotels." The Nathan Rayfield house (16243 Main Ridge) and the Peter S. Crockett house (16246 Main Ridge) together constitute the Chesapeake House. Sidney Wallace's house at 16408 West Ridge was built in 1904 and restored in 1995 as Shirley's Bay View Inn. The house was built from Wallace's own design by George Tawes, a carpenter imported for that purpose from Crisfield; Tawes later settled on Tangier and built other island homes.

Largest of all the new homes was the Methodist Parsonage, erected in 1887, a necessity after the Tangier congregation became a "station" with its own resident minister. The congregation shared its preachers with mainland congregations until 1883, when the Reverend C. C. Baker arrived to serve the Tangier church alone. With his arrival the islanders could, at last, count on preaching every Sunday.[13]

The year 1890 brought a bank, a hotel and a lighthouse. The Bank of Tangier is thought to have operated out of the Old Post Office at 16200 Main Ridge, and was still functioning in 1907. The hotel of Crockett & Thomas was a boarding house at 16199 Main Ridge. The Tangier Rocks Light was a square "screwpile" lighthouse, essentially a house sitting on stilts half a mile south of the island at the entrance to the deepest channel of Tangier Sound. It cost $25,000, and with the Watt's Island Lighthouse to the east made a more clearly marked entrance into the sound.[14]

The flourishing town attracted a physician, but the island's first

**The Tangier Rock Lighthouse**

experience with a resident doctor ended in tragedy. Young Dr. L. Thomas Walter settled on the island in May 1883, but by fall was stricken with typhoid and had to return to the Eastern Shore to recuperate. In his absence Dr. James Dennis Pitts substituted for him, and the two shared the medical practice after Walter returned in early 1884. Pitts, however, had his own problems, including an addiction to morphine. On May 17, 1884, he accosted Walter in the West Ridge house where they were boarding, argued with him over the fees they had agreed to charge, then suddenly drew a pistol and shot him four times. Walter died of four gunshot wounds, some of them inflicted as he was trying to escape. Convicted of second-degree murder, Pitts was sentenced to 18 years, but pardoned in 1888. He died in Nebraska in 1890. By then Tangier had a new physician in Dr. James F. Newman, who also operated a "beautiful drug store" on Main Ridge.[15]

Not all of the growth was on Main Ridge. By 1873 Henry L. Crockett was operating a "fish factory" offshore in Steamboat Harbor atop the shell pile. Menhaden, a small inedible fish from which industrial products could be obtained, existed in great quantities in the Chesapeake; a group of New Englanders visiting the region in 1866 found the waters so thick with them that "one enthusiastic member of the party jumped into the water and with a dip-net threw bushels of fish upon the beach." At the Crockett & Company factory menhaden were first boiled, then compressed for the extraction of "fish oil" which was useful in paint and cosmetics. The remainder was then dried, ground into "chum," and mixed with guano for the manufacture of fertilizer. When in the fall of 1876 Crockett docked his schooner *William Turner* at Onancock with a cargo of "fish manure" from his factory, mainland farmers were eager to purchase it for fertilizer. By 1883 there were as many as six such "factories" on the island, most or all of them on the beach at the southern end of the island, and in addition to Crockett the islanders who at various times owned and operated such establishments included Joseph Cooper, Lewis Crockett, and Richard Spence. [16]

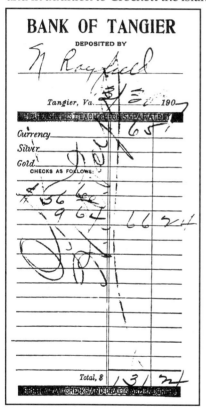

**The Bank of Tangier**

A rare artifact from the short-lived bank: the record of Nathan Rayfield's deposit of $131.24 on March 30, 1907

Canaan Ridge, or "Uppards," was by the end of the century the second most populous ridge on the island, and had its own store, church, and school. In Canaan the Methodists were operating a Sunday school as early as 1874, and the county a public school, the second on the island, by 1883; both efforts shared the same small building. This northern end of the island was linked to Main Ridge by a footbridge that crossed "the Creek" where the County Dock is now located. Though for the waterman Canaan provided ready access to his work, it was the most distant of the settled ridges, a full mile overland from Main Ridge, and many considered it a lonely place. Capt. Peter Dise, among the most prominent residents of Uppards, moved his family to 16230 Main Ridge in the late 1800s, and took his house with him. Others would follow his example in the next century.[17]

West Ridge was largely farmland, inhabited principally at its northern end, when during the decade of the 1880s the break-up of several large parcels of land resulted in smaller lots, and an increasing population. It too had its own school, in

**The Old Road to Canton**

operation by as early as 1893; a building was constructed for it in 1896, but where it stood is not known.[18]

By 1886 all the ridges, with the exception of East Point, had been connected by a series of roads and bridges built "at the expense of the inhabitants." An old photo of the road to Canton shows that a Tangier road could be little more than a wooden walkway only three planks wide. Yet in 1892 the county was maintaining a "Road Machine Manager" on the island.[19]

Politically speaking, the island was simply a portion of Accomack County, with no town government. Yet, boasted Thomas Crockett in 1890, "we have a Justice of the Peace, a Constable, also a Notary Public" — Joseph Cooper, Addison King, and Patrick Connorton, respectively. Three years later Dr. Newman, advocating Joseph L. Cooper as Justice of the Peace, urged the Democratic voters of Accomack to remember Tangier's unique situation: "We are...an isolated people. Our place (although it should be) is not incorporated. We have no municipal government and under the circumstances our magistrate is our only preserver of the peace."[20]

By the turn of the century Tangier was one of the largest communities of Virginia's Eastern Shore, its population having more than doubled between 1870 and 1900, from 412 to 1,064.[21] The island had come a long way from its days of isolation, and was looking increasingly like a modern community.

On Tangier Island, as throughout the region, much of this prosperity was built largely on the crown jewel of the seafood industry, the oyster.

Tangier had both tongers and dredgers, usually more tongers than dredgers, for dredging required a substantial outlay of funds for a larger boat and equipment. Even so, there were 52 dredging boats on the island in 1890. Zachariah Crockett II (1831-1878) was a tonger, while Peter Dise (1854-1910) owned no fewer than 12 schooners with which he dredged oysters from both Tangier and Pocomoke Sounds, using crews from Norfolk. Though most of Tangier's oysters went to Crisfield, Harrison Crockett chose to take his to Washington, D.C., on his pungy *Transport*. After 1905 oystermen had another option, for in that year Tangier had two shucking houses of its own, run by W. E. Phibbs and A. P. Ford, and both of them were running to full capacity.[22]

The oyster season lasted from fall to spring, those months whose names contain the letter "r" and which are, by tradition, the best months

**Oyster Pirates Dredging at Night**
from *Harper's Weekly*, March 1, 1884

for eating oysters. A Chesapeake winter could be hard on both tongers and dredgers, but especially brutal on the dredge boats, which mined the deeper waters and often stayed out for weeks or months or even the entire season.

The fixing of the boundary in 1877 did little to ease the Oyster Wars, for watermen from both states frequently crossed the line in search of the valuable bivalve. Virginia dredgers were doing so by December 1883, meeting a storm of bullets from outraged Maryland tongers. Ten years later it was the Marylanders who were "pirating" oysters in Virginia waters. In the winter of 1893-94 Somerset waterman Robert Wharton was arrested by the Virginia oyster militia for gathering oysters in Pocomoke Sound. After refusing to pay a $500 fine, Wharton sat in jail while his friends appealed to Annapolis for his release. In the heated legal confrontation that followed Maryland argued that her watermen were guaranteed access to the Sound by a compact with Virginia dating back to 1785, while Virginia's position was that the Pocomoke Sound was a "separate and distinct body of water" not covered under the 1785 agreement. Unable to resolve the matter, the two states submitted the matter to the U.S. Supreme Court in the spring of 1894.[23]

Meanwhile a second confrontation was brewing on Tangier Sound. On February 17, 1894, Marylanders dredging Woman's Marsh on lower Smith Island were intercepted by the Virginia police boat *Tangier* and told to withdraw; they answered with gunfire. In the battle that ensued two Virginia boats, *Tangier* and *Chesapeake*, were arrayed against 150 Smith Islanders in 30 vessels. Most of the Marylanders escaped northward across the boundary, but two schooners were captured and their crews lodged in the Accomack County jail.

**Oyster Pirates**
from *Harper's Weekly*, 1892

A month later the *Tangier* was patrolling Horse Hammock, also on the Virginia portion of Smith Island, when she was fired upon again. The *Tangier* replied with a salvo from its cannon, but was no match for twenty-five Marylanders with repeating rifles firing 500 rounds of ammunition from behind hastily prepared "forts and breastworks." Outnumbered, Capt. A. J. Read and his crew sailed the *Tangier* back to Onancock. "The Marylanders have sworn to kill the whole crew of the police schooner," he reported to an outraged Virginia newspaper, "so that they cannot be witnesses against them."

These violent encounters quickly generated dueling editorials in newspapers throughout the region. Each state appointed a special committee to confer about the lawlessness in the Bay, and Governor Charles O'Ferrall, accompanying the Virginia committee to Tangier, took a well-publicized side trip to examine the "oyster waters of the Commonwealth." A week later, on April 23, 1894, the Supreme Court ruled in *Wharton v. Wise* in support of Virginia's position on Pocomoke Sound. Outraged Marylanders launched a campaign to pay Wharton's fine and to continue the struggle against Virginia's claim to Pocomoke Sound.[24]

Greed as well as violence punctuated the insatiable pursuit of the oyster. Among the captains of the dredging boats were unscrupulous men who recruited crews with promises of fair wages, then mistreated them under conditions amounting to virtual slavery. Many crewmen were not recruited but "shanghaied," some were murdered, and a number were "paid off at the boom" — deliberately knocked overboard by the swinging boom of the ship's sails when they were no longer needed, and not yet paid, at the end of the season. Reports of such practices reached Baltimore as early as 1881, and over the next quarter century several Tangier skippers were among those accused of shanghaiing.

In 1893 James E. Hall, age 15, was in Norfolk when he joined the crew of the oyster schooner *Fillhope*, under Captain Vick, with the promise that he would be paid, and the boat would return to port, every Saturday. Instead he was taken to Tangier, detained "without clothes and without the means of escape," and subjected to "treatment unknown even to human slavery." His mother in North Carolina learned of his plight from another sailor who managed to escape from the island, and she appealed directly to Virginia Governor Philip McKinney for his release. McKinney, arguing that he had no authority to intervene, gave Hall's mother advice on how to secure her son's liberty, but what came of her efforts, or of Hall's plight, is unknown.[25]

In early November 1906, Deputy U.S. Marshal H. W. Miller arrived in Tangier and placed Capt. West Williams under arrest for shanghaiing a man named Walter Everett. Williams was taken to Norfolk, where at his hearing witnesses against him failed to show up, but one witness who did show up was an employee named E. Lee Jackson who had come to speak for him. After Jackson claimed to have worked on one of Williams' boats with Everett, and offered himself as evidence that he was not worked involuntarily and was free to come and go, Williams was released on bail.

The following Saturday two U.S. marshals were back in Tangier, where this time they arrested Capt. John Pruitt on the same charge. After his appearance before the U.S. Commissioner on Monday the case against Pruitt, as well as that against West, was promptly dismissed.

Within a week's time a third islander was in custody. Andrew A. Crockett, captain of the schooner *James A. Whiting*, surrendered to authorities after nine members of his crew accused him of cruelty and were removed from his vessel by marshals. Crockett's crew included three Italians who were unable to speak English, and two white and seven black men who arrived in Norfolk "very poorly clad" and bearing "other evidences of destitution." Though a number of prominent islanders went to Norfolk to vouch for him, Crockett was convicted in Federal Court in late November and fined $500. "We know nothing of the merits of this case," commented the *Accomack News* upon his conviction, "but...we are inclined to think that there is a possibility that Capt. Crockett may not be the monster his crew represented him as being, and that instead of him having 'shanghaied' his crew, the crew [with] this trial may have shanghaied him."[26]

Behind the greed and violence, behind the conflict between tongers and dredgers, Virginians and Marylanders lay the obvious but seldom considered fact that the number of oysters in the Bay was finite, and the supply steadily decreasing because of careless and rampant over-harvesting. In 1884, fifteen million bushels of oysters were harvested by Chesapeake watermen, and after that peak year the decline began, though oysters were still plentiful for a number of years. Almost a century of dredging had not only removed most of the oysters but also destroyed the "rocks" on which they grew. The shells which young oysters needed to attach themselves to had not been replaced, but used to pave roads, or ground for lime or poultry feed — "not a single shell was returned to the beds." Pollution, pests, and disease accelerated the decline. By 1905 Tangier was reporting that "quite a number of our oystermen have left [the Chesapeake Bay] for the Seaside and other places to oyster." By 1908 oysters were so scarce that Chesapeake dredge boats were working a hundred miles up the Atlantic Coast in Sinepuxent Bay near Ocean City, Maryland.[27]

In 1889, as the decline in the annual harvests was getting under way, Virginia passed a new law that allowed individuals to lease "oyster flats," hoping that industrious watermen would be encouraged to replenish the stock within their own private areas. The law flew in the face of the widespread tradition that the Chesapeake belonged to everyone, its bounty there for the taking, and it provoked further controversy.

There was oyster planting at Fox Island even before the passage of this law. In 1885, John B. Blizzard of Crisfield purchased the island and took up residence there with two goals in mind: "to engage largely in the planting of oysters and the soft crab business, and [to] open a first class summer resort." Blizzard attended to the second goal more promptly than to the first. He obtained a liquor license, and for at least two years operated a popular saloon. It is said that he consistently violated local liquor laws by claiming first that his establishment was in Virginia, then in Maryland, as occasion demanded.

The next owner of Fox Island was more serious about the planting of oysters. In 1892, after Blizzard's death, William Ellinger of New York took up residence, and soon had in operation an extensive "oyster farm" just east of the island. Ellinger guarded his oyster beds zealously, and on one occasion shot a Maryland crabber through the ear for trespassing on them, only to have the misfortune of encountering the man later in Crisfield while on his weekly shopping trip to the mainland. As Ellinger headed back to his boat, a watermelon under each arm, the offended waterman knocked him to the ground and walked away without a backward glance. Several people who witnessed the attack did nothing to help the unpopular Ellinger, who staggered to his launch and sailed home without pressing charges, and without watermelons.[28]

In 1904, Joshua Crockett was granted a lease on 200 acres near Tangier on which to "plant oysters," and he quickly learned how unpopular the idea was with the other islanders. To the watermen of Tangier, "the [area] was a source of livelihood...as they caught many oysters, fish and crabs from these waters, and as it had belonged in common to their ancestors for centuries they were violently opposed to its lease. They declared that their living was dependent upon it, and as long as a Tangier man lived the ground would never be rented out."

In August when the police steamer *Rappahannock* brought county surveyor Ernest Ruediger to the site to lay out Crockett's flat, he was met by a crowd of protesters who had come out in a swarm of boats to prevent the survey from taking place. "As fast as a stake would be set it would be pulled up by the islanders amid cheers and howls of defiance from their comrades." When it was clear that the survey could not proceed, the *Rappahannock* sailed back to the mainland.

Two weeks later Ruediger was escorted back to the site by the entire Oyster Navy of Virginia, "the ships *Rappahannock*, *Accomack*, and *Pocomoke*, with flag flying, gunners at the posts and everything ready for action." This time they were met by another crowd — said to number almost 500 men and women — whose boats quickly surrounded the fleet. "Armed only with a righteous cause," the islanders again attempted to sabotage the survey. This time the stand-off lasted through the night, during which "by shrewd work" Ruediger succeeded surreptitiously in plotting the area. But the confrontation ended in victory for the islanders the next morning, when Crockett informed the authorities aboard the fleet that he was abandoning his lease.

Dr. John W. Bowdoin, Eastern Shore physician who was Chairman of the Virginia Board of Fisheries, had supported Crockett's right to lease the flat, and angrily brought an indictment against thirty of the protesters. Their case came to trial in Accomac in January 1905, and they were found guilty. The fine imposed was "one dollar on the entire number, about three cents apiece."[29]

It was when oysters began to decline that crabbing emerged as an important part of the island's commercial seafood industry. The ways of the crab had long been familiar to Tangier's residents, who caught them for their own tables, and used them for bait. Yet as late as 1886 only one man on the island was crabbing for commercial purposes. Ten years later crabbing furnished "fairly remunerative employment for many of our oystermen from May to September," and a local newspaper reported that "the crabbing industry in this section of Virginia amounts annually to $60,000." One observer counted 800 crabbing boats in Tangier and Pocomoke Sounds in a single day in 1893.

When crabbing began, buyers from Crisfield purchased directly from the watermen. Then in 1905 the islanders began building their own "crab houses," and crabs were packed in boxes with grass and ice before being shipped to Crisfield or on the Baltimore steamboats. In 1898 Lewis C. Dize of Smith Island patented a "crab scrape bag," a kind of toothless dredge for gliding along the eel grass where crabs hide to molt, but Tangier watermen continued to use the old trot-line and net for harvesting for more than a decade.

Crabbing was done during the months not devoted to oystering, a portion of the year in which islanders had previously tended gardens and small farms. As crabbing grew, island men shifted away from agriculture, and Tangier became increasingly less able to produce its own food supply, more dependent upon importing foods it had previously grown. Yet crabbing also provided money that made this dependence viable.[30]

The violent Oyster Wars became deadly Crab Wars as watermen from the two states soon sparred over the thousands of acres of shallow water between Tangier and Smith Island, not a prime site for oysters but, in season, filled with eel grass and crabs. In August 1901 fifteen-year-old John T. Evans of Smith Island was shot and killed in his skiff by the Virginia police, who believed him to be illegally harvesting soft crabs. Smith Islanders always insisted he wasn't even crabbing that day, but had simply strayed across the line.[31]

For all its progress during the last half of the nineteenth century, Tangier was still located on an island in the middle of a bay famous for its changing weather, and was still very much vulnerable to the whims of weather.

On April 10, 1889, a storm blew across the island from the east, bringing with it waves that "submerged all the living places." Islanders took refuge in the upper stories of their houses, "where they remained for nearly forty-eight hours in mortal terror of being swept away by the water." By approaching from the east, the storm unleashed its full fury against Steamboat Harbor. "All the vessels laying here were driven ashore," and the pungy *John Scarburgh* was sunk, a total loss. Henry Crockett's fish factory was destroyed, the shell pile on which it was located "was in a great part swept away," and the beach "terribly washed and torn to pieces." Oldtimers insisted that they had never seen such strong wind and high water.[32]

The dangerous weather of January 1893 was of a different sort. A heavy snowfall blanketed the Eastern Shore, 12-14 inches deep in the town of Accomac. The creeks along the bayside froze with ice 8-10 inches deep, while the Bay itself was sufficiently frozen that three young men were able to walk across the ice from Chesconessex to Watts Island. On Tangier Island conditions were nothing less than alarming. With steamboat connections severed, food and fuel supplies dwindled, even as the population was increased by the presence of drummers who were unable to leave. Hundreds of crewmen from the dredging boats were stranded in the Crisfield region without food, shelter, or money, so many that some were temporarily housed in the jail. As in 1889, the oldest inhabitants declared the weather to be "the most severe and protracted they have ever known."[33]

In January 1896 it was not storm but simply a shifting wind that caused a tragedy that became part of the island's lore. Captain Harrison Crockett was returning from Washington in the *Transport* when a "furious northwest wind" struck the pungy just as she drew abreast of the Tangier Lighthouse. The boat capsized, and Crockett and his crew — son-in-law Tubman Pruitt and two black crewmen — were thrown into the frigid waters. Only "Tub" Pruitt was not drowned immediately. He managed to climb to the top of the mast, where his cries for help were heard at the lighthouse, but neither the lighthouse keeper nor the police boat were able to get to him before the pungy settled on the bottom. When they reached the scene "nothing was to be seen but the wild waste of roaring waters."

From this disaster two tales entered the lore of Tangier. One is that the lighthouse staff started to the rescue, but turned back because their wives were in the lighthouse, against regulations, and insisted the men not risk their own lives — an accusation that seems belied by newspaper accounts of the event.

The other concerns the bodies of Crockett and Pruitt, and the immense esteem in which the islanders held the pastor who was serving at that time. Neither body was recovered for months. Eventually Pruitt's body washed ashore on Dameron Marsh on the Northern Neck, but Crockett's was still not to be found months after the event. His widow, fearing that her husband would never have a decent burial, sought consolation from Rev. Charles P. Swain (1859-1900), and the minister told her that he had been in earnest prayer for her husband to come home, and was sure that his prayers would be answered soon.

A few days later the captain's body was found — floating in the little gut behind his own home, drifting slowly towards the landing behind the Crockett house.[34]

Twenty years after the erection of Mariner's Bethel in 1870, the Methodists had outgrown their building yet again.

The last quarter of the nineteenth century was a good one for the Methodists of Tangier. Sunday school at Mariner's Bethel was flourishing, with as many as 100 "scholars," while a second Sunday school was in operation in Uppards. There were camp meetings in 1876 and 1883, smaller than the late great camp meeting of the earlier part of the century, but even so one of them resulted in 18 conversions. When in 1896 the church sponsored a picnic on the beach, it erected a tent to accommodate 1,000 people, almost the entire population of the island. There were flourishing local chapters of the Good Templars Lodge and the Women's Christian Temperance Union, civic organizations that shared Methodism's concern about the dangers of alcoholic beverages. During local option elections Tangier consistently voted "dry," and claimed to have saved the county from "the curse of a licensed grog shop" in 1896. Though unable to do so again in 1898, the island nonetheless voted 150 to 5 against the sale of liquor in that election.[35]

C. P. Swain

In 1890 revival again swept the island, 150 people were converted, and the building which had seemed so large in 1870 was crowded. The building was lengthened by 12 feet in that year, but after another revival and 200 more conversions in 1896 the congregation voted to build an even larger structure. An island-wide campaign raised $5,500, the first dollar of which was subscribed by 14-year-old Thomas Walters, and ground was broken, on the old site just south of Mariner's Bethel, on July 23, 1897.

This time, under the leadership of the charismatic C. P. Swain, the congregation spared no pain or expense, and the large new building was equipped with the very latest in furnishings and equipment —stained glass windows, slate roof, acetylene lights, steam heat — until the initial projected cost was doubled. The last nail was driven on February 4, 1899, and the following day guest preacher J. D. C. Hanna of Wilmington preached the dedicatory sermon despite weather that was "as gloomy a sky as ever covered the heads of men, [with] rain in torrents driven by gusts of wind [that] made the temperature especially unpleasant." For his

## The Churches of Tangier, 1899
Left, Swain Memorial (1899); right, Mariner's Bethel (1870)

second sermon that evening Hanna's topic was "Warm with the Fire of the Holy Ghost," and just as he was getting wound up the new acetylene lights flickered, dimmed, and failed, and most of the congregation rushed out of the building, fearing an explosion. Yet at day's end the remaining debt on the building had been subscribed by a proud membership.[36]

A year later a new minister came and Swain, like Joshua Thomas, moved to Deal Island. There, suddenly, he became ill, developed pneumonia, and died on May 22, 1900, not quite 41 years old. "When the news reached Tangier, the whole Island was in mourning. Young and old wept as if the home were bereft of some loved one." The grief was compounded when "a fearful rainstorm" prevented the islanders from attending the funeral two days later. Within a short time the name of the new church, which had been "Lee's Chapel," was changed to Swain Memorial Methodist Episcopal Church.[37]

Unlike its several predecessors, the church of 1899 proved ample for its congregation, and has been in use for over a hundred years. Its steeple commands almost every vista of Tangier Island from every direction, while in front of it, less noticed by passers-by, is a stone that bears the name of the preacher who built it.

But the stone is simply a memorial, a cenotaph erected by the admiring islanders of Tangier. Charles P. Swain does not lie there, but in a grave near the church on Deal Island, not far from the grave of Joshua Thomas.

# 8
# Remotely Modern

Tangier Island at the beginning of the twentieth century was a lively mixture of the old and the new, the traditional and the progressive, of continuing isolation and increasing involvement in the outside world.

The new church was the pride of the community, and behind it stood an even newer school, erected in 1905, which was "a model for any town." Telephones were the "rage" that year, and a number of stores put them in after an underwater cable was run from the mainland. In 1910 electricity, supplied from individual generators, lighted the church and a few of the stores, by which time "moving picture shows" had been shown in the Tangier Opera House recently erected at 4447 Hilda Crockett Road. Oysters were selling well, shucking houses full, a new seafood canning house operating on the beach, and boats powered by gasoline were "fast taking the place of the sail-boat."[1]

In 1907 the steamboat company built a proper new wharf on the remnants of the shell pile in the harbor. The new dock was 70 foot square, with 12-foot boardwalks surrounding a freight house that was topped with a cupola. The roof of the freight house projected out to shade the boardwalks and to protect the produce that accumulated between the comings and goings of the boats. There was a derrick to lift heavy freight, and a bell in the cupola for use in foggy weather. Because the whole structure sat out in the harbor unconnected to the island itself, it was fitted with "steps to let passengers in[to] the small boats without exposure."[2]

Four times a week the whistle of the steamboat set off a whirl of activity as merchants and their employees descended upon the wharf to claim the merchandise that would fill their stores, while "drummers" and visitors sought the small boats that would take them ashore, and islanders departed for or returned from the city. At such times the steamboat wharf was undoubtedly the busiest place on the island, and it is surprising that no photograph of it has been preserved.

Tangier, which had already set itself apart from Accomack County to create a separate school district in 1904, got its own town government two years later. On March 14, 1906, the state legislature granted a charter for the incorporation of the Town of Tangier. William E. Parks was appointed Mayor, and six others — Cary Crockett, Joseph J. Daley, Peter S. Crockett, Edward L. Crockett, Joshua T. Pruitt, and Travis A. Crockett — were appointed to the Town Council, which was given the authority to appoint a "Town Sergeant" to enforce the law. All of the new officials were residents of Main Ridge, because only Main Ridge was incorporated. The rest of the island remained outside the town limits, which accounts for the fact that Tangier's population appears as only 698 in the

**The Second Tangier School**

census of 1910, even though ten years before the island had over 1,000 inhabitants.[3]

Yet for all the "spirit of advancement" visible on Tangier, the island also had another, less progressive side. Cattle still grazed on the marshes that separated the settled areas. Most of the island's water came from shallow wells or from rainwater funneled into barrels or cisterns, and there was neither a community water supply nor an up-to-date septic system. Refrigeration was unknown, ice far more rare than in comparable mainland towns, and to keep food cool islanders stored it temporarily under the front porch, or down a well. Influenza killed 17 people in the early part of 1900, putting Dr. James Newman himself into a hospital on the mainland, and when another sickness swept the island in 1905 a doctor had to be brought in to handle more than 50 cases that were potentially deadly — the papers do not name the disease that killed "one [person] for every fourteen days" in the spring of that year. Influenza swept Tangier again in 1918 and a young doctor named Charles Gladstone

(1880-1968) came to the island to help; he stayed for almost 40 years. As late as 1923 a county health officer, after visiting the island with a nurse, observed that there was still "a great work to be done" in matters of public health.[4]

The greater the distance from Main Ridge, the more the island seemed rooted in a simpler time. Canaan Ridge in 1915 was a small community of 25 or 30 houses and a single store operated by John "Jackie Ed" Parks. Methodists and the public school shared the same one-room building, and in 1919 a dispute arose as to which should purchase a stove to warm the 22 week-day pupils. The matter was settled by compromise: the school trustees bought the stove, and the Methodists paid for the fuel. Meanwhile the condition of the road to the ridge was a factor in Canaan's continuing difficulty in securing a school teacher, since "no lady teacher can travel the road," and the patrons of the school could not pay the higher salary — as much as $50 a month — that a male teacher could command. Over on West Ridge the school ceased to function altogether after 1903. East Point's few residents abandoned their distant ridge about 1905, and the houses left behind burned shortly thereafter.[5]

Weather, of course, continued to remind Tangier's residents of their unique and vulnerable location. The Chesapeake froze over in January 1900, interrupting the rounds of the steamboat *Pocomoke* and marooning two Tangier school teachers on the mainland. During another freeze in

**The School at Canaan Ridge**
c. 1914

February 1905, the schooner *Mary L. Colburn* collided with the lighthouse as the ice began to break. The lighthouse tender *Maple* was sent to relieve keeper John T. Jarvis and his staff, whose situation was "perilous in the extreme.... The sea now raises and throws the wreck against the piling with terrific force." Another storm the following year downed houses, drowned animals, and dislodged coffins from their graves.

Charles A. Sterling was keeper of the Tangier lighthouse when on the evening of May 30, 1909, the five-ton bugeye *Blanch B*, bound from Solomons Island to Pocomoke City, sank in heavy seas two miles to the west. Hearing a cry of distress, he rushed to the scene and found John E. Wilson clinging to the bottom of his boat "almost gone from exposure." Wilson was rescued, one of many persons saved by Sterling during his long career. Keeper Edward L. Thomas was less successful on February 7, 1914, when his assistant William Asbury Crockett capsized in heavy, frigid seas while returning from a routine trip to pick up the mail from Main Ridge. By the time Thomas reached him, Crockett was dead of hypothermia, and "standing straight up in the water." He was brought ashore, laid out on an oyster culling board, and carried to his home with "a solid flock of people following."

This tragedy came close to repeating itself a few weeks later when another winter storm struck the island, ripping off roofs and uprooting trees while covering the island with snow. Barney Thomas, the new assistant, was headed to the island from the lighthouse when a gale turned into a blizzard, swamped his boat, broke its mast, and swept it southward towards the open Bay as he lay soaked and unconscious in it. Fortunately John and Lewis Cooper had seen his plight, set out in a motorboat, overtook his disabled boat two miles from the island, and succeeded in towing him in to Little Watts Island, where with the lighthouse keeper they were able to revive him. Thinking the storm was over, the three set out for Tangier, ran out of gasoline, and ultimately reached home only by abandoning their boats to the storm and wading ashore.[6]

When the Chesapeake froze yet again in December 1917, "it wasn't like we weren't use to being frozen in," remembered Elmer Crockett, "but no one expected fifty-two days of it." Food supplies dwindled as the freeze lingered into February 1918 and livestock and chickens succumbed to the cold. After lard, butter, sugar, and cheese were used up, many islanders were reduced to only canned and salted meat, and at such times John Wallace, who owned the biggest store and was able to supply the others, carefully rationed the food that he made available. Even the wildfowl the hunters brought home were "hardly fit to eat...they were so poor." Though no one starved during the freeze, Tangier's dependence upon imported food was painfully obvious. The one islander who did die during the freeze could not be buried in the hard ground, and was left in a deserted house in Canaan until the ground thawed.[7]

Even though the town had grown to be the third largest community in Accomack County, progress did not come easily or evenly to Tangier.

The telephone cable connecting it to the mainland quickly deteriorated, leaving the island without telephones for another three decades. John Strigle opened a wireless station in June 1909, but it too was discontinued in 1913. The handsome new school offered only seven grades. When Clara Shores rose to the eighth grade in 1916, she was the only one at that level, and the school trustees, fearful that attempting to offer an additional grade would harm the lower ones, "tried to prevail with her & her mother to go into the 7th grade [again] as two more books had been added this year." Nor was Tangier's school without its discipline problems, as its teachers could testify. In 1917 Miss Nellie Parks found vulgar graffiti written on the building with chalk. In 1913 a boy in Miss Harris' room pulled a revolver and pointed it at the other pupils.

Not even the new town government proved to be a great step forward. On March 16, 1910, only four years after creating it, the legislature dissolved the Town of Tangier. No records of its meetings or its accomplishments, if any, survive, and no one knows why it was so short-lived.[8]

In 1915 the citizens tried again. Granting a petition from 33 islanders, the Circuit Court of Accomack ordered the second incorporation of the Town of Tangier on February 6, 1915. This time the town included Canton and West Ridge in addition to Main Ridge, but not the more distant sections of Oyster Creek and Canaan. An election was set for March 27, but who was chosen Mayor is not recorded. In fact, the Court was surprised to learn nine years later that there had been no regular election of the members of the Town Council or the Mayor since that first one in 1915, even though in the interim Edward T. Murphy and Patrick Connorton had served as Mayor, and John Crockett and Decker Crockett as Town Officer. Accordingly, on April 8, 1924, the Court appointed five men to the Town Council to serve until the next election.[9]

"War" came to Tangier even before the United States entered World War I.

On February 15, 1911, the USS *San Marcos* was towed to a location several miles southwest of Tangier and moored within view the island. Built in 1895 as the great battleship *Texas*, the giant vessel was now to end its career as a target ship for the U.S. Navy.

The shelling began less than a week later. On March 21-22, the *San Marcos* was subjected to the practice gunfire of a dozen ships, including 42 salvos from the *New Hampshire*. On March 27 naval inspectors boarded the ship and declared her a "total wreck." The *San Marcos* was eventually stripped of everything useful, stricken from the naval register, and abandoned near Tangier, resting on the bottom of the Chesapeake with a good part of her superstructure above water.

The following year, in September 1912, ten battleships of the Atlantic fleet used her again for target practice. It was a "war" that Tangier would witness a number of times over the next several decades.[10]

Europe was already at war, the United States cautiously watching, when on Saturday, April 1, 1916, a large and unknown vessel appeared off the island, dropped anchor in Steamboat Harbor, and sent out a smaller vessel filled with uniformed officers. The little boat landed briefly at Banty's Wharf, then quickly returned to the mother ship.

The islanders — without telephone or wireless, unable to communicate directly with the mainland now that the steamers had already paid their weekly visit — were uncertain who the visitors were, but unwilling to take chances. If they were Germans, coming to blow up the island, or to occupy it like the British a hundred years earlier, there was no defense except to gather the family into the house, shut the door, and pray.

Later that day a larger party emerged from the vessel, rowed over to Banty's Wharf, and started up Main Ridge, and the islanders, true to their plan, scurried into their homes. One of the visitors later described that day from their vantage point:

"We transshipped to the tiny boat, landed on a wooden 'dock' and made our precarious way over a single plank which led to dry land at one end of the small street that composed this quaint little town. On either side were neat little one-story houses, each with a tiny front garden, surrounded by a picket fence. The yards contained the family graves marked by simple headstones.

"We walked the entire length of the village, and, although by this time it was nearly noon we saw only closed doors and drawn blinds; not a person in sight. It truly seemed a city of the dead."

**Banty's Wharf**
from *Harper's Monthly Magazine,* 1913

**Main Ridge**
from *Harper's Monthly Magazine*, 1913

Puzzled by the eerie quiet, the visitors returned to the dock, but were unwilling to leave without solving the mystery of the missing inhabitants. "Let's go back again and see if we can find out what this means," said their leader.

As they walked again up Main Ridge, "about the nearest houses we found no sign of life as before, but at the far end of the street our return had taken the inhabitants by surprise. The people were all outside. But the moment they saw us they sped back into their houses and closed and locked the doors. Only one man stood his ground, peering at us through his glasses.

"My husband lifted his cap. 'Good morning, sir,' he said. 'I hope we are not disturbing your quiet homes here.'

"The old fellow stood agape and, slowly removing his own hat, he said, 'Isn't this the President?'"

It was indeed. The unknown ship was not from Germany but was the presidential yacht *Mayflower*, all the way from Washington, D.C. The uniformed men were not German but American officers, some of them Secret Service staff. The leader of the group was no foreign invader but Woodrow Wilson, President of the United States.

The following week the *Accomack News* described the remainder of that day on Tangier:

**Woodrow Wilson**

> *President Wilson and Party*
> *Visit Tangier Island*
> On Saturday, April 1st, the yacht *Mayflower* arrived in this port and about 3 P.M., President Woodrow Wilson and Mrs. Wilson were seen on the streets of Tangier, Va. The streets were crowded so no one could hardly get by. Old Glory was displayed on most every building and the school children sang many songs of cheer for our President.

Eighty-three years later two Tangier residents recalled that day. Annie K. Parks was 15 when the President came to Tangier, Ruth Wallace Clarke was 9, and both had vivid memories of the hearty welcome the townsfolk gave him, even where they stood when they saw the President and shook hands with him. Neither, however, had any recollection of the earlier part of the day, when the doors of the town were closed to him because his entourage was thought to be German.

That part of the story comes from Edith Bolling Wilson, the President's second wife, in the autobiography which she published 22 years later. She alone records the conversation with the old man who recognized the President:

"'...Isn't this the President?'

"When Mr. Wilson replied, 'Yes, I have that honour, sir,' the old man broke into a hearty laugh and then told us that early that morning they had seen a big ship anchor outside in the [harbor], then some men in uniform put out in small boats for their island. This gave them great alarm for they decided that the officers were coming to blow up the island. They had been greatly relieved however, when the men did not land and thought they were safe — until a second time the same boat put out and headed for their abode.

"The old fellow added: 'Well, sir, when I saw your lady with you I kinder felt she wouldn't be with Germans; so I thought I'd just stay out here and she would see there was no harm in me.' Then he begged to go and tell his friends. In a moment the street was filled and every one wanted to shake hands with the President."

What brought Wilson to Tangier was his own curiosity. While taking a brief holiday aboard the *Mayflower* he saw "a tiny speck" called Tangier on the ship's maps, and asked to go there. As Mrs. Wilson reports, "Captain Berry said...he would send the launch over to see what the conditions were." So the "German officers" whose appearance so unnerved the islanders were simply scouting out whether there was a way for the

President to come ashore.[11]

Three days after his return to the capital, the *Washington Post* carried an article about the "quaint" and "odd" little island which had "interested the President immensely." Of particular interest to Wilson were the graves and tombstones in the yards of the island's homes. "The yards are small," reported the *Post*, "not larger than two good-sized rooms. But in each of them are graves, here four or five and there nine or ten, with elaborate monuments and customary headstones. The lawns are green and well kept, with neat walks and fences."[12]

The *Post*'s account of Tangier almost certainly derives from a description given reporters by Wilson himself. Over the years the island has always been uncomfortable with the fascination of many visitors with its front yard burials — a practice which is, in fact, hardly unique to the island, and not uncommon on the Eastern Shore. It is arguable that the world's notice of the practice began with no less a person than the President of the United States.

Exactly one year after his departure from Tangier, Woodrow Wilson, who had been re-elected because "he kept us out of war," appeared before Congress to ask for a declaration of war against Germany. Thirty-one men from Tangier served in the war. William L. Crockett was the first Eastern Shoreman to die in the Argonne Forest. Less than three weeks before the armistice Tubman Crockett died in Portsmouth Naval Hospital of influenza, which claimed the lives of more Eastern Shoremen than all those killed in battle.[13]

By the time of the First World War, Tangier's seafood industry was thriving, though the uncontested dominance of the oyster was slipping. In 1915 Tangier had not only licensed oystermen — 91 tongers, 62 dredgers, 3 patent tongers — but also crabbers — 75 "netters" and 40 "scrapers" — as well as fishermen — 13 of them, plus 43 pound fishermen. Most watermen were licensed for more than one of these pursuits, so oystermen might also be crabbers and fishermen. The island had eight crab packing houses in that year, and eight people who were licensed to rent oyster grounds.

The state was now more actively engaged in policing the oyster industry. The schooner *Pocomoke* patrolled Tangier Sound and "guard[ed] the Maryland-Virginia line to prevent citizens of Maryland from trespassing in Virginia territory." Joseph Daley was the local Oyster Inspector, responsible for enforcing state laws that prevented the harvesting of "culls," oysters under a certain age and size. When the dredging season of 1915-16 proved especially successful, the oyster rocks having "struck young growth," a local newspaper gave much of the credit to Daley and to William T. Murphy, mate on the *Pocomoke*. Schooners still loaded oysters at Tangier, but in the same week of 1915 that the *Minnie May Kirnan* left Tangier with oysters for Baltimore, the *William J. Townsend* headed for Norfolk with a cargo of shells, and later in the year when the steamer *Nellie E. Rawson* of Solomons Island put into Tangier it was to pick up a cargo of fish.

Fishing remained the viable occupation it had been for centuries. There were no fewer than 152 pound nets staked out around the island, and an island fisherman would typically work more than one such net, harvesting them in the morning and taking the catch directly to Crisfield. For some, fishing was a year-round profession, but the best time for it was from February to May, and for many it was seasonal work. Still plentiful in the Bay, but a rare catch, was sturgeon, highly prized for its caviar; a single sturgeon could weigh hundreds of pounds and be sold for an amount equal to several weeks' income. More likely to be found in the nets was herring. A cargo of herring roe was loaded in May 1916 by the Davis-Palmer Company, owners of the fish factory on Tangier Cod. In 1920 the factory and the beach were purchased by the Beach Packing Company; at that time the facility included a fish packing house and a bottling plant. How long it continued in operation is uncertain.[14]

Crabbing got a real boost from the introduction of the gasoline engine, for crabbers could not depend upon wind and sails to get their perishable product to market. Though netters still outnumbered scrapers, many watermen were using the motorboat with the crab scrape, both of which began to be used on Tangier at about the same time. But the growing use of the motorboat also exacerbated the ancient problem of the lack of a harbor. Landing facilities were poor, and some of the island's earliest motorboats had to be anchored off the high marsh north of Canton.

The lack of a real harbor had long plagued the island and hampered its commerce. "Shallow water is our greatest inconvenience," wrote Sidney Wallace in 1921, advocating a channel from the deep water of Tangier Sound to the island. The wharf in Steamboat Harbor lacked a direct land connection, and was not designed for the many working boats of the islanders. Some larger vessels anchored off East Point and were loaded and unloaded from small boats that plied back and forth to a landing on "the Creek" at the northern end of Main Ridge. At that time the water's edge was much closer to the church than it is now, and islanders made use of a small landing in front of the church that was "not very much better than many other places on the island."

In 1917 a government dredge, which the locals dubbed the "mud-sucker," deepened the water just off the northern end of Main Ridge, creating a boat basin, and threw the "spoil" from the bottom up next to the Ridge, creating new land. Watermen had, at last, one place where deep water was adjacent to good high land. Then in the fall of 1921 the French Dredging and Wrecking Company, under a government contract, dug a channel from deep water in the Sound northeast of East Point to the new basin, creating more new land and, for the first time in the island's history, a real harbor. Though the steamers continued to use the wharf in Tangier Cod, the northern end of Main Ridge became, almost immediately, the new center of activity and commerce, and became in time the

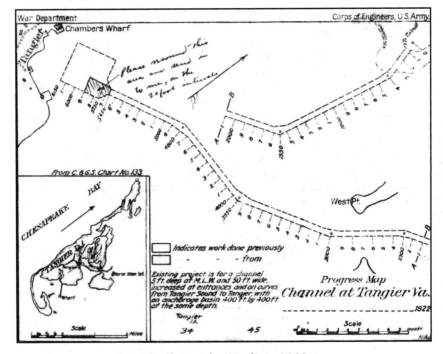

## Dredging the Harbor, 1922
### U.S. Army Corps of Engineers Map

island's "downtown."[15]

Though seafood was the main source of livelihood, it was not the only one. In a town the size of Tangier there was ample room for private enterprise and creativity. John Strigle tried a number of businesses — Opera House, wireless station, "oyster saloon" — but moved to Baltimore after they failed. Noble Dise, despite a withered right hand, was a merchant who also sold and distributed licenses, did correspondence and writing for the islanders, served as Registrar of Vital Statistics and correspondent to the mainland newspapers, and peddled from a pushcart which he wheeled around the island. E. L. Crockett ran a "hotel" in his home at 16199 Main Ridge, Susan Crockett a millinery shop in hers at 16255 Main Ridge. Emily Pruitt made her living repairing the canvas sails of local schooners, and often sat in the yard of her home at 16394 West Ridge happily sewing.[16]

Among the island's several successful merchants was Sidney S. Wallace (1884-1939), son of John Wallace, who after his father's retirement in 1921 shared the operation of the island's biggest store with his brother Elwood and opened a movie theatre in one end of the building. A few islanders had government jobs. The position of lighthouse keeper was a civil service appointment often held by an outsider, but islander Edward

**The New Harbor, c. 1929**

L. Crockett served not only as its keeper but also on the state police boat *Pocomoke*. William Asbury Crockett, who was the assistant keeper when he drowned in 1914, had previously served as the lighthouse keeper at Solomon's Lump, Holland's Island, and Smith Island in Maryland. J. T. Anderton, captain of the *Pocomoke*, also lived on the island, as did the assistant keeper of the lighthouse Barney Thomas.[17]

A shirt factory that opened in 1919 at 16276 Main Ridge provided rare jobs for women; later it moved to a new site south of Factory Road, to which it gave its name. In 1915 some islanders found seasonal employment on the mainland, picking berries in the spring, working in a canning factory at Hunting Creek in the fall. Seasonal employment for the men often meant hunting for waterfowl, not simply to put meat on their own tables but also to supply the demand for game in the cities. Such legal "market gunning" ended in 1918 when new laws prohibited the interstate sale of migratory waterfowl. "Outlaw gunning," which thereafter became a way of life in many Eastern Shore communities, seems to have been practiced by only a few in Tangier. Nor, surprisingly, did the islanders produce the carved decoys that later became an admired folk art, despite — or perhaps because of — the proximity of Crisfield, a major source of them.[18]

It was during the first quarter of the twentieth century that people began to "discover" Tangier, and perhaps during that time that the island gained a reputation as a place that was suspicious of outsiders.

Perhaps the world first learned of the island from the "drummers" who came to the island to sell their wares. In 1915 they included a jeweler and watchmaker, a photographer from Buffalo, N.Y., and a New York City businessman. In 1914 the island welcomed the James Adams

Floating Theatre, a troupe of actors and performers whose theatre was a barge that traveled from port to port pulled by the steamboat *Elk*. Edna Ferber once spent a week aboard the barge, and from her experiences came the musical *Show Boat*. When the theatre played at Tangier in June 1914, the *Elk* could not get close enough to the island to tow the barge in, so a small fleet of local boats waited for high tide and brought the theatre to dock at the Robert Williams pier behind today's electric plant. One of the theatre's attractions that the islanders particularly remembered was a bear in a cage.[19]

**The Williams House**
Looking east from Janders Road (no longer standing)

In 1921 the island welcomed its first Chautauqua, a traveling "show" whose emphasis was more on education than entertainment. There were several Chautauqua companies, and the one that toured the Eastern Shore that spring was generally a three-day affair with a different program of lectures and music each day. On Tangier it played in a traveling tent on the site now occupied by the New Testament Congregation.[20]

Not so welcome was the "movie camera man" who arrived on the island on May 5, 1920, only to be so roughly handled by islanders that he had to be rescued by the Methodist preacher. He had the misfortune to discover that the recent incident he had come to publicize was not one that the island wanted broadcast to the world.

On Sunday, April 11, 1920, Charles C. "Bud" Connorton, Town

Sergeant and Deputy Sheriff, shot and wounded 17-year-old Roland Parks while trying to enforce a town ordinance that forbade "loafing on store porches and streets on Sunday." Residents were required by town law "either to be in church during the hours of service, or in their homes." According to the report that made the newspapers, Connorton discovered Parks on the streets when he should not have been, was cursed by Parks when he tried to arrest him, and fired during a scuffle after Parks resisted arrest. Many islanders insisted that the newspapers had it wrong. Parks had gone to the store which his family operated to get some ice cream for his invalid mother when Connorton saw him opening the store, and warned him against it (stores were, of course, closed on Sundays).

**Main Ridge, c. 1920**

Angry words were exchanged as Parks entered the store, got the ice cream, and walked home with it, the Town Sergeant at his heels. When he got to the door of his home at 16338 Main Ridge, Parks turned before entering it and taunted Connorton, daring him to shoot. Connorton fired, and the bullet passed through the boy's chest and lodged in the front door.

The shooting electrified the community, particularly when it seemed to many islanders that much of the publicity given to it gave a false impression of their community. So when "a representative of a motion picture company" arrived a few weeks later to film the island where the shooting had occurred, "he was warned...against taking any pictures, and when he ignored the warning was handled roughly." His camera was taken from him and destroyed, along with the reels of film he had taken, and "but for the intervention of Rev. W. F. Godwin, pastor of the only church on the Island, [he] would have fared worse." The cameraman was given until midnight to leave, and promptly secured a boat to take him to safety on the mainland.

Connorton, who surrendered to the county authorities the day after the shooting, was tried on June 18 and sentenced to a year in prison. He appealed to the State Supreme Court, but was taken to the state penitentiary in October. There he served only a brief time before being pardoned by the Governor. He returned to Tangier, and resumed his old position as Deputy Sheriff. Months later, while he was seated in an oyster house on Main Ridge, he was fatally shot through an open window by an assailant who was never identified. Roland Parks survived his wounds, spent his adult years running the family store that still operates at 16315 Main Ridge, served on the Town Council, and died peacefully in 1973.[21]

Years later, in April 1931, five boaters from New York docked at Tangier on a Sunday afternoon and set to work "in a manner that didn't sit well with the residents." When told of the fate of the cameraman, they quickly departed. It is not unlikely that incidents such as these — and perhaps even Woodrow Wilson's initial reception — formed the basis of the often-repeated assertion that Tangier Islanders tended to be distant from and suspicious of strangers. Yet, as one islander commented after the New Yorkers left, Tangier residents "are always glad to have visitors, and treat them with every courtesy, but in return they expect tact and judgment."[22]

By 1920 there were two target ships in the Bay off Tangier. The *San Marcos* had been joined by the *Indiana*, and the "war" against them was about to resume.

World War I demonstrated the military possibilities of the airplane, but in the years after the war the Army and the Navy were at loggerheads over whether and how to use it. Foremost among the advocates of the airplane was General William "Billy" Mitchell (1879-1936). Colorful, vocal, and able to command the nation's headlines, he contended vigorously that the airplane could destroy any battleship, rendering the conventional Navy obsolete, and he pursued the idea so relentlessly in military circles and the press that at last the government agreed to arrange an experiment to test his theory. The Navy was ordered to make ready a series of target ships and give Mitchell the chance to destroy them from air. The tests were to be held in two locations: in the Atlantic off the coast of the Virginia capes, and in the middle of Chesapeake Bay.

In February 1921, Mitchell and his crews, based at Langley Field in what is now Hampton, began making practice flights up and down the Chesapeake to bomb the old *San Marcos*. When hazy Chesapeake weather sometimes made it impossible for the Army flyers to orient themselves, Mitchell prevailed upon Lawrence Sperry to solve the problem, and Sperry quickly created the "artificial horizon," a device that has aided aviation ever since.

The first phase of the test began in the ocean off Cape Charles on June 21, 1921, when the targets were German ships captured during the war.

Over the course of a month Mitchell's flyers bombed away, gradually working their way up from submarines to battleships. When the supposedly unsinkable battleship *Ostfriesland* was quickly dispatched by Mitchell's bombers, an observer remarked, "A bomb has been fired that will be heard around the world."

In preparation for the second phase of the test, Mitchell and his crews continued their practice runs up and down the Chesapeake, and during one such run in late June two flyers died in a mid-air collision. The body of Capt. Howard T. Douglas was not found until two weeks later, and was taken to Tangier and transferred from there to Army authorities.

**Gen. BIlly Mitchell**

In September the test resumed, this time in the Chesapeake, where a third battleship, the *Alabama*, had been moored not far from the *San Marcos*. On September 23, Mitchell watched from a motor launch as his flyers covered the ship with a smoke screen and then bombarded it with small bombs and tear gas. At 11:00 p.m. there was a night attack, the first ever, and 300-pound bombs set the ship afire. Finally on September 26 one-ton bombs were dropped from 2,500 feet, and within half an hour the *Alabama* was resting on the floor of the Chesapeake. Mitchell had proven his point, and there in the Bay southwest of Tangier — within the range of the eyes and ears of the islanders — a major chapter in the technology of modern warfare had begun to unfold.

It was not simply from the air and motor launch that Mitchell observed the "war." During the days when the *Alabama* was being shelled, he came ashore several times to Tangier. Islander Frank Dize (1914-1991) remembered him as "a very friendly man [who] passed out candy to the local kids."[23]

In 1924 the remains of the *Alabama* and the *Indiana* were sold for salvage and removed. The old *San Marcos* proved immovable, and remained in place for a number of years to come.

On Wednesday, August 15, 1923, Tangier held its first Homecoming. It was a grand day. Congressman S. Otis Bland and State Senator G. Walter Mapp came over on the state boat *Marguerite*, and "all...turned out for the occasion." After a "sumptuous dinner," the islanders assembled at the church where Mapp addressed them in the afternoon and Bland in the evening, and music was furnished by the Crisfield Band. It was the first of many homecomings, which remained an annual event for a number of years and by the 1930s was held on the beach. Afterwards it became more occasional, and was held first on the vacant lot on Main Ridge opposite the church, then after 1946 on West Ridge at what is now

**A Direct Hit on the Alabama**
September 23, 1921

the northern end of the landing strip.

By the early twenties it took a deliberate "homecoming" to assemble the islanders, for over the years Tangier's growing population had outstripped the island's ability to contain it or to provide a livelihood for everyone. Islanders could name at least 125 Tangier families who had left to live elsewhere.[24] There were pockets of Tangier people living in Crisfield, on the Northern Neck, and on the Eastern Shore of Virginia, especially in the region of Onancock, Deep Creek, and Cape Charles. Most of them, though scattered, retained strong ties to the island, and a strong sense of being Tangier Islanders.

Any returnees who had not seen the island in a number of years might well have been surprised at how Tangier was looking in 1923. One arrived at the new harbor and stepped directly out of the boat to a pier connected to a busy part of the island. Electric lights glowed from a few of the larger buildings, thanks to individual generators. Movies were showing at the Wallacedale on West Ridge. Scattered among the older women in their sunbonnets were young girls with their hair bobbed in the latest fashion.

For any who returned at the end of the decade there was even more modernity to admire. There were now two theatres showing the latest "talkies;" Gordon Daley's new Grand Theatre opened at 16171 Main Ridge in 1929, and it and the Wallacedale together could seat 500 people. James Thorne owned a passenger car, the first on the island and only the second motor vehicle ever to be seen there. (The first had been a truck barged over to the island to haul a new piano to one of the homes.) The tiny streets were lined with stores that sold "everything from a coffin to a pin," and with people selling fresh produce from stands or wheelbarrows. Tangier was "on the map," and had even been filmed by "moving picture men" who visited the island in February 1928 to put "the story of this famous community on the silver screen."

Most important, Tangier now had electricity. On March 23, 1928, the islanders approved the expenditure of $10,000 to establish an "electric works." A generator was purchased and installed at 16276 Main Ridge, the old post office and former shirt factory, and from it was strung wires to 70 of the island's 240 homes. Now the town could have street lights, and the residences electric lights, radios, irons — but not refrigerators, for the "electric works" provided direct current only part of the day. The current was turned on at 5:00 p.m. and turned off at 10:30 p.m.[25]

By 1930 Tangier Island had 1,120 residents, and Main Ridge was *the* place to be. It was on Main Ridge that the watermen gathered to talk in late afternoon after work, and young girls in their Sunday finery walked up and down the street before church. It was to Main Ridge that the men from other parts of the island came to sit around the stove in the store for an evening of conversation. It was on Main Ridge that the vegetables grown in Canton were peddled from wheelbarrows, and both substantial stores and insubstantial sheds offered eats from oysters to ice cream.

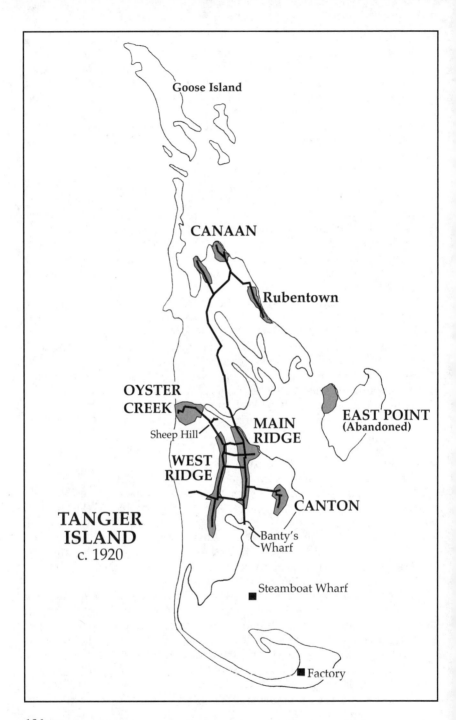

Goose Island

CANAAN

Rubentown

OYSTER
CREEK

Sheep Hill

MAIN
RIDGE

EAST POINT
(Abandoned)

WEST
RIDGE

CANTON

TANGIER
ISLAND
c. 1920

Banty's
Wharf

Steamboat Wharf

Factory

Things were happening on Main Ridge, and the people who lived on the more distant parts of the island felt, by comparison, "kind of under."[26]

As Main Ridge flourished, Canaan and Oyster Creek declined, not because they were washing away — although Oyster Creek would eventually erode into the Chesapeake — but because these communities were distant, lonely, and increasingly uninviting. Oyster Creek, half a mile from West Ridge over a road that was only a few inches above normal high tide, had no school, no store, and no electricity. Its citizens began to move away about 1917, and by 1931 what had once been a community of 20 homes had only two houses still occupied. By the following summer one of them had been abandoned, and by 1939 all that was left was the ruins of six empty houses.[27]

The demise of Canaan Ridge was equally as swift. After years of struggle, the school closed in 1921, and the superintendent urged "the upper end patrons that the only thing & the best thing to do was to hire some one to take the children to school No. 1 [Main Ridge] & back to their homes, this method used on the mainland & other places." Faced with this difficulty and expense, the residents chose instead to move their entire families to Main Ridge, and by 1928 Canaan was completely abandoned.

Some of the people who moved from these parts of the island took their houses with them. Two houses once located in Oyster Creek are still standing elsewhere on the island, at 16140 Main Ridge, and at 16338 West Ridge.

Five houses on Main Ridge are known to have been moved from Uppards: 16084 Main Ridge, 4411 and 4413 Chambers Lane, the Peter Dise House at 16230 Main Ridge, and the Henry Parks House at 16338 Main Ridge. Most of those left behind were demolished by the great storm of August 1933.[29]

Meanwhile Watts Island, like the distant ridges of Tangier, was also declining. The island had been the home of the Parkers since 1743, but in 1908 Harry and Arinthia Parker Doremus, the last remaining residents, moved to the mainland. Dr. Daniel Hardenberg of Jersey City, a nephew, bought the island, and in 1910 his brother Charles took up residence in the abandoned Parker home.

Charles Hardenberg (1875-1937) was a native of New Jersey, son of a well-to-do northern family, a scholarly man with a law degree from Princeton. His health was not good, and when he became convinced that life in the city would harm it even further, he wagered with his college chums that instead of practicing law he would retire to an island and live the life of a hermit. His friends scoffed, perhaps not knowing that his brother owned an island in the middle of the Chesapeake.

When Hardenberg arrived on Watts Island, he came with farming equipment and several horses, but his horses soon died and his hopes of cultivating the still-fertile soil were soon abandoned. Instead he fed him-

# Going to the Movies
## On Tangier Island

In its day Tangier had not one but two moviehouses.

Sidney S. Wallace opened the Wallacedale Theatre in the J. E. Wallace & Co. store on West Ridge in 1921. While his brother continued the general store in the eastern end of the building, Wallace converted the western end into an auditorium, and with his own hands built stage, benches, and booths, installed a single projection machine, and opened the island's first movie theatre.

**Grand Theatre**

In its early years the Wallacedale (see photo, page 75) showed silent movies, which Wallace's daughter Ruth accompanied on the piano, and there were occasional stage shows and live plays. Soon after "talkies" became available, a salesman from Fox persuaded Wallace to install sound equipment, and "King of Kings" played for two weeks straight after the new equipment was in.

Despite its name, the Grand Theatre, built by Gordon Daley in 1929, was a small building covered with tin that sat opposite the Methodist church. Together the two theatres could seat approximately 500 people, but they operated simultaneously for less than a decade. Wallace suffered a stroke in 1931, and though his theatre was still operating in 1936, it closed shortly thereafter and was torn down in the early 1940s.

On conservvative Tangier, mixed couples, even married people or those within the same family, were almost never seen going into the theatre together. Women went with women, girls with girls, boys with boys, and men singly or in groups — though after entering separately, young couples would often rendezvous inside.

After the demise of the Wallacedale, the Grand offered mostly westerns, with admission ranging from 10 to 35 cents "depending on the picture and whether or not there is a comedy." There were no late shows, because in those days the island's electricity was turned off at 10:30 p.m. By 1956 the Grand was open only irregularly, and by 1963 it had been closed for some time. By then many island homes had television.[28]

self by fishing and crabbing, and by harvesting figs and other fruits from the orchards left behind by the former residents. In 1913 the government abolished the position of lighthouse keeper on nearby Little Watts, installed a gas lamp in the lighthouse, ran a pipeline over to the big island, and hired him to keep the gas tanks filled. Thereafter life on Watts Island was exactly what he wanted it to be: ample time for reading from the crates of books he had brought with him.

**The Watts Island Lighthouse**
Charles Hardenberg (right) and
an unidentified visitor,
c. 1936

Hardenberg was a friendly man with a cheerful disposition, well liked by the few people who came into contact with him. He sailed occasionally over to Crisfield or Onancock to stock up on supplies and books, and his first visit of each year was a sure sign to Crisfielders that spring had come. A number of Chesapeake boatmen were on friendly terms, and would stop in occasionally to leave mail or supplies, or to cash his checks. One winter when the Bay froze over and his food supply dropped to the danger point, Hardenberg managed to signal his distress to Tangier, and before long there were visitors from that direction, pulling a sled over the ice laden with supplies.

After ten years of contented exile, Hardenberg suddenly sold his belongings and in 1920 moved to Georgia, only to return a few months later to find his house on Watts Island demolished. So he took up residence in the lighthouse keeper's manse on Little Watts. His brother, perhaps to accommodate him, purchased Little Watts from the government in 1924, except for the 30-foot circle in which the lighthouse stood.

It was during this second, longer residence on Little Watts Island that Hardenberg achieved unwanted publicity as "the Hermit of Watts Island." A playwright named Willard Robinson happened by the island, and later used him as the model for a character named Charley Watts in a play entitled *The Sea Window*. Cartoonist John Hix featured him in his strip "Strange As It May Seem." And in 1930 he granted an interview to newspaperman Albert A. Richards, whose article about him was published in the *New York Sun* and eventually reprinted by over 800 newspapers nationwide. Marriage proposals began pouring into the Onancock post office, one of them from a Jersey City woman he had known as a child. In the spring of 1931 she came down to Onancock to visit him, and on August 26, 1931, he and Katherine Seipel were married. When he took her home to Watts Island, she stepped ashore carrying a typewriter with plans of her own for writing a novel.

Two years later the great Storm of 1933 struck their island, and the Accomack County authorities insisted upon their removal to safer lodgings on the mainland. They moved to Harborton, but within months Charles was back on Little Watts. Katherine, unwilling to live on the island again, moved to the county almshouse.

Charles Hardenberg again lived alone on Little Watts Island until 1936, his vegetable garden well-tended, his bed made, and the house uncluttered except for the stacks of magazines that lay everywhere. He wore big rubber boots and indulged in not shaving until a boat would stop offshore and friends, or the merely curious, would start scrambling into a rowboat to pull towards his pier. He would then dash inside to make himself presentable, greet his guests with the grace of an educated gentleman, and grant them full run of his tiny domain, except for the lighthouse tower. He abandoned his hermit's existence only when ill health forced him back to Jersey City. He died there in the home of his brother on February 26, 1937.[30]

When the stock market crashed in late 1929, only one man on Tangier Island owned stock, and it was not until the end of summer in 1931 that the Great Depression really began to be felt. By then a new school had already been authorized and funded (by the school board of Accomack County, for the island's separate school district ended in 1923), and the new building, which was used until the present school was built in 1998, was opened on September 8, 1932. In the winter of 1931-32 oystering did little more than cover the expenses of some families, and the man who earned a dollar a day on the water was thought to be doing well. Disposable income for luxuries like movies and ice cream, and for ordering from the mail-order catalogs, diminished drastically. Yet like many rural communities that "lived close to the land," Tangier lived close to the water, and no one went hungry.[31]

A major casualty of the Depression was the steamboat line, which had filed for bankruptcy in 1927 and ended service on March 1, 1932, a victim of improved highways and competition from trucks. Tangier's vital link with Baltimore was suddenly severed, its only regular contact with the outer world now a daily mailboat from Crisfield. Only days after this loss, a storm of rain and snow pummeled the island, blowing over trees and electric poles, scattering boats from their moorings, and knocking the house of Frank Williams completely off its foundation. Water covered West Ridge, and in other places on the island "it was almost impossible...for the occupants of homes to leave their abodes." Deep in the night before the wind subsided, the home of E. L. Landing caught fire, and was saved only by an emergency bucket brigade.[32]

That summer the man whom some of the nation blamed for the Depression came to Tangier. President Herbert Hoover was in the declining days of his term when he took a three-day fishing trip on the Chesapeake, and on August 16, 1932, went fishing in Tangier waters from the yacht *Sequoia* and the motorboat of John Crockett, whom he engaged as a guide.

This time the entourage accompanying the Chief Executive included a Cabinet officer — Patrick J. Hurley, Secretary of Commerce — businessman Clarence Woolley and author Will Irwin, all of whom toured the island while the President spent every possible moment fishing. Photographers snapped Hoover, attired in white trousers, blue coat, and Panama hat, as he sat in Crockett's boat, pole in hand. Newspapermen interviewed Crockett and labeled him a "tall, grizzled fisherman" who "drawled" when he spoke. The President caught 15 trout, one of them three feet long, and gave Crockett at $10 tip.[33]

**Herbert Hoover**

By the beginning of 1933 the island had ten stores, three barber shops, a millinery shop, and nine places on Main Ridge to buy ice cream, but hard times were beginning to tell. Tangier crabbers were working Dameron Marsh on the Western Shore, and "what was caught wasn't bringing much money." The number of crab houses in operation was down by 20 percent from the previous year.

Economic difficulties seemed even to threaten the island's long tradition of lawfulness. The chief topic of conversation at the Homecoming of 1931 was the three young men who stole the safe from William Crockett's store on West Ridge in August. Two of them were sentenced to three years in the penitentiary, and the youngest placed in the care of the public welfare authorities. Mayor George Cooper's enforcement of the laws against public intoxication landed him in the hospital with a gunshot wound that same year. Participants in the 1937 Homecoming had another incident to talk about. Only weeks before the event Mayor William Crockett was stabbed in a fight while attempting to board an islander's boat to investigate a report that liquor was being sold from it. His assailants were sentenced to fines of $500 and nine months in jail.

Not all of the island's difficulties stemmed from the economic crisis. Fronia Crockett's store in Canton was destroyed by fire in the summer of 1933, and after the fire as she was searching through the rubble the chimney toppled over and killed her and two neighborhood girls.[34]

Then nature added its fury. On August 22-23, 1933, a devastating hurricane swept up the Eastern Shore causing immense damage. On Tangier

**Main Ridge, c. 1932**
Looking north; on the left, the Old Post Office at 16200 Main Ridge

Island, breaking seas crashed upon the houses, destroying household furnishings and forcing families to seek safety upstairs. Schooners sailed over the main street "without so much as a drag on the bottom." A single spot in Canton was the only place on the island not covered by tide. Some island children "had only to jump out of windows to go swimming."

When the great Storm of 1933 was over, Tangier's boats were scattered or lost, its crab shanties demolished, chickens drowned, gardens ruined, and the shade trees that had lined the narrow streets were uprooted. Tide had carried away the steamboat wharf, and a number of houses had been swept into the Bay. There was almost nothing left standing on Canaan Ridge, and some parts of the island itself had eroded away overnight. As the long and expensive recovery began, some islanders put their houses on scows and moved them to higher ground. A number of islanders moved away to the Western Shore.[35]

In February 1936 yet another freeze locked in the island, while the Eastern Shore lay blanketed with 15 inches of snow. Some watermen reached home by walking across the ice, and one man died while trying to get supplies to Tangier. But food shortages were averted when a "blimp" delivered 1,800 pounds of food to the islanders, and the Army Air Corps dropped both food and medical supplies. "We watched in fascination," recalled one islander, "as the bomb-bay doors swung open and sacks of Red Cross food came tumbling down. We had never dreamed we would enjoy being bombarded with beans."[36]

The oyster industry of Tangier Sound never fully recovered from the Storm of 1933. Heavy flooding throughout the region swelled the rivers that fed the Chesapeake, which then spilled millions of gallons of muddy fresh water into the Bay. Thousands of acres of oyster beds were destroyed, and the oysters that were harvested sold at deflated prices. During those same years Tangier's pound fisheries suffered severe losses, beset by tumbling prices and the rising cost of maintaining and working the big nets. Meanwhile steady jobs at good wages beckoned from shipyards in Baltimore and Newport News, even as the life of the waterman turned ever harder and less promising.

The scarcity of jobs turned suddenly around when the United States entered World War II. The Coast Guard sent teams of recruiters to the island to sign up the sons of its watermen, many of whom, by virtue of their familiarity with water and boats, entered the service directly as coxswain petty officers. The number of Tangiermen who served in the armed forces was 139, fully a hundred more than had served in World War I. Tangier was "fiercely proud" of its boys in uniform, and is said to have purchased more war bonds per capita than any other community in Virginia. Eight islanders gave their lives in the conflict.[37]

With the coming of the war, the old *San Marcos* was again used for target practice, and shortly before the United States entered the war she claimed a victim of her own. The last steamer to serve the Eastern Shore of Virginia was the freighter *Lexington,* which was still making occasional runs between Onancock and Baltimore. On March 27, 1940, the *Lexington* was pulling abreast of Tangier Island when she struck the hulk of the partially submerged *San Marcos* and sank, a total loss. Built prior to the Spanish-American War, the *Texas/San Marcos* never sank a ship in battle, but managed just before the Second World War to take down the last of the Baltimore-based steamboats to the Eastern Shore of Virginia.[38]

**Mailboat at Tangier Dock**

# 9
# A Wider World

In February 1943, while the United States was at war in Europe and the Pacific, a Connecticut couple traveling in Virginia found their vacation twice interrupted, in Fredericksburg by sleet and ice, in Williamsburg by swarms of military personnel.

"We were certain that somewhere in this area there must be a quiet spot the Army and Navy hadn't taken over, a place where we could vacation for a few days. So we got out a map and studied it closely. What we eventually found was a small island, shaped like a fishhook, almost in the middle of the Chesapeake Bay: 'Tangier Island.'"

A few days later Henry and Ann Jander stepped from the mailboat to the Tangier dock, intending to stay only a few days. Instead they found themselves captivated by the island, so much so that a few months later they sold their home in Westport, packed up their four children and two cats, put the city behind them, and headed for a new home on Tangier. Once installed in the old Severn Crockett house at the southernmost end of West Ridge, looking out over the lovely but lonely stretches of the Chesapeake, they named their new home "Crab's Hole."[1]

Robert Arthur Jones had an altogether different experience on Tangier. He visited the island the year before the Janders to write an article for *The Saturday Evening Post*. Jones sought the acquaintance and aid of a number of islanders — Mayor Ray Crockett, Rev. J. H. Billingsley, Capt. Willie Moore, Joshua and Amanda Pruitt — but managed nonetheless to overstep the bounds of hospitality by photographing some of the island's front-yard graves. When islanders objected, he took quick passage back to Crisfield aboard the *King Tut*, the boat of undertaker John Bradshaw. His article, which appeared in September 1943, between the Janders' first visit to Tangier and their acquisition of the house, insisted that he "barely escaped with hide intact" from Tangier.[2]

To many of the outsiders who visited the island, or read about it in magazines, Tangier in the 1940s seemed "quaint," a time-forgotten place where people drove bicycles instead of cars, housewives wore old-fashioned bonnets, and the chief excitement of the day was meeting the mailboat from Crisfield. Islanders seemed to sense when they were being remarked upon as oddities or curiosities, and often met outsiders who did so with reserve.

Yet to visitors without preconceived notions, Tangier Islanders could respond with hospitality that knew no bounds, as Henry and Anne Jander discovered. A successful building contractor and a schoolteacher, the Janders were college-educated, urbane and sophisticated, lovers of classical music, friends of artists and sculptors, accustomed to the cultural and ethnic diversity of New York. They too were initially regarded with suspicion, especially since the war was on and they were rumored to be Germans, but in a relatively short time they were accepted by the islanders and became a vital part of its community. Henry Jander (1895-1951) quickly became a catalyst for change and progress, and had a major impact on the island by his leadership in the effort to obtain modern electricity. Anne Jander (1905-1962) promoted a library, and led islanders on forays into far-off New York City. Her memoir, *Crab's Hole: A Family Story of Tangier Island*, published by her children after her death, is a charming account of life on Tangier Island in the 1940s.[3]

**Henry Jander**

In 1943, when the Janders arrived, there were still two Tangier Islanders who "farmed" their land and a great many fig trees growing in places that had once been farms. Most homes had not wells but cisterns or barrels that collected rainwater from the roofs. West Ridge had a road that was still unpaved, and Canton a single small store. On Main Ridge the land between the Methodist church and the harbor was low and undeveloped, with the result that in many pictures of that decade the church appears to stand virtually beside the water. The cemetery at the back of the church had not yet spread to the side yard, and facing it, down the lane that leads to the school, stood the lodge of the Daughters of America. The Town Council met behind the electrical plant in a small tin building that also doubled as a jail. A few doors up the street stood the old home of Peter S. Crockett which, in 1944, Hilda Crockett (1907-1974) turned into the Chesapeake House, a boarding house with four guest rooms and a dining room on the front porch where a family-style meal cost $1.25.

Tangier now had telephones — four of them, installed in 1940 and linked to Crisfield by radio. An islander who wished to phone the mainland could go to Homer Williams' store — or to the Parks Store, the

**Hilda Crockett**

115

**The Methodist Church seen from the Harbor, c. 1940**

electrical plant, or the home of Alfred Benson — pick up the receiver, and automatically be connected to a mainland operator who would complete the call. Each phone was equipped with a key which, when turned, made it possible to call one of the three other phones on the island.

Tangier also had electricity, at least from 5:00 in the afternoon until 10:30 p.m., when with a single warning blink of the light the electrical plant would shut down. The poles that carried the wires were low, and frequently fell over during storms. A farm tractor, the only one on the island, was kept in readiness to supply current from its batteries during those not-infrequent times when the aging generator failed.

In 1944 Tangier's primitive electric generator wheezed its last, and failed utterly and finally.[4] It had never supplied the whole island, and so undependable had it become that "few tears were shed" at its demise, and many islanders were content not to replace it. But new resident Henry Jander, soon to be elected to the Town Council, envisioned the benefits that a proper electrical facility could bring to the island, not only radios and refrigeration for homes but also businesses not previously possible — regular movies, beauty salons — and even the drilling of deep wells for better water.

Rebuffed by the Rural Electrification Administration, which surveyed the island and found the population too small to merit a government-built electric plant, Jander led the campaign for a town-owned facility. An "Electric Fund" was created, shares were sold, and by 1946 the town owned two electrical generators, obtained from government war-surplus stock, and a new electric plant on the south side of the harbor east of the church. The new plant sat idle, brand new poles in place all over the island, as Jander searched in vain for the transformers needed to make it all work. Months later, in May 1947, the R.E.A. ruled that Tangier and Smith Island together had enough people to qualify for its assistance. Islanders quickly formed the Chesapeake Islands Electric Cooperative, obtained a $207,000 loan to light both islands, and by December of that year experienced for the first time the full benefits of modern electricity.[5]

In the same year that the old electric generator ceased to function another important light fell dark. In the late fall of 1944 a hurricane engulfed Little Watts Island, swirling the waters of the Bay around the base of the lighthouse. The tower, severely weakened, collapsed a few weeks later, and before the year's end was replaced with a blinking light atop a structure of steel pipe located just off the remnants of the island.[6]

In 1945, when the war in Europe and the Pacific ended, Tangier's "boys in uniform" were not the only ones who found their way back home. In April of that year the island's first foreign missionary also returned after eight years in the mission fields of South Africa.

Stella Thomas (1905-1992) returned to Tangier with a faith much more intense than the one she possessed when she left, having become convinced that the Christian, for whom Christ died on the cross, must also become dead to sin. As she shared her experiences with other islanders, none were more impressed than James C. Richardson (1914-2006), the young pastor who had been serving Swain Memorial Church since 1943. Moved by her example, Richardson also became convinced that the modern church and its people were in need of a deeper commitment and a greater spirituality, and soon experienced his own "crucifixion with Christ." As his parishioners noticed a decided shift in his preaching, a number of them joined him in regular prayer and Bible study, and a revival seemed to be in the making. But others in the congregation saw the emphasis on "death with Christ" as new doctrine, and by August 1946 the congregation was seriously divided.[7]

In October, when Richardson was given a new assignment by the Methodist bishop, he elected to withdraw from The Methodist Church and remain on the island. As Robert Bryan, the new minister, moved into the parsonage, Richardson moved his family into the house at 16386 West Ridge, and on November 10, 1946, convened the first service of worship of a new church, the New Testament Congregation, in a rented store building at 16131 Main Ridge.

The schism rocked the island, though the

**James C. Richardson**

117

new congregation was small — originally only four men and a number of women at a time when the Methodist church had over 400 members. The day after the first convening of the new congregation, Richardson found his boat sunk. A few months later a brick was thrown through his window.[8]

On August 13, 1947, forty-two members of the New Testament Congregation gathered on the western side of the island and were baptized — re-baptized, according to Methodist teaching — and thereafter the public reaction became more intense. The rented store that served as a church was repeatedly vandalized, hymnbooks torn, chairs broken, screens and doors ripped away, furniture tossed on the roof, graffiti scrawled on the walls, and the organ thrown overboard. On August 31 the Congregation, unable to meet in their vandalized building, worshiped at the home of John Parks, and shortly thereafter the building in

**New Testament Congregation**

which he stored his nets was destroyed by fire. Richardson appealed to the Town Council, and in October addressed a letter to the entire community, but the vandalism continued. The Methodists insisted that such actions were not done by any of their number; Richardson himself believed that the culprits were most likely young servicemen recently returned from war.[9]

On October 13, 1947, Tangier's religious troubles gained national attention when they were covered by *Newsweek* magazine, and at that point the authorities on the mainland became involved. Two weeks later a grand jury convened in Accomac, and a number of islanders were sub-poenaed to give testimony. Though no indictments were issued, Judge Jefferson F. Walter delivered a stern "charge" to all present that any fur-ther such actions would be prosecuted, and thereafter the "disorders" ceased.[10]

The division in the island's church was, in a theological sense, not a wide one. Methodism on Tangier was hardly liberal in the 1940s, and the schism insured that the island would be served by not one but two con-servative churches. The event was far more divisive socially. For more than a century religion had been a uniting factor among the islanders. After 1946 husbands and wives, homes and families were divided by reli-gious differences, and no single church could claim to be the gathering place for the entire community. Though after 1947 the two churches co-existed peacefully, the "disorders" that accompanied the schism may well indicate the extent to which some islanders feared, at first, that religious division threatened the entire way of life of the island and the very fabric of its community.

When the "disorders" ended, the New Testament Congregation abandoned its rented building and worshiped thereafter in Richardson's home on West Ridge. The Congregation adopted an apostolic model of church government and, at Richardson's insistence, a shared "priesthood of all believers" instead of a professional clergy. By 1949 Richardson had founded a second New Testament Congregation on the Eastern Shore in Deep Creek, where a number of former islanders lived.

In 1958, by which time the New Testament Congregation was wor-shiping in its new building at 16289 Main Ridge, the Methodists invited a "wise old patriarch of the Church" to conduct a revival. The Reverend Andrew Johnson was a colorful and forceful speaker, at one time a can-didate for Vice President of the United States on the Prohibition Ticket, and at Swain Memorial he took as his theme the very "deeper life" issues that had divided the community in the 1940s. When he preached "the doctrines of the deeper life so clearly that it would have been difficult for anyone to misunderstand," a revival occurred that leapt across the lines of controversy, and members of both churches worshiped together fra-ternally for the first time in twelve years. Relations between the two churches grew steadily more cordial after that year.[11]

Except for its brief moment of publicity in *Newsweek* in 1947, Tangier passed through the decade after World War II in quiet obscurity.

In many ways the island's way of life was unique, still shaped by the age-old rhythms of drawing a livelihood from the water. Each November through March found the oyster boats at work, thirty-four of them in 1947, when the average daily harvest of 25 bushels per boat pumped $152,000 into the local economy. Crabbers in that year harvested 6,500 barrels of crabs, worth $65,000, and 15,000 dozen soft crabs, worth anoth-er $12,000. The crabber's tools now included not simply trotline, net, and scrape but also the crab-pot, designed and patented in 1928 and popular among the islanders by the early 1940s.

From time to time the Crab Wars flared, as on July 5, 1949, when Virginia Fisheries deputy David Acree boarded the workboat of Earl Nelson two miles south of the boundary and accidentally shot him in a struggle for control of the boat. Nelson, a father of four from Crisfield, was the last person to die in the centuries-old struggle. The weather continued to be a force with which to reckon; a northeaster in November 1947 submerged the docks and brought 18 inches of water to the doorstep of the Methodist parsonage. An occasional vessel still collided with the *San Marcos* wreck — a yacht from Urbanna in 1948, the oysterboat *T. H. Anderson* in October 1949.

In other ways Tangier was like many another small American town far from the water. At Homecoming in 1947 the festivities included fireworks, a minstrel show, the crowning of Miss Tangier, the unveiling of a monument in honor of World War II veterans, and a visit from Governor William M. Tuck. The Grand Theatre showed movies two nights a week, "the rest being taken up with church work." Rowdyism was not unknown. Many of the younger men congregated at the poolroom above a grocery store on Main Ridge, and there in 1946 Albert Crockett used a billiard cue to quiet a disturbance and eject Lawrence Dise. Three years later, on August 31, 1949, Dise took his revenge by shooting Crockett five times in the back of the head. He was sentenced to life imprisonment.

The more progressive of the islanders, spurred by their success at obtaining electricity, dreamed of an airport, and persuaded the legislature to grant permission for it and the Corps of Engineers to use "fill" from the dredging of the harbor to build up ground for it. But that dream was delayed, perhaps in part because of the sudden death of Henry Jander, the tireless advocate for progress who died in 1951 while rushing to meet the mailboat. Islanders were more successful in lobbying the county school board, and in 1955 a combination gymnasium-auditorium-cafeteria was added to the island school, the first of its kind in the county. The drilling of deep artesian wells, made possible by electricity, began in 1958.[12]

The unlikely person who thrust this quiet community into the public spotlight in the mid-1950s was its beloved town doctor. Charles F. Gladstone was 74 and had practiced on the island for 36 years when in 1954 he announced his impending retirement. Gladstone agreed to stay until a replacement could be found, but had chosen to retire at the very time when small-town doctors were becoming increasingly hard to find, and it took three years to replace him. Islanders appealed for help to the Virginia Council on Health and Medical Care, and as its "physician referral service" swung into action Tangier's plight captured the attention of the *New York Times*, which ran several stories that were picked up by the wire services. Within a short time reporters and photographers from the television networks and from metropolitan newspapers were visiting the

# Charles F. Gladstone
## 1880-1968
### Island Doctor

Before Charles Gladstone, the doctors of Tangier came and went swiftly, seven or eight of them in the twenty-five years prior to his arrival. Gladstone came to the island in the fall of 1918 during an epidemic of Spanish influenza, and stayed for almost

40 years. A native of Northampton County, Virginia, he earned his M.D. at the University of Maryland, went almost immediately to Tangier, and never really practiced anywhere else.

Three of his predecessors had lived in "the Doctor's House" at 16251 Main Ridge, each selling it to his successor when the medical practice changed hands. He purchased the house from Dr. G. Bache Gill in 1919, yet never lived there. Instead he lodged in a single room next door, upstairs in the house of Sidney and Florence Crockett. His office, the same one used by his predecessors, still faces the back yard of the Doctor's House.

Gladstone was the very embodiment of the small-town doctor, and greatly beloved by the islanders. It is said that he "never lost a baby," and at least one island boy was named after him. He charged no fees, but instead was paid a flat $1.50 per month by each family on the island, though it is said that often some were able to pay as little as 25¢.

Gladstone announced his retirement in 1954, and the search to replace him, nothing short of worldwide, brought Tangier a great deal of publicity. He stayed on the island until Dr. Mikio Kato, a native of Kobe, Japan, arrived on April 15, 1957.

A bachelor for most of his life, Gladstone was 82 when he married widow Frances Sturgis Belote of Exmore, former educator and novelist. His marriage was said to have broken the heart of one special admirer who was still waiting for him back on the island.

Gladstone died at 87 in 1968, and is buried in Onancock. The U.S. Congress honored him with a citation for "faithful and loyal service," the islanders by naming the health center at 16155 Main Ridge for him.[13]

island to file stories about the search, and people from all over the country were learning about Tangier.

In 1957 the call was answered by Dr. Mikio Kato, a specialist in obstetrics and gynecology who had practiced in his native Japan and in New England. When Dr. Kato arrived on the island on April 15, 1957, the church bell tolled, about half the population gathered at the harbor to greet him, and *Life* magazine reported the event. Meanwhile Oscar J. Rishel, pastor of Swain Memorial Church, had been leading a strong effort to establish a health clinic for the new doctor's use, and the Gladstone Memorial Health Center was dedicated two weeks after Kato's arrival.[14]

When Kato ended his island practice — in the fall of 1958, after marriage to islander Emma Sue Crockett — the publicity was even greater. Once again magazines, newspapers, and metropolitan radio stations featured Tangier, and amateur radio operators, invited to the island from Richmond, broadcast a continuous "call to anyone listening." Mayor Alva Crockett and several others appeared on a major network television program, narrated by newscaster Douglas Edwards, and were seen by millions. As before, nationwide publicity did not yield immediate result. Not until November 1961 did North Carolina physician John Edward Parks (no relation to anyone named Parks among the islanders) take up residence, after learning about Tangier's need from *Modern Medicine* magazine. He ended his practice in December 1964, and the radio appeal that followed his departure was nothing less than worldwide. Dr. Oscar M. Watson, Jr. of Denver "happened to hear something on a radio broadcast about a lonely island in Chesapeake Bay" and took up residence on Tangier in July 1965. This time the island offered the new doctor not only the use of a clinic but also of a new home, built to his specifications at

**Gladstone Memorial Health Center**
Dedication ceremonies, April 28, 1957

16472 West Ridge, and a car, which turned out to be "an elderly Volkswagen which had lost several disputes with fenceposts." Watson was the last resident doctor of Tangier, and by the time of his departure the island's new airstrip made a doctor's presence less critical.

The publicity surrounding the island's recurring need for a doctor helped to put Tangier "on the map." After the television program that followed Kato's departure, letters poured in from every state in the Union requesting information about how to get to Tangier and where to stay. By the end of the decade Tangier had been featured in the Sunday supplements of the principal newspapers of Baltimore and Washington, in *Life*, *Americas*, *National Geographic*, *Commonwealth*, *Flying*, and *Yachting* magazines, and had been the fictionalized scene of a paperback romance about the arrival of a new doctor on a Chesapeake island. It was undoubtedly because of such publicity that even before the arrival of Dr. Watson a new industry had established a foothold on Tangier Island: tourism.[15]

Meanwhile out in the Chesapeake southwest of Tangier the old *San Marcos* still rested on the floor of the Bay, more of a navigational hazard than ever now that rust and ice had broken her down to the point where she was barely visible at low tide. By 1957 seven ships and boats had sunk after colliding with her, costing the government $100,000 in damages and prompting a reporter to observe that "this is a far better record than the *Texas* had in the Spanish-American War, when it not only failed to sink any enemy ships, but nearly rolled over each time it fired a salvo."

In November 1958 the Navy undertook the final demolition of the wreck, but after three weeks and the use of twelve tons of explosives succeeded only in reducing it to 13 feet below the water's surface. In February 1959 a new tack was tried: a Navy demolition team blasted a deep trench next to the wreck, then blew the hull into the trench. The *San Marcos* lay, at last, a safe 20 feet beneath the waves, still marked on maps of the Bay, but no longer a serious hazard.

Yet Tangier's years as a site for target ships were far from over. A 1947 government plan to establish a restricted target area in Tangier Sound was abandoned after stiff opposition from the islanders, but on June 16, 1958, the Navy opened a new target range on the Chesapeake side of the island to provide bombing training for carrier-based flyers. Two control stations were built on West Ridge, one at the southern end (the site now under water), the other at the northern end near today's airstrip. The first target was a billboard "ship" made of wooden slats 2.3 miles out in the Bay; it was later replaced by two more vessels resting on the Bay's floor, the *American Mariner* and the *William L. Davidson*. Naval flyers from Chincoteague, Oceana, and Patuxent practiced their skills on the Tangier targets, as many as 80 flights a day, more than 227,000 bombs by 1970. Initially a staff of six islanders monitored the range, but by the time the effort ended in April 1982 there were only two "spotters" still at work.[16]

In 1961, shortly after the Navy took up business on Tangier, the

Tangier Lighthouse was dismantled. In its place, resting on the structure that had supported it, was left an automated light flashing every six seconds. The light removed from the lighthouse was preserved at East Point.[17]

The tourboats first came in the summer of 1964, from Deltaville on the Western Shore, "intermittently scheduled" excursions arranged by a travel agency of Urbanna. Tourists boarded the boat at 8:00 a.m., arrived at Tangier at 11:30, dined at the Chesapeake House, returned to the boat by 2:15, and were back in Deltaville by 5:30, a round-trip fare costing $10, not including Hilda Crockett's "immense midday meal." The first excursion boats were small enough that "the winds and resultant waves" could force the cancellation of the trip, but subsequent summers found the larger *Suntan* docking at Tangier's harbor. Tour boats arriving from the Western Shore had, at first, to circle south around the island and approach from the east, for the North Channel connecting the harbor to the Chesapeake was not dredged until 1967.

In 1968 islander Eulice H. Thomas (1898-1981), operator of the mailboat between Tangier and Crisfield since the 1920s, entered the business by founding Tangier Lines Inc. to ferry passengers to and from the island. Within two years the *Captain Thomas* was in operation between Fairport, near Reedville, and Tangier. The names of the ever larger and newer tourboats that plied to Tangier — *Captain Thomas, Captain Eulice, Captain Thomas, Steven Thomas* — testify to the prominence of the Thomas family

**The *Suntan* approaching the Tangier Dock, c. 1965**

in Tangier's tourist industry. After the *Captain Thomas* was sold to Stanley Bowis in 1971, the tourboats from Reedville, including the *Chesapeake Breeze*, were operated by his family, which was allied by marriage to the island family.[18]

By 1974 as many as 15,000 people were visiting Tangier during the summer tourboat season, and tourism had become an important new industry on the island. Hilda Crockett expanded the Chesapeake House to accommodate 168 at a sitting, and became famous for her giant seafood meals cooked from "scratch." Evelyn Day opened the Tangier Nautical Museum two doors up the street. Frank Dize, retired waterman turned historian, met the boats at the dock to peddle his two books, *Something Fishy from Tangier* and *Something Fishy from Tangier and Corny Too*. Vernon Bradshaw (1922-1993) sold his own drawings of the island from his Little Shop for Discriminating Souvenir Collectors at 16240 Main Ridge.

Yet the hundreds of visitors always came at midday, when most of the men were on the water, and were gone by supper time, and the face of Tangier itself remained steadfastly unaffected by the daily influx. Not only did Tangier remain visibly "un-touristy," but its residents also continued to pursue their own ideas of progress, and given the opportunity to enjoy the benefits of modernization usually did so with little regard for whether outsiders would find the results picturesque or appealing. The narrow streets, once shaded and lined with picket fences, were widened when pick-up trucks were introduced to haul groceries, and motorcycles and scooters became popular. Chain-link fences, better able to withstand being brushed by such vehicles, were replacing picket fences even before

**Main Ridge in the Morning, 1965**
Picket fences are still to be seen, and tourists stroll in Bermuda shorts

the advent of tourism. The precedent for the chain-link fence was set in 1958 by the Methodist Parsonage; by 1962 there were 35 such fences around the island, and within a few years picket fences were the exception instead of the rule, much to the lament of many visitors. The first mobile home on the island, moved into place at 16226 Main Ridge in 1959 — not without a great deal of difficulty, a number of "close calls," and the sawing of neighboring tree limbs — was soon followed by others. The old radio telephone system was replaced in 1966, complete with a fully modern and highly visible microwave tower. A new Recreation Center, much needed but hardly beautiful, opened on West Ridge in 1976. Fully modern water and sewage treatment facilities were installed in 1983, and the buildings that housed them placed where needed, regardless of the view. The island's several bridges were reconstructed in the 1990s to enable them to accommodate the fire engine housed at the new firehouse erected in 1983.[19]

One of the most important improvements was the airstrip on West Ridge, a long-awaited project built with state and Federal funds. On August 7, 1969, Governor Mills E. Godwin and a host of state dignitaries flew in to dedicate it, and within a year it had been used by people from as far away as California and Alaska seeking a meal at the Chesapeake House. In April 1971 Jinx Holton, wife of the Governor, flew in for a day's visit with a number of other wives of Republican governors, among them Judy Agnew of Maryland (with her Secret Service agent; her husband was then Vice President), and Nancy Reagan of California. They dined at the Chesapeake House, but were not allowed to serve the sherry they had brought with them — "You're not going to have that stuff in my dining room," insisted Hilda Crockett, who permitted no alcoholic beverages of any kind at her establishment. Among the other celebrities who later flew into Tangier were actress Elizabeth Taylor, whose husband John Warner was elected Senator in 1978, and two novelists who wrote mysteries set in Tangier: Phyllis Whitney (*The Ebony Swan*, 1992), and Patricia Cornwell (*Unnatural Exposure*, 1997, and *Isle of Dogs*, 2001).

Islanders found the airstrip a boon in many ways. Five months after it was dedicated it proved its worth when ice filled the harbor and food supplies had to be flown in. Tangier's recurring problem of the lack of a doctor became less urgent because patients could be airlifted to mainland hospitals. By the late 1970s two doctors who were also pilots were making weekly flights to the Tangier health center, which nurse Helen Landon staffed several days a week after her return from the missionary field in 1970. Less welcome were the planes that descended in January 1976 as helicopters, airplanes, outboards and cabin cruisers converged upon the duck-hunting camp of Kenneth Pruitt at Uppards on the northern end of the island. The raid was the largest ever conducted up to that time by the U.S. Fish & Wildlife Service, and resulted in four felony counts against Pruitt.[20]

The islanders' own attitudes about their home took an important turn in November 1973, when Tangier was featured in a 26-page article in *National Geographic* written by Harold G. Wheatley, island native and principal of the local school. Photographer David Alan Harvey spent six weeks on the island preparing for the article, and when the project was done invited the townsfolk to the school auditorium to see the beautiful color photographs he had taken. As the slides were shown, "an atmosphere — a hush — went over the auditorium," remembered Helen Landon. "Suddenly they understood what a unique culture we have, and that it is worth saving." Islanders who had always resisted being labeled "funny" and "different" now saw their home as "rare" and "valued." "It was a very important thing to happen," observed Landon, "for a description of our culture to go all over the world."[21]

Two decades later when Bell Atlantic chose Tangier as the site for a commercial to be aired on television, islanders eagerly lined up for a spot in it. "It's a wonderful opportunity to show our unique island and its closeness," commented Postmaster Fern Tyler. The commercial, in 30-second and 60-second versions, was shown for 13 weeks from Pennsylvania to Virginia in 1995. Narrated by actor James Earl Jones, it juxtaposed attractive vignettes of the island with watermen selling their wares by computer and a history teacher beaming her lesson from the mainland into an island classroom. The islanders' "lilting accent," for all the times it had been described as difficult to understand, was apparently comprehensible to millions of television viewers.[22]

The winter of 1977 was the worst Tangier had seen since 1936. Two January storms in a row left the island surrounded by ice. A fearsome combination of tide and frigid 50-mile-per-hour winds created great floes of ice that smashed like matchsticks the poles that carried the electric lines north to Smith Island, and rammed up against the western side of the island in piles twenty feet high. As the ice thawed, the black-topped surface of the island's streets gave way underfoot, and watermen wondered how extensively the intense cold had damaged the Bay's oysters.

Once again the new airstrip proved its worth as food and supplies were brought in by air, but this vital link with the outside world was located in the very part of the island most vulnerable to the ultimate damage a storm could wreak upon Tangier: erosion. Had the airstrip been built in the same place a century earlier, it would have been approximately 1,000 *yards* distant from the Chesapeake. A government map of 1968, the year before its completion, shows it located 1,000 *feet* from the Bay at the furthest point. In 1976 the runway was lengthened to 3,600 feet, making it able to accommodate a DC-3, but bringing its southern end even closer to the water; a stone breakwater was erected at that end to protect it, but even before the project could be completed a storm washed a ten-foot corner out of the runway. In March 1984 another storm damaged over 700 feet of the runway.[23]

The vulnerability of the vital airstrip was the most graphic illustra-

**The Great Freeze of 1977**
Charlie Pruitt demonstrates the height of the ice floes
behind his home on West Ridge, February 1977

tion of the fact that Tangier Island was eroding at an alarming rate. A 1975 report of the Virginia Soil and Water Commission recommended the construction of a stone breakwater along the western edge of the island, tied in with the "jetty" then being built, but estimated the cost at a prohibitive $2.8 million. Fourteen years later the cost had risen to $3,594,000, and by then the situation was so urgent that even that higher figure no longer seemed prohibitive. To meet their share of the funding Tangier Islanders agreed to a 400% raise in local taxes. One conservationist observed that the cost amounted to $6,925 per resident of the island, or between $25,000 and $35,000 per family, and argued that "it would be more sensible to give this money to the Tangierines for a new start on the mainland." Nonetheless construction began on March 22, 1989, and the "seawall" — 5,700 feet long, 50 feet wide, 73,000 tons of stone — was completed in 1990. It was for most of its length over six feet high, designed to withstand "the worst storm every 25 years."

Though the seawall appeared to stabilize the western edge of the island, erosion elsewhere continued unabated. A second breakwater, 430 feet long and 62 feet wide, was proposed to prevent erosion around the North Channel and to protect the harbor, and in 1996 Congress approved the idea. A year later the funds for the project had still not been appropriated.[24]

**Preparing Seaweed for Market**
Sinclair's Dock, Tangier Beach, 1970s
(Photograph by A. Aubrey Bodine)

One person seemingly undaunted by the prospect of erosion was Robert Sinclair, a successful businessman from Hampton who began spending summers on the island in the 1960s. In the early 1970s he bought the beach at the southern end of the island and had it surveyed and divided into 48 vacation homesites which he hoped to develop as "Tangier Shores." With his own hands he erected a "surprisingly sturdy" building on the beach which served as both his home and a store, and to provide a visual center for his development he secured the *Edward J. McKeever Jr.*, an old menhaden boat, which he half-sank in the sand nearby. Always the entrepreneur, Sinclair also obtained a grant for determining whether seaweed gathered from around the island could be marketed as fertilizer, and purchased the old post office/electrical plant building on Main Ridge where he opened a gift and craft shop. His seaweed experiment proved unsuccessful, and most islanders scoffed at his attempt to develop the beach, for it was well known that this part of the island shifted and changed shape from time to time.[25] Sinclair sold no lots on the Tangier beach, and after his death both his store and his moored boat burned. Remnants of each are still visible on the shifting sands.

More successful at transforming a part of Tangier was G. R. "Randy" Klinefelter, a Pennsylvania businessman who in 1959 purchased the island containing East Point Ridge. Klinefelter renamed his purchase Port Isobel Island, planted tens of thousands of trees, built three lodges, a pier, and a barn, and "developed" it into "one of the finest natural areas on the Bay." In 1962 he also purchased Watts Island, and later rescued the gravestones from its eroding cemetery by removing them to Port Isobel. In 1988 he donated his showcase island to the Chesapeake Bay Foundation, which used it as an education center and in 1992 added a new "main hall" to its several buildings.[26]

The decades that brought progress and change, publicity and tourism to Tangier also brought devastating blows to its seafood industry. The oyster beds of Tangier and Pocomoke Sounds were again damaged in October 1954 when Hurricane Hazel poured millions of gallons of fresh water into the Bay. The latter part of that decade witnessed a number of attempts to replenish the stock, among them that of Charlie Pruitt (1916-1982), whose *Ruth S* brought boatloads of seed oysters for replanting in Cod Harbor. But even as he worked a deadlier enemy was on its way.

In 1957 a mysterious disease — Multinucleate Sphere Unknown, or "MSX" — was discovered in Delaware Bay, and within a few years the oyster industry of that region was

**Transplanting Seed Oysters in Tangier Sound**
from the *Ruth S*, 1958

decimated. The single-celled protozoan, which shriveled the meat of the oyster to an unpalatable mass, found its way into the Chesapeake in 1959 and, thriving on high levels of salinity, struck first the oysters of Virginia, then those of Maryland further up the Bay. As the disease spread the number of marketable oysters plummeted, and the oyster industry of Chesapeake Bay, like that of Delaware Bay, was devastated.[27]

Though severe, the blow to Tangier was not fatal, for among the islanders diversity had always been the key to drawing a living from the waters around them. Crabbing, previously a summer occupation, quickly became the mainstay of the island's income. By 1966 the region produced 97 million pounds of crabs, an all-time high. Even though the crab harvest could fluctuate widely — in 1973 the harvest was little more than half that of 1966 — Tangier by the end of the 1970s was producing more crabs than any other single locality in the Chesapeake Bay region.

Nor was the crab the only alternative. Some island men found summer work with the menhaden fleets out of Reedville, Salisbury, or even further afield. Tangiermen continued to catch trout, striped bass, croaker, spot, flounder, and bluefish for market, and in some cases sold them right at the waterfront in Washington, Baltimore, and other cities. By the early 1990s a small commercial clamming industry had emerged, as watermen tonged for clams as they once had for oysters. And there were still viable professions related to the seafood industry: three island men continued the long tradition of building boats.[28]

But the worst was still to come. In 1985, after years of MSX, continued over-harvesting, and drought, Virginia closed the Tangier and Pocomoke Sounds — traditionally the state's most prolific source of the bivalve — to oystering altogether. In addition, the crab harvest began to decline as more and more watermen were forced into crabbing as the other possibilities became more constricted.

The 1990s found the island's seafood industry surrounded by regulations that were unpopular among watermen steeped in the tradition that the bounty of the Bay belonged to the person who went after it. Concerned that the crabbing industry was over-capitalized — so many people involved in it that most of them could not make a full-time living from it — Virginia in 1996 began a new policy of capping the number of licenses issued for crabbing. Unlike those in most other localities, Tangier watermen tended to be "full-timers," but the new policy of limiting licenses threatened the potential for the island's young people to "follow the water" like their fathers before them.[29]

There was still, perhaps, a future for oystering. Throughout the ban Tangier watermen had always insisted that there were good oysters in the Bay, and they brought to the attention of state officials oysters so large that they were believed to have survived MSX and to be, therefore, resistant to it. In 1997, the Virginia Marine Resources Commission oversaw the removal of 2,500 bushels of such oysters from the waters between Tangier and the Eastern Shore and their replanting as "brood stock" on an experimental "reef" in the Great Wicomico River on the Northern Neck. The process was repeated the following year, when the "strike" of good oysters was the largest in many years. The Commission remained hopeful that such cultivation would result in the eventual re-introduction of oystering to the Chesapeake, although it seemed unlikely that the industry would ever again reach pre-1960s proportions. The promise of the future seemed to lie not in the kind of massive harvesting for shucking and canning that had once dominated the industry, but in supplying smaller specialty and quality markets, such as oysters on the half-shell.[30]

Tangier was already known as a religious and highly moral community when in 1987 it became the only town on the Eastern Shore of Virginia to vote against the establishment of a state lottery. The following year it became one of only four to vote against pari-mutuel betting. In the other three communities the vote was close, but not in Tangier: 281 against, 87 for. By the 1990s Tangier was still officially dry, one of the few communities in the state where lottery tickets could not be purchased, and its residents could count on one hand the number of divorces that had occurred on the island in the past quarter-century.[31]

At the end of the twentieth century, religion was still very much at the center of life on Tangier Island. Though many American communities could only claim to remember such a time, most people on the island were members of one of the two churches, and most members — 66 percent of the Methodists in 1998 — attended church regularly. For Tangier Islanders, religion was not a matter of convenience but of conviction, and righteousness and sin stood out in clearly, even sharply defined distinction. "On Tangier you're either a Christian or a sinner," observed one islander, and most of the island's residents not only identified themselves as Christians but also participated in the life and the lifestyle defined by their church.

One measure of the church's influence is the number of islanders who became ministers. Like other small Virginia communities, Tangier produced its share of professionals who "made good" in the outside world. Willie Davis Crockett (1921-1996) practiced dentistry in Richmond, taught at Virginia Commonwealth University, and garnered a number of awards for excellence in both endeavors. Vernon Gladden Spence (1924-1989) earned a doctorate in history, taught at two universities, and wrote three books on the history of the American West. Island natives David Shores, an authority on Chaucer, taught at Old Dominion University, while Willie Crockett became a successful artist. William A. Pruitt served as Commissioner of the Virginia Marine Resources Commission, and Robert Crockett served as Sheriff of Accomack County. Yet no fewer than 16 people entered the Methodist ministry from Swain Memorial Church, and another six islanders from both churches served as ministers in other denominations. One island native, Dr. Gerald Wheatley, taught at Prairie Bible College, and from the two churches six women entered the foreign mission field. In addition, four ministers who served the New Testament Congregation itself did so while also working at secular professions — a total of 33 islanders who, by 1997, had entered some form of the Christian ministry.[32]

In 1995 yet another religious revival swept the island, the latest in a long series throughout the island's history. Both churches traditionally held revival meetings each year, but the services at the New Testament Congregation in March 1995 were followed by "cottage meetings" which continued unabated until the Methodists began their own annual revival. Thereafter the two congregations met together for nightly services that frequently lasted as long as three hours, most of them led by laymen from each of the churches. The results were dramatic: over 200 people, some of them previously unchurched and some of them long-term churchgoers, answered the altar call for conversion. Over 60 people were baptized on the beach, a new Sunday school class of young adults was formed at the Methodist church, and religion became the topic of conversation in home, store, and school.[33]

So when in the late 1990s issues concerning tourism and seafood once again brought Tangier into the public eye, it was hardly surprising, given the prominence of the church in the island's life, that religion helped to shape the outcome of each.

In early 1998 scouts from Warner Brothers came to Tangier seeking a "location" for an upcoming Hollywood movie. *Message in a Bottle*, with stars Paul Newman, Kevin Costner, and Robin Wright Penn, was described as a "poignant romantic drama" set in a waterfront community, and the island won the nod as the setting for some of the movie's scenes. Scripts were distributed to the members of the Town Council, whose approval was needed for the movie to use municipal property in the harbor area, and excitement among the locals mounted. But after reading the script council members voted unanimously on March 9 not to permit the filming unless parts of it were revised. Explaining the vote, Mayor Dewey Crockett cited scenes with cursing, drinking, and sex. "We realized the movie would have an economic impact on the island, but it would also be undermining what we have stood for all these years.... Based on our religious values, we felt the movie was in conflict with the way we live."

The decision stunned the island, and divided its residents — "It's not as if we don't already have drinking and cussing on Tangier," commented one citizen. "I teach the children not to compromise with their religious beliefs," said another, "and to vote for the movie would be a compromise." The following night 200 islanders packed the school auditorium for an open meeting, and the 27 people who spoke were "almost evenly split between those who supported the council's decision and those who opposed it." Council members received a petition signed by 200 citizens requesting a reconsideration of the matter, promptly rejected it, and stood by their decision.

# The Tangier Class Meeting

Long before a church stood on Tangier, or there was preaching on Sundays, Tangier Methodists were gathering for the "class meeting." Beginning under Joshua Thomas in 1805, following the

model established by John Wesley himself, island Methodists met weekly to sing, pray, read the Bible, and "work out their salvation" by encouraging and admonishing one another to keep up the effort to make religion a vital part of daily life.

They are still doing so. By the late 1800s, when the class meeting was withering away in most American churches, no fewer than five "classes" were functioning among Tangier's growing congregation. By the late 1900s, when the gathering was known to most Methodists, if at all, only from the history books, Tangier's class meeting was not only still operating, but also thriving.

"Class meeting" convenes in the South Room of Swain Memorial at 9:00 a.m. every Sunday morning, an hour before Sunday school, two hours before "preaching." The minister is not expected to be present, and the gathering is completely led by the laity of the church. After a reading from scripture, members speak, share personal "testimonies," or break into song as the Spirit may lead.

Though it is no longer, as originally, a small group — typically as many as 100 attend, including a few youth — the interaction and sharing are often uninhibited. Participants speak openly of salvation and eternal life. The sick are prayed for, thanksgivings offered, and not infrequently people offer face-to-face apologies to one another for past wrongs or slights, and share words and signs of forgiveness. Requests for prayer, handshakes, "Amens," spontaneous singing, and affirmations of "Praise the Lord" abound.

After an hour a bell rings, and most participants move on to the other events of Sunday morning. Sunday school, at 10:00, is a more recent practice dating only from 1856. "Preaching," at 11:00, has been an every-Sunday event on Tangier only since 1883. More so than these others, the class meeting is Tangier's vital link to its early Methodist origins, and may be the last surviving example of this eighteenth-century practice in American Methodism.[34]

Once again Tangier found itself in the media spotlight. Newspapers far and near reported the event, radio talk shows fielded comments, and internet users debated the decision. For weeks readers expressed their opinions to their editors, either lauding or condemning the decision — "God is surely smiling on Tangier," wrote one Eastern Shoreman; "self-righteous, egotistical," wrote another. The Accomack County Board of Supervisors weighed in with a commendation of the council for "standing on their principles" and "exemplifying their religious beliefs."[35]

The debate had not died down when on March 18 actor Paul Newman visited Tangier. Having planned to see the island even before the council's vote, Newman chartered a boat, took a walk around the island with the charter boat captain, and with his sunglasses and baseball cap was, as he wished, recognized by no one. Only Rudy and Beth Thomas, who had circulated the petition, were introduced to him. The actor had planned to feast on crab cakes but discovered that the island's restaurants were closed, so the party dined on hot dogs microwaved on the boat. After seeing the island, Newman stated that "it's a sad thing that the movie isn't taking place on Tangier," for "it's the ideal location."

Tangier was not the only place to turn down the movie. Chilmark, Massachusetts, on Martha's Vineyard also nixed the opportunity, citing the fragility of its sand dunes. *Message in a Bottle* was eventually released in early 1999. A *Washington Post* reviewer labeled it "90 minutes of melodrama," adding, "there's only one thing to do with this 'Bottle': Put a cork in it."[36]

In February 1998, even while Hollywood was scouting out Tangier, the islanders were making news of their own: many of Tangier's watermen had pledged publicly to stop polluting the Bay and the island and, citing their religious beliefs, formed a covenant to abide by all existing civil laws regarding seafood and the environment. To seal the covenant, the islanders had formed two groups: the Tangier Island Watermen Community Stewardship Initiative, and a women's group named F.A.I.I.T.H., Families Actively Involved in Improving Tangier's Heritage.

In one sense, the sudden emergence of environmental concern among the islanders came to many as a surprise, for Tangier, like other Chesapeake Bay communities, had for centuries operated on the principle that the Bay was common ground to be used by all, that it would continue to sustain the waterman without needing sustenance itself, and that it was acceptable to turn an occasional blind eye to any attempt to regulate the waterman's right to live off its bounty. Yet in another sense Tangier was also a profoundly religious community. The catalyst behind the new covenant was an outsider who came to the island hoping to draw the two concerns together, and to demonstrate that environmental stewardship could thrive if it drew its impulse from a community's religious beliefs.

An evangelical Christian with experience in negotiation and conflict resolution, Susan Drake read about Tangier's revival while serving as a part-time professor at the University of Wisconsin, and arrived in Tangier in 1996 hoping to bring her convictions from hypothesis to reality. Shortly after her arrival two storms flooded parts of the island, and trash dumped on the marshes floated into the streets and yards of the town. Given the opportunity to speak at both churches, Drake used the event to advocate her concept that stewardship of the environment was not only a wise investment but also a matter of faith. Her message found ready acceptance, and 58 men came to the altar to dedicate themselves to being "good stewards of God's creation."

Within weeks of the covenant, many Tangier watermen were flying red ribbons from the antennas on their boats, islanders had picked up truckloads of litter, and public school and Sunday schools were stressing the importance of conservation. A three-day symposium brought together a hundred people, including scientists, Federal and state regulatory officials, and representatives of the Chesapeake Bay Foundation, an agency typically unpopular among the watermen. At this and other meetings, the islanders hammered out a "long list of goals and strategies" for cleaning up the island, developing its economy, and maintaining its seafood industry.

Yet the new environmental movement was not universally popular. Most of the island's 175 licensed watermen had not signed the covenant, and its economic ramifications for the individual waterman remained a high concern. Some expressed concern that the movement ignored the Tangier Island Waterman's Association, or that differences on economic or environmental strategies might now be interpreted as differences between the saved and the unsaved.

For the covenanters, it was a matter of personal faith that the new stewardship offered long-term gain despite any economic loss from "playing by the rules." "Our watermen have [received] a bum rap," observed school principal Dennis Crockett. "They're perceived as people who would catch the last crab, the last clam, the last oyster. But the watermen themselves have produced a plan that says we're not like that." Indeed, "Tangiermen are not the only fishermen who [have been] abusive" of the environment, observed waterman Philip Pruitt, who suggested that if the watermen of Tangier could make it work, the island's model of faith-based environmental stewardship might well spread to other communities.[37]

As the twentieth century drew to a close, it was the pursuit of the blue crab that shaped much of Tangier's life. A typical workday found the waterman up at 3:30 a.m. and the harbor alive with lights and noise well before dawn. The "crab houses" that lined the harbor were essentially "shedding pounds" where the molting of the crab could be monitored and the crab packed in grass and ice for shipping at just the right moment after shedding its shell. The morning mail boat left with the result of the waterman's pre-dawn labor: hard crabs packed in baskets and soft crabs in boxes, bound for dealers in Crisfield or even New York's Fulton Fish Market. After hours in the crab house, the waterman then spent hours in his boat scraping for crabs or gathering the day's catch from his crab pots, taking the harvest to Crisfield or to his crab house before returning home for an early supper.

Meanwhile back in the village, families lived by the schedule shaped by the crab; even classes at the Tangier Combined School began early, at 7:30 a.m., synchronizing the island's next generation with a daily routine unique to this unique community.[38]

**Crab houses, Tangier Harbor, 1999**

# 10
# Tangier Today
## A Walking Tour

To the passengers who line the decks of the tourboats, cameras at the ready for a first glimpse of the island they have come to see, the view at Tangier harbor is, in one sense, a fine one. Boats wait in orderly fashion at substantial piers, and zip effortlessly over to crab houses that cluster like detached villages out in the water. To the north, beyond another row of crab houses, lies fully half the land area of Tangier Island, the once-inhabited Uppards, now a maze of marshland and water that, from the tourboat, looks peaceful and unspoiled. To the east lies the islet once known as East Point, now Port Isobel, behind it, more distant on the horizon, Watts Island. To the south Canton rises handsomely in the distance, in recent years dominated by the biggest house on the island.

When the cameras point to the town itself, the view is less than picturesque. Petroleum tanks crowd the harbor's edge, and the vista across the docks to the steeple of the Methodist church is interrupted by the fences and towers that accompany the electric plant. In the foreground of the view towards Canton stands a quonset hut, a trailer, and a side of the harbor that appears abandoned and cluttered. The ubiquitous chain-link fence is much in evidence at the docks, and the buildings at water's edge seem almost defiantly utilitarian. Despite its dependence upon the Bay that surrounds it, Tangier turns its back to the water, disappointing any visitors who anticipated a town of picture-postcard beauty.

From the dock the passengers follow a wide lane, lined with chain-link fence, to the town's main street, known for many years as King Street, now Main Ridge Road. Here most of them turn left, headed for the Chesapeake House and its famously huge lunch. Here many engage the golf-cart "buses" that offer quick transit to the restaurant and a tour of the entire island. Here, three hours later, they will converge again as the boat prepares to depart. Most of them will have walked, or been driven, down Main Ridge, over the Hoisting Bridge to West Ridge, and back by one of the other bridges, perhaps even up to the Parsonage and the County Dock. Most will have stopped at one or more of the several shops. Most will remember the town as a whole, but probably not many will have noticed much about the individual homes and buildings. With a few exceptions — the Methodist church, the bed-and-breakfast inns, the school, the parsonage — the houses and structures of Tangier appear at first glance unremarkable.

Yet nowhere is Tangier's past more visible than in the individual homes and buildings that line its narrow streets. Many a Tangier address has its own place in the island's history, and its own story to tell.

The store on the corner of the lane to the docks, now a gift shop known as **Robin's What Not Shop [1]** *(16131 Main Ridge)* is the store that in 1946 became the first sanctuary of the New Testament Congregation. After being vandalized several times during the most difficult days of the island's religious schism, it was pictured in *Newsweek* magazine in 1947. Opposite it, on the site of the little ice cream shop, occurred the island's only unsolved murder; C. C. "Bud" Connorton was eating in an earlier building here when he was shot through an open window by an unknown assailant.

The houses on the east side of Main Ridge Road towards the church are of relatively recent vintage (1950s and later), because they stand on "new land," built up with shells and with fill from the dredging of the harbor. This was the "Homecoming Lot" for a number of years until that event was moved to West Ridge. The buildings on the west side of the street include an old **Oyster Creek House [2]** *(16140 Main Ridge)*, moved from that now-vanished ridge, and the **Double Six Sandwich Shop [3]** *(16146 Main Ridge)*, a favorite hang-out of local watermen that was depicted in the 1973 *National Geographic* article on Tangier.

The **Gladstone Memorial Health Center [4]** *(16155 Main Ridge)* was dedicated in 1957 and preserves the name of the island's most beloved physician. Behind it stands the **Electric Plant [5]** *(4443 Janders Road)*, the oldest part of which is the wooden front section, built in 1947. Opposite the Electric Plant is the storage building that from 1964 to 1983 served as the **Old Firehouse [6]** *(4444 Janders Road)*; here was kept the 3-wheeled Cushman "mini-engine" depicted in *National Geographic* in 1973. It was at a pier at the end of Janders Road that the James Adams Floating Theatre docked in 1914. The area behind the Electric Plant, though far from attractive, nonetheless houses a functioning "marine railway" where boats are repaired.

At what is perhaps the island's most prominent and historic site stands **Swain Memorial United Methodist Church [7]** *(16164 Main Ridge)*. The present building, substantially unchanged since 1899,

c. 1930

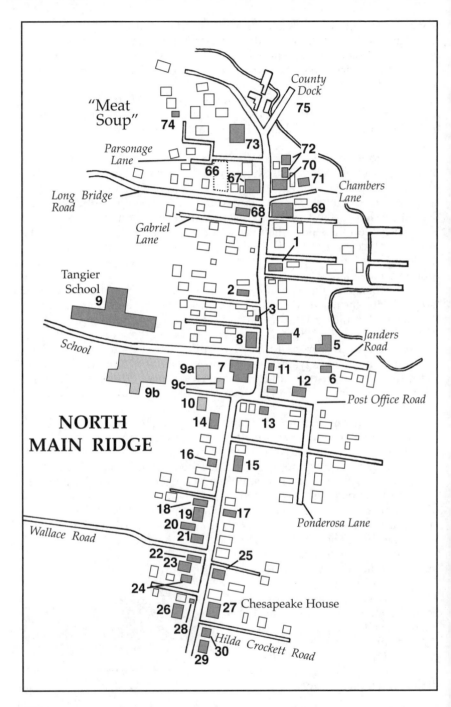

"Meat Soup"

County Dock
**75**

**74**

**73**

Parsonage Lane

**72**
**70**
**71**

Chambers Lane

Long Bridge Road

**66** **67**

**68** **69**

Gabriel Lane

**1**

Tangier School
**9**

**2**

**3**

**4**

**5**

Janders Road

School

**8**

**9a** **7**

**9c**

**11**

**12**

**6**

Post Office Road

**9b**

**10**

**13**

NORTH
MAIN RIDGE

**14**

**16**

**15**

**18** **19**

**17**

**20**

**21**

Wallace Road

**22** **23**

**25**

**24**

**27** Chesapeake House

**26**

**28**

**30**

Hilda Crockett Road

**29**

Ponderosa Lane

occupies the site of the island's second church, erected 1842. The **Hiram Benson Educational Building [8]** *(16152 Main Ridge)*, dedicated in 1963 and named for a prominent "pillar" of the Methodist Sunday school, occupies the site of the third church, "Mariner's Bethel" (1870). Prior to 1963 as many as 12 Sunday school classes were conducted simultaneously in the church sanctuary, while small children met in the "parish house," an old building that stood just north of the church. It is easy, by noting the dates of the tombstones, to see how the church cemetery expanded into its several sections over the years. In front of the church stands the cenotaph for C. P. Swain, the marker honoring island servicemen, and the state historical marker. The "class meeting" announced on the church sign may well be the last such gathering still functioning among the Methodists in America.

Behind the church on School Lane stands the **Tangier Combined School [9]**, dedicated in 1998, "combined" because it is attended by all the island students, Kindergarten through Grade 12. The location of the first school building (1871) is unknown, but the second (1905) **[9a]** stood behind the church, and the third (1932) **[9b]** opposite the present one. At least two other nearby buildings, no longer standing, also housed school functions: an old house **[9c]** that stood south of the church, where the cemetery is today, and the **Daughters of America Lodge [10]**. The Daughters of America was sponsored by the American Insurance Company, and was for many years an important force in the life of the island. Its building faced the lane that leads through the cemetery south of the church, and at various times housed church, school, and community events.

**Jim's Gift Shop [11]** *(16151 Main Ridge)*, on the corner opposite the church, is located in an old barber shop. In the front yard of the **Telephone Building [12]** *(16171 Main Ridge)*, erected in 1966, stood the Grand Theatre, opened in 1929 by Gordon Daley. Despite its name, the Grand was a small building covered with tin; it closed and was torn down in the early 1960s. The **Post Office [13]**, the island's fourth, was built in 1969 on the site of store operated by Alonzo Moore. After turning a right angle Post Office Road becomes Ponderosa Lane, named for the location of a TV western that was popular when this part of the island was developed; the "new land" on which its homes stand, built up with fill from dredging, was said by the islanders to be "as big as the Ponderosa."

Some of the island's oldest and largest homes line the street south of the church, among them the **Stephen Pruitt House [14]** *(16186 Main Ridge)* adjacent to the cemetery, and the **Edward Crockett House [15]** *(16199 Main Ridge)*, which at various times served as the home of Sugar Tom Crockett, a "hotel," and the office of Dr. W. O. Daisey. Two new shops operate where older ones once stood: an ice cream shop on the site of the **Old Post Office [16]** *(16200 Main Ridge)* of the 1930s, and a gift shop on that of the **Lewis Crockett Store [17]** *(16215 Main Ridge)*. The

**The Church Corner, c. 1936**
Looking east from behind the church
Behind the small tree at the left is the Grand Theatre

house at **16212 Main Ridge** [18] was once a barber shop that sat much closer to the street.

The **Joshua Pruitt House [19]** *(16216 Main Ridge)* is one of the island's oldest. Here Pruitt (1866-1949) and his wife Amanda, devout Methodists, took in boarders, especially teachers, and sometimes held worship services in the front yard. Pruitt is said to have traveled to Washington during the Depression to remonstrate with the President, knocked on the front door of the White House, and gained an audience with Franklin Delano Roosevelt. The **Connorton House [20]** *(16220 Main Ridge)* was the home of the town sergeant imprisoned in 1920 for shooting an island teenager. Next to it stands an **Old Store [21]** *(16222 Main Ridge)*, now a home.

On the corner of Wallace Road the island's first mobile home (1959) occupies the site of the old **Noble Dise Store [22]** *(16226 Main Ridge)*. Adjacent to it is the **Peter Dise House [23]** *(16230 Main Ridge)*, one of the oldest on the island, moved to this location at an unknown date from Uppards. Next to it is the late 19th-century **Ranford Spence House [24]** *(16234 Main Ridge)*. **Sandy's Place Gifts and Museum [25]** *(16233 Main Ridge)* is located in the old Milton Marshall House, and contains a roomful of Tangier artifacts gathered by Marshall's daughter Evelyn Day. Both the Dise and the Marshall house had wells in the yard; an old well in the yard of 16235 Main Ridge, adjacent to the Marshall house, was widely used before the advent of the town's modern water supply.

The famous **Chesapeake House** occupies not one but two old island homes. Hilda Crockett opened the business in 1944 in the **Peter S. Crockett House [26]** *(16246 Main Ridge)* with four guest rooms and a dining room on the front porch, then expanded by purchasing the **Nathan Rayfield House [27]** (*16243 Main Ridge*), where the dining room is now located. Both houses are late 19th-century, although the date of neither can be fixed with certainty. Down Hilda Crockett Road stood two short-lived businesses run by John Strigle: the Tangier Opera House where movies were first shown (1908) and the wireless station (1909-1913). The little gift shop opposite the Chesapeake House once bore the grand name

**Main Ridge, c. 1930**
Looking north from 16255 Main Ridge
The last house on the right (behind the electric pole)
is today's Chesapeake House

**Little Shop for Discriminating Souvenir Collectors [28]** (*16240 Main Ridge*).

At 16251 Main Ridge stands the **Doctors' House [29]**, owned consecutively by doctors Samuel Oglesby, Willard Daisey, Bache Gill, and Charles Gladstone. Gladstone, however, never lived here, but boarded next door in the **Sidney Crockett House [30]** (*16249 Main Ridge*). His office still faces the back yard of the Doctors' House, behind the **Susan Crockett House [31]** (*16255 Main Ridge*), whose owner operated a millinery shop in the rounded room at the front of her home (see map next page).

The new house on the corner of Garman Road occupies the site of the old **Peter S. Crockett Store [32]**, later Daughtery & Ward, later the Haynie Grocery. It had a two-story front porch which stands out in many old photographs of Tangier. A few doors down the street another new house stands on the site of the old **Nathan Rayfield Store [33]** (*16276 Main*

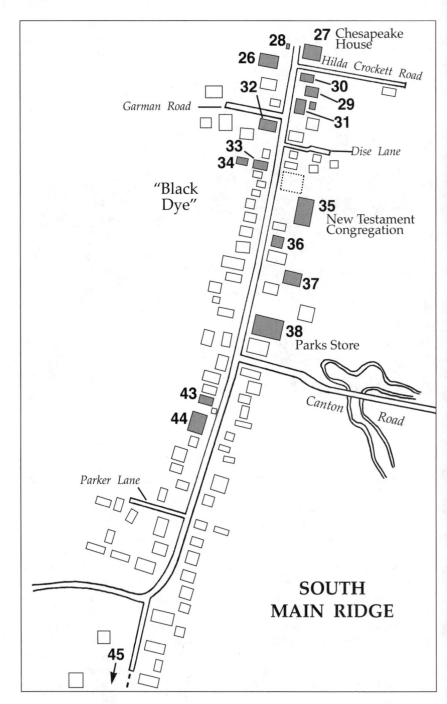

27 Chesapeake House
28
26
*Hilda Crockett Road*
30
32
29
*Garman Road*
31
33
34
*Dise Lane*
"Black Dye"
35 New Testament Congregation
36
37
38 Parks Store
*Canton Road*
43
44
*Parker Lane*

**SOUTH MAIN RIDGE**

45

*Ridge)*, a landmark that at various times housed the post office, the shirt factory, and the first primitive "electrical works." Though the store is gone, in the back yard can still be seen the old **Town Jail [34]**, a tin building where the town kept its lock-up cell. It is said that one of the last persons jailed there, convinced that the jailer had forgotten to bring him his mid-day meal, simply climbed out of the roof, went home for lunch, then climbed back in to resume his sentence. Town Council meetings were often held here prior to the opening of the Methodist educational building.

The southern part of Main Ridge, below the old Jail, is known locally as "Black Dye," a name whose origin is unknown. A number of homes in this part of town — among them 16269, 16270, 16278, 16282, and 16286 Main Ridge Road — are quite old, though they cannot be dated with certainty. Early photographs of Tangier streets often depict this part of Main Ridge. The building of the **New Testament Congregation [35]** *(16289 Main Ridge)* was first used for worship on Easter Sunday 1957, but for a number a years the congregation continued to use also the older house that was already on the lot when it was purchased in 1956. It was here that the Chautauqua pitched its tent in the 1920s. Two doors south of the church the congregation has renovated an old house for use as the **New Testament Mission House [36]** *(16299 Main Ridge)*; here at one time lived Alfred Benson (1893-1963), who taught at the Canaan Ridge school. Two

doors south of it stands the **Patrick Benson House [37]** *(16307 Main Ridge)*, the late 19th century home of Capt. Patrick Benson (1856-1940).

The **Parks Store [38]** *(16315 Main Ridge)* was established by Capt. Henry Parks (1862-1933) and is still operated by his descendants. It shares with the mailboat service, founded by Capt. Henry Thomas (1880-1947), the distinction of being the island's oldest continuous business still in the same family.

Just below the Parks Store, Canton Road leads eastward to the smallest of the ridges of Tangier, affording pretty vistas of Main Ridge, Canton, and Canton Creek. Though this was the first part of Tangier to be permanently settled, it is no longer possible to ascertain exactly where the house

**The Patrick Benson House**
16307 Main Ridge
Center: Delia Parks Benson
(1858-1930)

of the original Joseph Crockett stood. As recently as twenty years ago Canton still retained an air of antiquity, but today it is largely a place of substantial new homes. At its northern end stands the **Haynie House [39]** *(5053 Canton Road)*, erected 1994, the largest home on the island; in its front yard stood the last of Canton's small stores **[39a]**. The cemetery at the corner was, in the early 1900s, a place of well-tended gardens, the last of the "farms" of Tangier. Just inside the cemetery fence is the recent marker indicating the **Possible Site of "Lee's Bethel" [40]**, the island's first church. The house at **5085 Canton Road [41]** was built by Dr. Mikio Kato during his brief residence on the island. In the yard adjacent to 5104 Canton Road stood the **Fronia Crockett Store [42]**, which was destroyed by fire in 1933.

Back on Main Ridge, the owner of the Parks store lived several doors south of his establishment at the **Henry Parks House [43]** *(16338 Main Ridge)*, site of the shooting of his son by the town sergeant in 1920. The house is thought to have been moved from Uppards at the same time as the Peter Dise House. The small building in the front yard is an old barber shop. The **Tangier Volunteer Fire Department [44]** *(16344 Main*

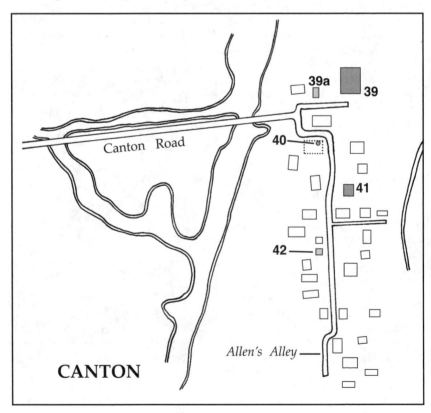

*Ridge)* was established in 1964 and moved to this location in 1983. South of it are a number of homes that are known to be old but which cannot be precisely dated.

From the southern end of Main Ridge, Banny's Road leads southward towards **Banty's Wharf [45]**, once the major landing point for the island, now the site of a few crab houses. Here President and Mrs. Woodrow Wilson came ashore in 1916 as did, probably, the British in 1814. Steamboat Wharf was located just offshore, and with the disappearance of the steamboats in the early 1930s Banty's Wharf fell into disuse; it lies today beyond the reach of the paved road.

Factory Road (see map next page), said to have been built by Henry Frazier, one of Tangier's few black residents, takes its name from the old **Shirt Factory [46]** which was located on the marsh between the two bridges in the 1920s. The factory burned about 1927, but part of its concrete foundation can still be seen. The first and larger of the bridges is the **Hoistin' Bridge [47]**, in local parlance pronounced "highston," over the "Big Gut." Now fixed, and wide enough to accommodate a modern fire engine, the bridge once had an opening in the center that allowed the masts of sailing vessels to slip through; a loose plank across the gap, removed for boats, was put back for pedestrians to cross — and not infrequently removed at night by pranksters. From the bridge can be glimpsed the beach at the southern end of the island and the remnants of Sinclair's beached menhaden trawler. The interesting view in the other direction displays the topography of much of the island, specifically the marshes separating Main Ridge from West Ridge.

The old store standing on West Ridge at the end of Factory Road is the **William T. Crockett Store [48]** *(16614 West Ridge)*, operated for many years by the island Mayor and site of a burglary that scandalized the

**The "Hoistin' Bridge"**
Looking towards West Ridge, c. 1960

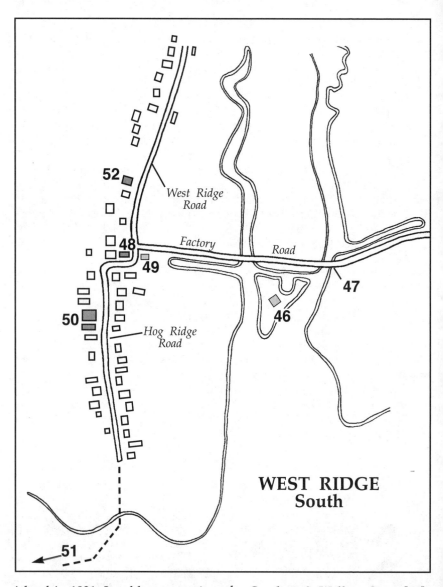

island in 1931. Its older competitor, the **Crockett & Wallace Store [49]**, once located across the street from it, is no longer standing.

Hog Ridge Road leads southward, past **Sunset Inn [50]** (*16650 Hog Ridge*), a bed-and-breakfast, to the southernmost parts of the island. Beyond the end of the road a series of paths, walkways, and bridges (not always easily passable during high tide) leads to where the northern end of Tangier Beach meets the southern end of **the Seawall [51]**. In this region was located "Crab's Hole," home of Henry and Anne Jander, now under water. From this point there is more than a mile of beach to the southernmost tip of Tangier Island, and then "the hook" bends sharply northward for an additional half mile. This is also one of the points at which the erosion that is threatening Tangier is most obvious; the houses on Hog Ridge Road were once more than a half mile from the Chesapeake.

West Ridge, except at its northern end settled later than Main Ridge, is not so crowded with houses, and a number of them are of recent vintage. The **Orville Pruitt House [52]** *(16588 West Ridge)* once served as a boarding house. The **J. E. Parks House [53]** *(16472 West Ridge)* was built in 1961 for the doctor who arrived in that year (see map next page). The large house at the end of Wallace Road is the **John Thomas House [54]** *(16448 West Ridge)*, one of the island's largest. Two families — Thomas and Wallace — owned much of West Ridge at the end of the nineteenth century, and the line between this and the next house was the boundary between their large properties.

The **J. E. Wallace & Co. Store [55]** *(16443 West Ridge)* faced Wallace Road at this corner, and Wallace himself lived across the street at 16443 West Ridge; his grave is behind the mobile home now at that address. In the store was located also the Wallacedale Theatre. Nearby stands the home named for the husband of Wallace's daughter Mary, the **Edward S. Pruitt House [56]** *(16428 West Ridge)*, and beyond that the home of Wallace's son, Mary's brother, the **Sidney Wallace House [57]** *(16408 West Ridge)*, one of the most admired and photographed homes on the island. Built in 1904, it was restored in 1995 by Wallace's grandson, and operates today as Shirley's Bay View Inn. Like many other Tangier houses, it once had rain gutters that directed water into a ground-level cistern at the back of the house, but even so Mrs. Wallace always insisted upon boiling water before using it for drinking or cooking.

Near neighbors of the Sidney Wallace House are the **Emily Pruitt House [58]** *(16394 West Ridge)*, home of the island's seamstress of sails, and the **Amanda Wallace Pruitt House [59]** *(16386 West Ridge)*, which became the home of Rev. James C. Richardson after his resignation from the Methodist church. Here the New Testament Congre-

**The Sidney S. Wallace House**
"Shirley's Bay View Inn"

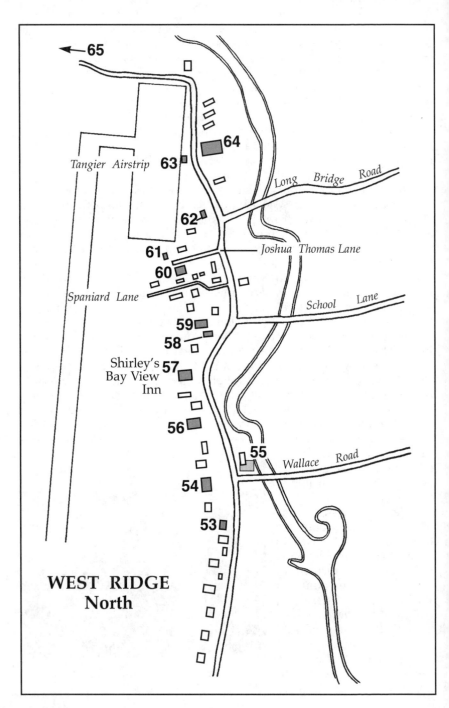

← **65**

**64**

*Tangier Airstrip* **63**

*Long Bridge Road*

**62**

**61**

**60**

*Joshua Thomas Lane*

*Spaniard Lane*

*School Lane*

**59**

**58**

Shirley's **57**
Bay View
Inn

**56**

**55**

*Wallace Road*

**54**

**53**

**WEST RIDGE**
**North**

gation met weekly from 1948 to 1956, when as many as 50 people gathered for worship in the living room and Sunday school students convened upstairs.

A modern house in the style of a chalet stands on the site of the **Joshua Thomas House [60]** *(4300 Joshua Thomas Lane)*, where the Parson of the Islands lived from 1799 until about 1825. The large old house which stood at this address until the present house was built was not that of the Parson himself but dated from the time of his grandsons Joshua II (1826?-1870?) or Lybrand Thomas (1838-1922). The small building opposite it is **Spotting Station [61]** *(4301 Joshua Thomas Lane)* for the Navy's target range, moved to this site from north of the airstrip, now owned by the Town of Tangier.

At its northern end, West Ridge Road once extended to Oyster Creek Ridge, and facing Long Bridge Road is an old **Oyster Creek House [62]** *(16338 West Ridge)* moved from that community. Just beyond is the entrance to the **Tangier Airstrip [63]**, dedicated 1969, extended 1976. This part of the island was built up by fill from dredging that began in 1946, and in recent years has served as the "Homecoming Lot." The Robert Bros. Circus of Sarasota, Florida, played here on July 16, 1977. The big building beyond the airstrip, on the westernmost side of the island, is the sewage treatment plant, built in 1983. The **Recreation Center [64]** *(16315 West Ridge)* was dedicated in 1976. Beyond it are a few homes and, at water's edge, **Pruitt's Boat Yard [65]**, where boats are built and repaired.

The northernmost of the four bridges over the Big Gut, once known as Mooney's Bridge, is today called the New Bridge or Long Bridge, and it leads back to the section of Main Ridge known, for reasons unknown, as "Meat Soup." On the left (see map page 140) is the **Old Cemetery [66]**, sold to the people of Tangier for $12 by Jesse Crockett in 1858 and filled with many of the island's most interesting old gravestones. At the busy corner on Main Ridge stands the **Fisherman's Corner Restaurant [67]** *(16329 Main Ridge Road)*, and on the right the **Peter Williams House [68]** *(16116 Main Ridge)*, one of the oldest and largest on the island, now bereft of the "gingerbread" that once adorned its eaves and porch. Williams was the original operator of **Daley's Grocery [69]** *(16115 Main Ridge)*, which was built by Charles Roland Parks and William Walters in the 1920s. The **Channel Marker Restaurant [70]** *(4409 Chambers Lane)* stands on the site of the earlier Nice's Store. Chambers Lane leads to the area once known as Chambers Wharf, site of the **John Chambers Store [71]** *(4417 Chambers Lane)* and the first post office (1881), now occupied by Lorraine's Snack Bar. Two houses on this lane, more easily viewed from Main Ridge Road, are old **Canaan Ridge Houses [72]** *(4411 and 4413 Chambers Lane)*, moved here in 1928.

The **Methodist Parsonage [73]** *(16094 Main Ridge)* was erected in 1887, and was the first house in town with a chain-link fence. At the far right end of Parsonage Lane stands the **Annie Parks House [74]** *(16084 Main Ridge)*, moved from Canaan Ridge in the 1920s. The **County Dock**

## The Peter Williams House
### 16116 Main Ridge Road

[75] juts into the harbor at the point where "the Creek" was once crossed by the bridge to Uppards. Canaan Ridge lay a mile north of this point, the site now abandoned except for the mobile homes that constitute the hunting "lodge" at Pruitt's Paradise.

Most of Tangier's daily visitors trickle back to the docks well before the tourboats are scheduled to depart, remembering perhaps the captain's warning when they debarked: "If you miss us, we'll be back here at the same time tomorrow." They climb to the upper deck, if the day is pleasant and bright, and a final flurry of clicking cameras accompanies their departure from the harbor back to Crisfield, Onancock, or Reedville.

Only the few visitors who have chosen to stay overnight witness what is perhaps the best time of the day on Tangier Island. "Supper," they discover, is early at the Chesapeake House, because the evening meal, tied to the routine of the waterman, is early everywhere on Tangier. Then as the afternoon fades towards evening the narrow streets come alive with islanders. It is a time when families stroll and neighbors talk, when small children grind up the street on their plastic "big wheels" or tricycles and their younger siblings are wheeled around town in their strollers or even the front basket of a bicycle. Though the gift shops are now closed, the Double Six is crowded with customers, perhaps as many outside as indoors, while Lorraine's Snack Shop is churning out snacks for the younger set and pizza for delivery. If it is Wednesday night, some of the traffic will be people headed for the churches, Bible in hand, for prayer meeting, as the sounds of a spirited gospel hymn drift out from the Methodist church across the corner of Main Ridge Road and School Lane. Teenagers, like their counterparts on any Main Street USA, endlessly "cruise," circling Main Ridge and West Ridge in golf cart or pickup or on motorbike amid laughter and chatter.

As darkness falls, and the lights in the windows of the houses seem to beckon the townsfolk indoors, those who have elected to stay at one of the bed-and-breakfasts on West Ridge can witness what is perhaps Tangier's greatest show, the sunset. From a second floor window, or the elevated deck at Shirley's Bay View Inn, the view across the Chesapeake is wide and magnificent, and the flashing lights in the ships' channel and on the Western Shore begin their work even while the sunset lingers. Darkness creeps in slowly, in shades of deep and deeper black, as a breeze arises, rustling the trees, and a distant ship blinks its way northward to Baltimore.

As the island settles down for the night, even the outsider can begin to sense its appeal, and understand why for centuries people might, indeed, choose to brave the Bay and its weather, the hard work and the uncertainty, the isolation and the constant near presence of their neighbors to live here, and to call Tangier Island their home.

Tangier Harbor, 1949

# A Pictorial Portfolio

**Joshua Thomas in *The Methodist***
The famous log canoe was not purchased until after
he had moved away from Tangier

## Two "Exhorters" of the Methodist congregation on Tangier

Severn Crockett II (left)
1823-1893

Zachariah Crockett II (right)
1831-1878

**"One of the Lakes at Tangier, Va."**
The "Big Gut" looking north, from an old postcard, c. 1910

**Main Ridge, c. 1910**

**The John E. Wallace House**
Once located at 16550 West Ridge Road, no longer standing.

**John and Lena Wallace and Their Children in Funeral Clothes**
*Left to right:* Amanda Wallace Pruitt; Mary Wallace Pruitt; Elwood
Wallace; Lena Thomas Wallace (1857-1921); John E. Wallace (1855-1926);
Estelle Pruitt Wallace. They are thought to be gathered for the funeral of
Estelle's husband Charles Wallace who died in 1918

**Main Ridge, c. 1915**
Looking south from 16216 Main Ridge; Wallace Road intersects Main Ridge
between the two porches on the right

**Students at the Canaan Ridge School, c. 1921**

**The Great Freeze of 1936**
A "blimp" delivers food to Tangier, from an unidentified newspaper

**John S. Wheatley**
1874-1956
Son of M. Ignatius Wheatley, the first Wheatley on the island. Behind him (right) is the old Lewis Crockett Store at 16215 Main Ridge; (left) the house at 16212 Main Ridge, which was at that time a barber shop

**Tangier High School Girls in Nursing Uniforms, c. 1938**

**Homecoming Day on the Beach, late 1930s**

**The Electric Plant, 1952**
*Left:* The mailboat *Doralena*

**New Members at the Methodist Church**
Front left: Rev. Oscar J. Rishel, pastor 1952-1957

**Main Ridge, 1958**
Looking north from in front of the New Testament Church.
On the left: the old Post Office, originally the Nathan Rayfield Store;
behind it, the two-story Haynie Grocery

**Main Ridge, c. 1960**
The lettering on the door of the building at the right reads "Bus Station"

**Albert Gingrich and the "New" Fire Engine, 1965**
Pastor of the Methodist church from 1964 to 1967, Gingrich was an avid tinkerer, and attempted to put the first fire engine in working order

**An Aerial View of Canton, c. 1960**
Looking east from above Main Ridge

**The Circus Comes to Tangier**
Pasha the Elephant leads the parade to the Roberts Bros. Circus, July 1977

Tangier Harbor, 1999

West Ridge from Factory Road, 1999

# Footnotes

## Notes to Chapter 1, "Russels Iles"

1   Philip L. Barbour, *The Complete Works of Captain John Smith* (Chapel Hill: The University of North Carolina Press, 1986), volume I, pp. 224-225.

2   Barbour, p. 224n.

3   William B. Cronin, "Tangier Island," *Chesapeake Bay Magazine* 18 #5 (September 1988), p. 38. Harold G. Wheatley, "This Is My Island, Tangier," *National Geographic* 144 #5 (November 1973), pp. 702-703. Barbour, p. 225n.

4   Gilbert Byron, *Early Explorations of the Chesapeake Bay* (Baltimore: The Maryland Historical Society, 1960), pp. 5-6. Donald G. Shomette, *Shipwrecks on the Chesapeake* (Centreville, Md.: Tidewater Publishers, 1982), p. 6.

5   See depositions of Somerset County residents taken in 1872 during attempts to settle the question of the location of the Maryland-Virginia boundary across the bay, in *Final Report of the Virginia Commissioners on the Maryland and Virginia Boundary to the Governor of Virginia* (Richmond: R. F. Walker, 1874), pp. 159-160, 162, 182, 187, 203, 205.

6   Thomas Crockett, *Facts and Fun: Historical Outlines of Tangier Island* (Berkley Daily News Print, 1890), p. 1. *Final Report*, p. 203. *Washington Post*, 2 June 1975, A-1, 23.

7   Crockett, p. 1. John Neely Mears, *Tangier Island* (Onancock, Va.: The Eastern Shore News, 1937), pp. 3-4. Stuart Lehmann, *Visitor's Guide to Tangier Island, Va.* (Tangier, Va.: Published privately by the author, 1976), p. 2. Rick Parks, *Tangier Island* (Parsons, W. Va.: McClain Printing Co., 1997), p. 18.

8   Maxwell Blake, Agent and Consul General of the United States in Tangier in 1938, quoted by Donald Downs in "The Moors of Delaware," unpublished manuscript (1960) at the Division of Historical and Cultural Affairs, Department of State, Dover, Delaware. C. A. Weslager, *The Nanticoke Indians — Past and Present* (Newark, Del.: University of Delaware Press, 1983), p. 226.

9   Gail M. Walczyk, *The Ancestors of Thomas L. Crockett, "Sugar Tom"* (Coram, N.Y.: Peter's Row, 1999), pp. 29-30, *passim*. Crockett, pp. 37-38; Part II, pp. 2, 14, 38-43, 68, 81. *Peninsula Enterprise*, 16 August 1883, 16 February 1884, 23 February 1884, 27 February 1904. *Accomack News*, 1 July 1905. *Virginia School Reports*, 1880, p. 33.

10   Ralph T. Whitelaw, *Virginia's Eastern Shore* (Richmond: Virginia Historical Society, 1951), p. 974. See maps in Russell Morrison *et al.*, *On the Map: Maryland and the Chesapeake Bay* (Chestertown, Md.: Washington College, 1983), pp. 27-29, 31.

11   Whitelaw, pp. 974-975. *Accomack Wills Etc., 1692-1715*, Part I, pp. 134-135.

12   Gail M. Walczyk and Rebecca F. Miller, *A Primer on the Crocketts of the Eastern Shore* (Coram, N.Y.: Peter's Row, 1995), p. 18. See use of the name "Tangiers" in Adam Wallace, *The Parson of the Islands* (Philadelphia, Pa.: Published privately by the author, 1861), *passim* including pp. 92, 101, 115, 136, 199.

13   Susie M. Ames, *Studies of the Virginia Eastern Shore in the Seventeenth Century* (Richmond: Dietz Press, 1940), pp. 32-36. Brooks Miles Barnes and Barry R. Truitt, *Seashore Chronicles: Three Centuries of the Virginia Barrier Islands* (Charlottesville: University Press of Virginia, 1997), p. 7.

14   Whitelaw, p. 973. Donald G. Shomette, *Pirates on the Chesapeake* (Centreville, Md.: Tidewater Publishers, 1985), pp. 70-71.

15   The patent that Robert Cager received in 1665 is identified by Gail Walczyk as the area at the northern end of Smith Island that is now the Martins Wildlife Refuge. Frances W. Dize, *Smith Island, Chesapeake Bay* (Centreville, Md.: Tidewater Publishers, 1990), pp. 25, 27. Whitelaw, p. 1278.

16   Nora Miller Turman, *The Eastern Shore of Virginia, 1603-1964* (Onancock: The Eastern Shore News, 1964), pp. 68-69. Whitelaw, pp. 652, 714, 736, 806-808, 845, 892, 955, 959, 1027. Elmer T. West, *Some Descendants of Anthony West of Accomack, Virginia* (Silver Spring, Md.: Published privately by the author, 1980), pp. 14-15.

17   Crockett, p. 3.

## Notes to Chapter 2, "No Man's Land"

1   Crockett, pp. 3-4. This is the earliest published version of the John Crockett tradition yet discovered, and it is possible that it is "Sugar Tom's" invention, the result of attempts to reconcile the seemingly contradictory facts available to him. Crockett knew of West's patent, and dates it "about the year 1666," only four years off the mark. Elsewhere he states that much of his information about the island's early history came from his grandmother Priscilla Tyler Crockett (1750?-1850), who was not a native of the island. If she insisted — correctly — that the Crocketts were on Tangier *from the first*, and he interpreted *from the first* to mean from the island's patenting, then the 1600s date required that he hypothesize a full century's worth of earlier Crocketts prior to Joseph in the 1700s. Yet in another place this writer identifies not John but Joseph Crockett as the man from whom "come all the Crocketts in the world," and notes striking similarities between the John of the 1600s and the Joseph of the 1700s (see part II, pp. 48-49).

2    Whitelaw, pp. 975-976.
3    Walczyk and Miller, *A Primer on the Crocketts*, pp. 18-19, 28. Whitelaw, p. 975. Only "Sugar Tom" Crockett identifies the wife of Joseph Crockett as Sally, see pp. 48-49.
4    Walczyk, *The Ancestors of Thomas L. Crockett*, pp. 7-8. A. Parker Barnes, *Local Government in Accomack County, 1634-1991* (Published privately by the author, 1994), p. 37. Crockett's pew in St. George's Church is documented in Gail M. Walczyk, *St. George's Parish Vestry Book, 1763-1787* (Coram, N.Y.: Peter's Row, 1998), p. 28.
5    Turman, p. 158. Gail Walczyk has supplied a more recent reading of this census, and traced the presence of Joseph Crockett and his descendants in it. The population of Tangier Island itself in 1800 was perhaps as few as 13.
6    As late as 1906 wells on Watts Island and Fox Island were deeper than most of those on Tangier Island; see Samuel Sanford, *The Underground Water Resources of the Coastal Plain Province of Virginia* (Charlottesville, Va.: University of Virginia, 1913), p. 132.
7    S. Warren Hall III, *Tangier Island: A Study of an Isolated Group* (Philadelphia: University of Pennsylvania Press, 1939), pp. 31-32. Crockett, p. 3. Walczyk & Miller, pp. 18-19, 28.
8    Wallace, p. 44.
9    Crockett, part II, p. 49.
10   Crockett, pp. 5-7, 9, 11. Hall, p. 51. Wallace, p. 75.
11   Crockett, part II, pp. 51-56.
12   Crockett, pp. 7-8.
13   Crockett, pp. 7, 9-10, 13-14.
14   Susie M. Ames, "The Revolutionary Era," in Charles B. Clark (ed.), *The Eastern Shore of Maryland and Virginia* (New York: Lewis Historical Publishing Co. Inc., 1950), vol. 1, p. 152. John R. Wennersten, *The Oyster Wars of Chesapeake Bay* (Centreville, Md.: Tidewater Publishers, 1981), p. 8.
15   Crockett, p. 10. Truitt, p. 30. Wallace, p. 51.
16   Crockett, p. 10. Hulbert Footner, *Rivers of the Eastern Shore* (New York: Farrar & Rinehart, 1944), p. 49. Charles J. Truitt, *Breadbasket of the Revolution: Delmarva in the War for Independence* (Salisbury, Md.: Historical Books, Inc., 1975), p. 219. Adele Hast, *Loyalism in Revolutionary Virginia: Norfolk and the Eastern Shore* (Ann Arbor, Mich.: UMI Research Press, 1979), p. 148. *Final Report*, p. 188-189.
17   Truitt, pp. 59, 63-64, 219.
18   Nora Miller Turman, "The Eastern Shore, 1775-1783," *Eastern Shore News*, 30 October 1975.
19   Donald G. Shomette, *Pirates on the  Chesapeake*, pp. 260-261.
20   Crockett, pp. 10-11. Gail M. Walczyk, *Four Generations of Parks on The Eastern Shore* (Coram, N.Y.: Peter's Row, 1997), pp. 15-17. Deposition of James Evans, 27 May 1872, in *Final Report*, pp. 175-176. Evans testified that he was told this story by Job Parks himself.
21   Rebecca F. Miller and Gail M. Walczyk, *Four Generations of Evans on The Eastern Shore* (Coram, N.Y.: Peter's Row, 1997), pp. 12, 14-16, 18, 49-50. Walczyk, *Four Generations of Parks*, pp. 12-13, 22.
22   Truitt, pp. 105-106, 129, 135, 179. Hast, p. 148. Shomette, *Shipwrecks on the Chesapeake*, pp. 50-51. Shomette, *Pirates on the Chesapeake*, pp. 262-263, 284-285. Geoffrey M. Footner, *Tidewater Triumph* (Centreville, Md.: Tidewater Publishers, 1998), p. 49. Maurice Duke (ed.), *Chesapeake Bay Voices: Narratives from Four Centuries* (Richmond: Dietz Press, 1993), p. 108.
23   See John Greenwood's account in Duke, pp. 106*ff.* Ames, "The Revolutionary Era," p. 165. Truitt, pp. 157, 167-168.
24   L. F. Shreve, *Tench Tilghman: The Life and Times of Washington's Aide-de-Camp* (Centreville, Md.: Tidewater Publishers, 1982), pp. 158-160, 164, 242n.
25   Truitt, p. 178-179. Shomette, *Pirates on the Chesapeake*, pp. 284-285.
26   Shomette, *Pirates on the Chesapeake*, pp. 292-293.
27   Ames, "The Revolutionary Era," p. 164. Turman, "The Eastern Shore, 1775-1783," *Eastern Shore News*, 10 June, 17 June 1976. Barton Haxall Wise, "Memoir of General John Cropper," *Virginia Historical Collections* 11 (1892), p. 30.
28   Truitt, pp. 108, 186-188.
29   Wennersten, p. 9. The fort built by the British on Tangier in 1814 was "planned in England," and the systematic manner in which the British occupied the island during the War of 1812 indicates prior knowledge of the Bay. See James E. Mears, "The Shoreline," *Eastern Shore News*, 22 July 1938.

## Notes to Chapter 3, "The Parson"
1    Wallace states (p. 49) that Martha Hall Thomas moved her family to "the island," citing the now-vanished "Prettyman manuscript" (c. 1840), which was the basis for the early part of *The Parson of the Islands*. While it has been traditionally assumed that "the island" meant Tangier, and that Joshua Thomas was raised there, the only residents of Tangier at that time were the family of Joseph Crockett. Martha Thomas' relatives lived on Smith Island, as did David Tyler to whom Thomas was later apprenticed. This account of his life contends that Joshua Thomas was raised on Smith Island, and first moved to Tangier as a married man in 1799, an hypothesis grounded in the genealogical researches of Gail Walczyk.

2    Wallace, 47-50, Crockett 11.
3    Wallace, 57-58, 61-62, 64.
4    Turman, p. 158.
5    Whitelaw, p. 973. Shomette, *Pirates on the Chesapeake*, pp. 70-71. Turman, p. 158.
6    Whitelaw, p. 1277-1278. *Peninsula Enterprise*, 8 August 1936, sec. 1, p. 4. *Final Report*, p. 188.
7    Whitelaw, p. 1276. Nora Miller Turman, *A Brief History of Saxis* (Unpublished manuscript, 1976).
8    Gail M. Walczyk, *Four Generations of Parks*, pp. 12, 14-15, 17. Dize, p. 27.
9    Woodrow T. Wilson, *History of Crisfield and Surrounding Areas   on Maryland's Eastern Shore* (Baltimore: Gateway Press Inc., 1973), pp. 231-232. Whitelaw, p. 1278. *Final Report*, pp. 162*ff* contains many depositions about the state boundary as it crossed Smith Island. *Accomack Deedbook (District Court)*, 1806-1830, pp. 60-62. Miller and Walczyk, *Four Generations of Evans*, pp. 43*ff* Hall, p. 36. *Final Report*, pp. 171, 208.
10   Gail Walczyk, "Smith Island, Crossroads of the Chesapeake Bay," *The Island Crabber*, October 1994. *Surveyor's Record* I, p. 77. *Accomack Deedbook* #29, p. 416.
11   Walczyk, *Four Generations of Parks*, pp. 15-16.
12   *Accomack Deedbook #11*, p. 287. See "Preliminary Chart of Chesapeake Bay (#4) from the Potomac River to the Entrance to Pocomoke Sound" (U.S. Coast Survey map, 1859), collection of the author. Hall, pp. 4, 31, 33. Lehmann, pp. 4-5, 13. Wallace, pp. 44, 84, 86. When the island's timber was depleted is not known; the virtual treelessness of the island dates from the twentieth century.
13   Crockett, part II, pp. 54-55.
14   Crockett, pp. 11-12, 48-54. This encounter undoubtedly occurred prior to Joshua Thomas' marriage and move to Tangier Island.
15   Crockett, part II, pp. 56-57.
16   Crockett, part II, pp. 54-61. Wallace, pp. 100-101, 187.
17   Wallace, pp. 57, 59, 65-68.
18   Kirk Mariner, *Revival's Children: A Religious History of Virginia's Eastern Shore* (Salisbury, Md.: Peninsula Press, 1979), pp. 29, 40-41.
19   Wallace, pp. 67-69.
20   Wallace, pp. 75-78. Mariner, *Revival's Children*, p. 45.
21   Wallace, pp. 84-85, 97-91.
22   Wallace, p. 92.
23   Wallace, pp. 93, 95-97.
24   C. P. Swain, *A Brief History of Tangier Island, Va., with a Review of the Rise and Growth of the Methodist Episcopal Church* ([n.p.], 1899), pp. 12-13. Wallace, pp. 98-100. Mariner, *Revival's Children*, pp. 30-31.
25   Wallace, pp. 108-109.

## Notes to Chapter 4, "Prisoners of War"

1    Gilbert Byron, *The War of 1812 on the Chesapeake Bay* (Baltimore: Maryland Historical Society, 1964), pp. 17*ff*, 27-29, 31, 45. Letter of William R. Custis to Governor James Barbour of Virginia, 19 September 1814, in *Calendar of State Papers*, reprinted by James E. Mears in "The Shoreline," *Eastern Shore News*, 12 August 1938. No original source dates the story of the almost-aborted camp meeting to 1813, but the year can be deduced from the fact that the Reverend James Smith served as Presiding Elder from 1812 through 1814; see Wallace, pp. 113-115.
2    Wallace, pp. 128-129.
3    Wallace, pp. 129-131. Walter Lord, *The Dawn's Early Light* (New York: W. W. Norton & Co Inc., 1972), pp. 52-53.
4    Mears, "The Shoreline," *Eastern Shore News*, 3 June 1938, 22 July 1938. Wallace, p. 131. Crockett, p. 18.
5    Mears, "The Shoreline," *Eastern Shore News*, 20 May 1938, 3 June 1938.
6    Frank A. Cassell, "Slaves of the Chesapeake Bay Area and the War of 1812," *Journal of Negro History* 56 (April 1972), p. 146. Mears, "The Shoreline," *Eastern Shore News*, 3 June 1938, 17 June 1938.
7    For a fuller description of the battle, see Bayley's letter to the Governor, 31 May 1814, in *Calendar of State Papers*, reprinted in Mears, "The Shoreline," *Eastern Shore News*, 10 June 1938; and A. Parker Barnes, *Pungoteague to Petersburg: Eastern Shore Militiamen before the Civil War, 1776-1858* (Onancock, Va.: Lee Howard Books, 1988), vol. I, pp. 88-93.
8    Mears, "The Shoreline," *Eastern Shore News*, 29 July 1938, August 5, 1938.
9    Crockett, pp. 18-19. Mears, "The Shoreline," *Eastern Shore News*, 3 June 1938, 22 July 1938. Wallace, pp. 132-133, 136-138, 139. Swain, p. 16.
10   Mears, "The Shoreline," *Eastern Shore News*, 1 July 1938, 15 July 1938, 22 July 1938.
11   Lord, pp. 42-43, 47, 50. Mears, "The Shoreline," *Eastern Shore News*, 3 June 1938, 5 August 1938.
12   Byron, *War of 1812 on the Chesapeake Bay*, pp. 48-54.
13   Wallace, pp. 143-146.
14   Byron, *War of 1812 on the Chesapeake Bay*, pp. 63-74.

15    Wallace, pp. 148-149.
16    Walczyk, *Four Generations of Evans*, p. 38. "Methodist Americana," *Together*, March 1960, p. 45.
17    Byron, *War of 1812 on the Chesapeake Bay*, pp. 81-82, 84, 90. Wallace, pp. 150-151.
18    Wallace, p. 151. Mears, "The Shoreline," *Eastern Shore News*, 1 July 1938. Woodrow T. Wilson, *History of Tangier Island, Virginia* ([n.p.], [n.d.]), p. 6.

## Notes to Chapter 5, "Place of Pilgrimage"

1    *Gazette & Ledger* [Norfolk, Va.], 24 May 1815, 26 May 1815, 31 May 1815, 19 June 1815, quoted in John C. Emmerson Jr., *The Steamboat Comes to Norfolk Harbor* (Portsmouth, Va.: Published privately by the author, 1949), pp. 1-4. William L. Tazewell, *Norfolk's Waters: An Illustrated Maritime History of Hampton Roads* (Woodland Hills, Calif: Windsor Publications Inc., 1982), pp. 61-62. M. V. Brewington, *Chesapeake Bay: A Pictorial Maritime History* (New York: Bonanza Books, 1956), pp. 43-45.
2    *Herald* [Norfolk Va.], 7 August 1820, *Beacon* [Norfolk, Va.], 6 August 1821, 18 August 1821, quoted in Emmerson, pp. 157, 197, 199. A. Hughlett Mason, *History of Steam Navigation to the Eastern Shore of Virginia* (Richmond: Dietz Press, 1973), pp. 1, 3.
3    Emmerson, p. 200.
4    Wallace, pp. 110-111, 112-113, 202.
5    Henry A. Wise, *Seven Decades of the Union* (Philadelphia: J. B. Lippincott & Co., 1872), pp. 94-97.
6    Crockett, pp. 24-25. Hall, p. 46. Wise, p. 97.
7    Crockett, pp. 20-21.
8    Wallace, pp. 215-219. Crockett, pg. 22, states that Joshua Thomas moved away from Tangier "in the fall of 1820," but the Parson's continuing presence in the records of the Accomack Circuit of the Methodist Episcopal Church through the summer of 1824 makes Wallace's "about the year 1825" seem more likely.
9    Swain, p. 23. Crockett, p. 22. Journal of the *Accomack Circuit, Methodist Episcopal Church*, 2 June 1821, p. 92; 5 July 1823, p. 99.
10    Walczyk & Miller, *A Primer on the Crocketts*, pp. 18-19. Wallace, pp. 99-100, 122, 124, 128-129. Swain, p. 25. Crockett, p. 22, 27. *Journal of the Accomack Circuit*, 22 March 1823, p. 98. *Accomack Wills 1828-42*, p. 502.
11    Crockett, pp. 23-24.
12    Hall, pp. 46-47, 51.
13    Footner, *Tidewater Triumph*, pp. 213-214. Wennersten, pp. 13-14. Tom Horton, "The Chesapeake Crab Wars," *Chesapeake Bay Magazine* 13 #8 (August 1992), p. 30. Robert deGast, *The Oystermen of the Chesapeake* (Camden, Maine: International Marine Publishing Co., 1970), p. 132.
14    Robert deGast *The Lighthouses of the Chesapeake* (Baltimore, Md: Johns Hopkins University Press, 1973), pp. 166, 169.
15    Crockett, pp. 28, 31. Hall, p. 47. Swain, pp. 59-60. The earliest known reference to a Dise on Tangier is found in Crockett, p. 22, Spence in *Record of the Methodist Episcopal Church for Northampton Circuit, 1858-1903*, p. 24. For the family tradition about Joseph L. Cooper, see Rick Parks, *Tangier Island*, p. 35. All other families are dated from the census records of the years cited.
16    Crockett, pp. 25-26. Swain, pp. 24-25.
17    Hall, p. 61. 1860 Census, p. 347.
18    Crockett, pp. 35, 38; part II, p. 2. *Journal of the Accomack Circuit*, 6 September 1845, pp. 204-205. Barnes, *Local Government*, p. 52. *A Brief History of Education in Accomack County, 1632-1963* (Accomac, Va.: Accomack County Historical Association, unpublished typescript, 1963), p. 6. Barton Haxall Wise, *The Life of Henry A. Wise of Virginia* (New York: MacMillan Co., 1899), pp. 120, 125-126. Swain, pp. 60-61, also lists Richard Corbett and Lybrand H. Thomas as instrumental in the organization of the Sunday school in 1856.
19    Crockett, pp. 28-30. Swain, p. 26-28. Hall, p. 31. Wallace, p. 333.
20    Crockett, pp. 34-35. Swain, pp. 59-60.
21    Wallace, pp. 41-42, 58.
22    Wallace, pp. 350-352.
23    Joseph F. DiPaolo, *My Business Was to Fight the Devil: Recollections of Rev. Adam Wallace, Peninsula Circuit Rider, 1847-1865* (Acton, Mass.: Tapestry Press, Ltd., 1998), passim.
24    Swain, p. 54. DiPaolo, pp. 151. *Christian Advocate*, 23 September 1840, 24 March 1841, 19 January 1842, 14 July 1847, 28 March 1848. Mariner, *Revival's Children*, pp. 98-100. Wallace, p. 352.
25    F. E. Marine, *Sketch of Rev. John Hersey, Minister of the Gospel of the M. E. Church* (Baltimore: Hoffman & Co., 1879), pp. 162-164. Mariner, pp. 18-20. Mariner, pp. 80-81.

## Notes to Chapter 6, "War and Pestilence"

1    Hall, p. 47.
2    James E. Mears, "The Eastern Shore of Virginia in the Nineteenth and Twentieth Centuries," in Clark, vol. II, p. 603.

3    Dize, p. 73. Wennersten, pp. 11-12. *Official Records of the Union and Confederate Navies*, Series I, volume 5, pp. 742-743, 761-762.
4    Mears, "The Eastern Shore...in the Nineteenth and Twentieth Centuries," p. 628n. Eva M. Watson, *Glimpses of the Life and Work of George Douglas Watson* (Cincinnati, Ohio: God's Bible School and Revivalist, 1929), pp. 25-27. Watson later became a successful evangelist and preached to large crowds in this country and abroad.
5    *Official Records* [Navy], Series 1, volume 5, pp. 767-777.
6    *Official Records* [Navy], Series 1, volume 5, pp. 73-74.
7    *Official Records* [Navy], Series 1, volume 5, pp. 73-74. Dize, p. 76. Mears, "The Shoreline," 26 May 1950, 1 November 1952.
8    *Official Records* [Navy], Series 1, volume 5, pp. 74, 761-762.
9    Swain, p. 29. Crockett, p. 34.
10   Mears, "The Shoreline," *Eastern Shore News*, 28 April 1950. Leonard W. Johnson, *Ebb and Flow: A History of The Virginia Tip of The Delmarva Peninsula, 1561-1892* (Verona, Va.: McClure Press, 1982), p. 165.
11   Crockett, pp. 33-34. Swain, p. 22. Mears, "The Shoreline," *Eastern Shore News*, 16 August 1940. Wallace, p. 41. *Accomack Deedbook #44*, p. 625.
12   The tradition about Henry Frazier is found in Rick Parks, *Tangier Island*, p. 31. For traditions concerning immigrations encouraged by Harrison Crockett, see Larry S. Chowning, *Barcat Skipper: Tales of a Tangier Island Waterman* (Centreville, Md.: Tidewater Publishers, 1983), pp. 66-76.
13   James E. Mears, *The Eastern Shore of Virginia during the Civil War and the Reconstruction Period* (Unpublished manuscript, 1957), pp. 375-380, from Records of the Provost Marshal, Eastern Shore of Virginia, Department of Virginia and North Carolina, Book 249 in the National Archives. Mears, "The Shoreline," *Eastern Shore News*, 13 December 1951.
14   Wilson, *History of Crisfield*, p. 249.
15   *Official Records* [Navy], Series 1, Volume 5, pp. 476-477. *Official Records of the Union and Confederate Armies*, Series I, volume 43, part 1, p. 927; part 2, p. 441.
16   Kirk Mariner, "The Rebel Raid That Never Was," *Eastern Shore News*, 12 February 1997.
17   Marshall S. Berdan, "The Pestilence that Walketh in Darkness: The Cholera Epidemic of 1832," *Virginia Cavalcade* 43 #1 (Summer 1993), pp. 15-16.
18   *The Sun* (Baltimore, Md.), 1 October 1866, 6 October 1866, 9 October 1866, 16 October 1866. Many islanders believed that the epidemic on Tangier came from hog cholera, which continued to be a problem on the island for many years; see Hall, p. 60.
19   *The Sun*, 17 October 1866, 24 October 1866, 23 November 1866.
20   *Accomack County Register of Deaths, 1853-1871*, p. 41. Jean M. Mihalyka, *Tombstone Inscriptions, Tangier Island, Va.* (Unpublished typescript, 1978), *passim*. Hall, pp. 21, 60. Crockett, p. 35.
21   *Christian Advocate*, 20 December 1866. Hall, p. 21.
22   Wilson, *History of Crisfield*, p. 7. For a fictionalized version of this tradition from the Cooper family, see Rick Parks, *Tangier Island*, pp. 38-44.
23   Crockett, p. 34.

## Notes to Chapter 7, "High Gear"

1    Wennersten, pp. 14-17. John C. Hayman, *Rails Along the Chesapeake: A History of Railroading on the Delmarva Peninsula, 1827-1978* (Salisbury, Md.: Marvadel Publishers, 1979), p. 67.
2    Wilson, *History of Crisfield*, pp. 28, 31. Wennersten, pp. 17-18.
3    Norman H. Plummer, *Maryland's Oyster Navy: The First Fifty Years* (Chestertown, Md.: Literary House Press/Chesapeake Bay Maritime Museum, 1993), pp. 7-8, 43, 47, 94n. B. Miles Barnes, *Readjusters, Funders, and Oysters: Economics and Politics on the Eastern Shore of Virginia During the Readjuster Movement* (Unpublished typescript, 1981), pp. 21-23. Dize, p. 89.
4    Louis N. Whealton, *The Maryland-Virginia Boundary Controversy, 1668-1894* (Baltimore: Albert J. Leon, 1897), p. 41. Wennersten, p. 48. Dize, pp. 90, 97, 103.
5    Mason, pp. 1-3. Hall, p. 25. Mears, "Eastern Shore of Virginia in the Nineteenth and Twentieth Centuries," in Clark, vol. II, p. 587. The earliest advertisement announcing stops at Tangier Island is found in *Peninsula Enterprise*, 30 August 1884.
6    *Peninsula Enterprise*, 22 October 1887, 31 October 1891.
7    Wilson, *History of Crisfield*, p. 53.
8    Kirk Mariner, *Off 13: The Eastern Shore of Virginia Guidebook* (New Church, Va.: Miona Publications, 1997), p. 95. *Peninsula Enterprise*, 8 June 1907.
9    Swain, pp. 3, 31.
10   *Accomack Deedbook #47*, p. 458. James C. Weaver, "An Epitomized History of Education in Accomac County," in *Report of the State Superintendent of Education* (Richmond, 1885), p. 50. *Virginia School Reports*, 1880, p. 33.
11   Barnes, *Local Government*, p. 58. Crockett, pp. 39-41. *Accomack Deedbook #72*, p. 232. John N. Mears, *Tangier Island*, p. 13.

12    Henry Pickering Walker, "Teacher to the Mojaves: The Experiences of George W. Nock, 1887-1889," *Arizona and the West* 9 #2 (Summer 1967), pp. 144, 148, 149. *Virginia School Reports*, 1894, p. 11. *Peninsula Enterprise*, 1 September 1894, 19 September 1896, 8 September 1900, 5 September 1903, 16 September 1922. Mihalyka, *Abstracts of Tangier*, 42. George W. Nock, "Tangier" (Unpublished typescript, c. 1895).
13    Hall, pp. 47, 84. Swain, p. 38.
14    Hall, p. 70. *Peninsula Enterprise*, 17 May 1890. deGast, *Lighthouses of the Chesapeake* , p. 168. Crockett, p. 40. Chowning, *Barcat Skipper*, pp 38-39.
15    *Peninsula Enterprise*, 17 May 1883, 4 October 1883, 13 December 1883, 24 May 1884, 20 September 1884, 7 January 1888, 24 May 1890. Jean Mihalyka, *Abstracts of Tangier* (Unpublished typescript, 1978), p. 6. Crockett, p. 4.
16    G. Brown Goode, *The History and Present Condition of the Fishery Industries* (Washington: Department of the Interior, 1881), pp. ix, 91, 169. John Frye, *The Men All Singing: The Story of Menhaden Fishing* (Norfolk: Donning Press, 1978), p. 157. *Peninsula Enterprise*, 15 September 1876, 17 May 1883, 12 February 1893. *Accomack Deedbook* p. 49. *Richmond Dispatch*, 11 April 1889.
17    Hall, pp. 29, 35. *Record of the Methodist Episcopal Church for Northampton Circuit, 1858-1903*, 24 January 1874, p. 83. *Peninsula Enterprise*, 17 May 1883. School records and newspaper accounts are not specific that the second and third public schools on Tangier were Canaan Ridge and West Ridge, respectively, as these paragraphs assume.
18    Hall, pp. 33, 99. *Peninsula Enterprise*, 9 September 1883. *Accomack Deedbook #70*, p. 481.
19    *Peninsula Enterprise*, 23 October 1886. Barnes, *Local Government*, p. 65.
20    Crockett, p 41. *Peninsula Enterprise*, 22 April 1893.
21    Hall, p. 47.
22    Crockett, pp. 35, 41. *Peninsula Enterprise*, 29 February 1896. *Eastern Shore Herald*, 1 December 1905.
23    Wennersten, pp. 48-49, 93-94.
24    *Peninsula Enterprise*, 24 February 1894, 10 March 1894, 17 March 1894, 24 March 1894, 14 April 1894. Wennersten, pp. 48-49, 94-95. Dize, p. 105.
25    *Peninsula Enterprise*, 18 November 1893.
26    *Accomack News*, 10 November 1906, 17 November 1906, 24 November 1906, 1 December 1906. *Peninsula Enterprise*, 17 November 1906. Wennersten, pp. 55-56.
27    Wennersten, pp. 49, 55-56, 90, 95. deGast, *Oystermen of the Chesapeake*, p. 133. *Accomack News*, 4 March 1905.
28    *Peninsula Enterprise*, 18 April 1885, 9 May 1885, 19 February 1887, 4 February 1888. *Accomack Deedbook #61*, p. 208, #64, p. 508, #65, p. 156. William I. Tawes, *God, Man, Salt Water, and the Eastern Shore* (Cambridge, Md.: Tidewater Publishers, 1967), pp. 38-39.
29    Wennersten, p. 84. *Eastern Shore Herald*, 18 November 1904, 6 January 1905. *Accomack News*, 14 January 1905. *Eastern Shore Herald* , 20 January 1905, states that the fine of one dollar was levied on 16 residents of Tangier for unlawful assembly.
30    Hall, pp. 51, 55-56, 63-64. Crockett, p. 40. Chowning, *Barcat Skipper*, pp. 12, 52. *Peninsula Enterprise*, 14 April 1894, 29 February 1896, 8 June 1907. Paula J. Johnson, *The Workboats of Smith Island* (Baltimore: Johns Hopkins University Press, 1997), p. 16.
31    Tom Horton, "The Chesapeake Crab Wars," *Mid-Atlantic Country* 13 #8 (August 1992), p. 30. Dize, p. 104.
32    *Richmond Dispatch*, 11 April 1889.
33    *Peninsula Enterprise*, 21 January 1893.
34    *Peninsula Enterprise*, 4 July 1896. Chowning, *Barcat Skipper*, pp. 26-30.
35    *Peninsula Enterprise*, 26 July 1883, 23 October 1886, 4 July 1896. *Record of the Northampton Circuit of the Methodist Episcopal Church, 1858-1903*, 16 August 1876, p. 130. James E. Mears, *The Temperance Movement on the Eastern Shore of Virginia* (Onancock: Eastern Shore News, 1966), pp. 36-37. Swain, pp. 6-7.
36    Swain, pp. 31-45.
37    From Swain's "Memoir" in the annals of the Wilmington Annual Conference, quoted in John Pruitt, *Beacon of the Soul: A Centennial Remembrance of Swain Memorial United Methodist Church* (Tangier, Va.: Swain Memorial United Methodist Church, 1997), pp. 16-19.

## Notes to Chapter 8, "Remotely Modern"
1    *Accomack News*, 29 April 1905, 20 May 1905, 22 June 1907. *Eastern Shore Herald*, 1 December 1904. *Eastern Shore News*, 7 July 1935. Hall, pp. 40, 102. J. N. Mears, p. 18.
2    *Peninsula Enterprise*, 8 June 1907. *Accomack Deedbook #87*, p. 419.
3    *Acts of Assembly*, 1906, p. 301. Hall, pp. 46-47.
4    Swain, p. 2. *Accomack News*, 29 April 1905, 20 May 1905, 22 June 1907, 19 May 1923. *Peninsula Enterprise*, 26 May 1900. Chowning, *Barcat Skipper*, pp. 12-13, 32-33. For water resources on Tangier at this period, see Sanford, *Underground Water Resources*, pp 131-132. *Eastern Shore News*, 28 March 1968.
5    *Tangier [School] District Book of Records*, 8 September 1919, p. 39; 11 September 1920, p. 40; 8 October 1921, p. 46. The last record of the West Ridge School is among the listing of teachers for 1903 in *Peninsula*

*Enterprise*, 5 September 1903. The description of Canaan Ridge is from the reminiscences of Annie Kelso Parks, born there in 1901. Hall, pp. 29, 36.

6       *Peninsula Enterprise*, 13 January 1900. deGast, *Lighthouses of the Chesapeake*, p. 168. *Accomack News*, 11 March 1905, 12 June 1909. Connie Whealton, "Tangier Island," *Eastern Shore News*, 1 November 1951. Chowning, *Barcat Skipper*, pp. 38-41. Pat Vojtech, *Lighting the Bay: Tales of Chesapeake Lighthouses* (Centreville, Md.: Tidewater Publishers, 1996), pp. 93-97.

7       Chowning, *Barcat Skipper*, pp. 43-44. Ruth Wallace Clarke is the source of information about her grandfather's rationing food during times of emergencies.

8       J. N. Mears, p. 18. *Tangier Book of Records*, 14 January 1913, p. 8; 25 November 1916, p. 26; 22 September 1917, p. 34. *Acts of Assembly*, 1910, p. 391.

9       *Peninsula Enterprise*, 28 November 1914. *Accomack News*, 17 June 1921. *Common Law Orders, 1914-1916*, pp. 74-75; *1920-1922*, pp. 204, 346; *1922-1924*, p. 349; *1924-1925*, p. 40. The boundaries of the Town of Tangier described at the time of its incorporation in 1915 are not the same as those shown on more recent maps. Though they included West Ridge, Main Ridge, and Canton, plus the marshes between them, the original boundaries stopped at the western edge of high ground on West Ridge and the eastern edge of high ground on Canton, leaving unincorporated the western and eastern shores of the island which are now within the Town. The early records of the Town of Tangier are missing, and it is not possible from other sources even to reconstruct a list of the Mayors and their terms. *Minute Book 2*, beginning 28 September 1946, is the most complete record book, but even it is not continuous from that date. A few more records, written in school notebooks in the 1960s and 1970s, are in the possession of Lewis Parks of Richmond, having been rescued from the dump. It is arguable that the nonchalance in attention to municipal record-keeping stems from the fact that until the late 1940s the Methodist church, as much as or more so than the Town Council, was the functional locus of local decision-making.

10     Gary Gentile, *Shipwrecks of Virginia* (Philadelphia, Pa.: Gary Gentile Productions, 1992), pp. 139, 141-143. Robert Burgess, *This Was Chesapeake Bay* (Cambridge, Md.: Cornell Maritime Press, 1963), pp. 26-27. *Accomack News*, 6 September 1912.

11     Edith Bolling Wilson, *My Memoir* (Indianapolis: Bobbs-Merrill Co., 1938), pp. 96-98. *Accomack News*, 7 April 1916.

12     *Washington Post*, 5 April 1912.

13     A. Parker Barnes, *Young No More: The Tragedy of 1918* (Privately published by the author, 1994), pp. 62, 126, 130.

14     *17th Annual Report of the Commission of Fisheries of Virginia* (Richmond: Superintendent of Public Printing, 1916), *passim. Accomack News*, 6 March 1915, 27 August 1915, 10 December 1915, 26 May 1916. Chowning, *Barcat Skipper*, pp. 13, 56-57, 64. *Accomack Deedbook #96*, p. 95; *#119*, p. 408. Hall, p. 58.

15     Hall, pp. 31, 40. *Accomack News*, 11 March 1921, 9 September 1921.

16     J. N. Mears, pp. 18-19. *Accomack Deedbook #96*, p. 424. *Eastern Shore News*, 25 June 1964. *Accomack News*, 14 January 1921, 4 February 1921.

17     *Accomack News*, 10 December 1915, 10 November 1916. *Peninsula Enterprise*, 21 February 1914. deGast, *Lighthouses of the Chesapeake*, p. 168.

18     *Accomack News*, 21 May 1915, 17 September 1915. *Peninsula Enterprise*, 6 December 1919. Hall, pp. 68-69. *Accomack Deedbook #132*, p. 203.

19     *Accomack News*, 16 July 1915, 19 November 1915, 26 November 1915. C. Richard Gillespie, *The James Adams Floating Theatre* (Centreville, Md.: Tidewater Publishers, 1991), pp. 46-47. Mason, p. 32. Ruth Wallace Clarke believes that the theatre played in Tangier more than the single time listed by Gillespie.

20     *Accomack News*, 29 April 1921, 3 June 1921.

21     *Peninsula Enterprise*, 17 April 1920, 22 May 1920, 26 June 1920, 9 October 1920, 16 May 1931, 2 September 1949

22     *Eastern Shore News*, 30 April 1931.

23     Burke Davis, *The Billy Mitchell Affair* (New York: Random House, 1967), pp. 73, 94-95, 97-101, 107-108, 111, 124-125. *Accomack News*, 3 September 1921. E. Frank Dize, *Something Fishy from Tangier* (Published privately by the author, [n.d.]), p. 10.

24     *Peninsula Enterprise*, 18 August 1923. J. N. Mears, p. 24.

25     Kirk Mariner, "The Movies: Tangier," *Eastern Shore News*, 15 April 1992.

26     J. N. Mears, pp. 18-19. *Peninsula Enterprise*, 18 August 1923. *Common Law Orders, 1928-1929*, pp. 32, 58. J. Norwood Hamilton, "Electricity Changes Life on Tangier," *Sunday Star Magazine*, 24 February 1952, p. 4. Anne Hughes Jander, *Crab's Hole: A Family Story of Tangier Island* (Chestertown, Md.: The Literary House Press, 1994), p. 84. *Eastern Shore News*, 17 February 1928.

27     Hall, pp. 30-31.

28     Hall, pp. 34, 47.

29     *Tangier Book of Records*, 8 October 1921, p. 46. Hall, p. 35, 37-38. Robert E. Jones, "Crab Island," *Saturday Evening Post* 216 #13 (15 September 1943), p. 26. Annie K. Parks and Ruth Wallace Clarke helped to identify the houses moved from Oyster Creek and Canaan Ridge.

30     Kirk Mariner, "The Hermit of Watts Island," *Chesapeake Bay Magazine* 12 #10 (February 1983), pp.

29-30. Wilson, *History of Crisfield*, pp. 251-252. Calvin H. Robinson, *Along the Shoreline* (Onancock, Va.: Published privately by the author, 1931), p. 27. *Peninsula Enterprise*, 29 August 1931. *Eastern Shore News*, 15 August 1930, 10 October 1930, 28 August 1931, 4 September 1931, 5 March 1937. *Accomack County Register of Marriages #5* (1926-1936), p. 28.
31   Hall, p. 70. Chowning, *Barcat Skipper*, p. 90. *Tangier Book of Records*, 18 May 1931, p. 243. *Peninsula Enterprise*, 25 August 1923. *Eastern Shore News*, 2 September 1932.
32   *Eastern Shore News*, 26 February 1932, 11 March 1932. Mason, p. 2. Mears, "The Eastern Shore of Virginia in the Nineteenth and Twentieth Centuries," pp. 586-587.
33   *Peninsula Enterprise*, 20 August 1932. *Washington Post*, 17 August, 1932. Baltimore *Sun*, 17 August 1932. It is not clear from the Associated Press reports of Hoover's visit that he actually set foot on the island. Tangier traditionally voted Republican, and in the 1928 Presidential election preferred Hoover 55-11 over his Democratic opponent Al Smith; see *Eastern Shore News*, 9 November 1928.
34   Chowning, *Barcat Skipper*, p. 89. Hall, pp. 63-65. *Peninsula Enterprise*, 15 July 1933, 10 July 1937. *Eastern Shore News*, 15 May 1931, 14 August 1931, 16 October 1931, 9 July 1937, 13 August 1937, 29 November 1937.
35   *Peninsula Enterprise*, 26 August 1933. *Eastern Shore News*, 25 August 1933. Jander, p. 73. Jones, p. 26. Wheatley, p. 705. Pruitt, p. 62. Chowning, *Barcat Skipper*, p. 97.
36   Wheatley, p. 725.
37   Wennersten, p. 104. William W. Warner, *Beautiful Swimmers: Watermen, Crabs, and the Chesapeake Bay* (Boston: Little, Brown and Company, 1976), p. 239. "Tangier: A World Apart," *Rural Virginia*, 15 #9 (July 1960), p. 10. Jones, "Crab Island," p. 72.
38   Mason, pp. 2, 40. Mears, "The Shoreline," *Eastern Shore News*, 3 Sept 1959. Robert H. Burgess and H. Graham Wood, *Steamboats Out of Baltimore* (Cambridge, Md.: Tidewater Publishers, 1968), p. 146. Gentile, pp. 143*ff*.

## Notes to Chapter 9, "A Wider World"
1   Jander, pp 1-23.
2   Jones, "Crab Island," pp. 26-27, 72.
3   Jones, "Crab Island," p. 26. Jander, pp. 4, 24, 109.
4   Dize, *Something Fishy from Tangier*, p. 10. *Washington Post*, 18 June 1972. J. N. Mears, p. 19. Jander, pp. 4, 8, 24, 44, 58, 84. Jones, "Crab Island," p. 72.
5   Jander, pp. 84-87. *Peninsula Enterprise*, 25 October 1946. *Eastern Shore News*, 12 September 1947. "Tangier: A World Apart," *Rural Virginia* , p. 9.
6   Burgess, *This Was Chesapeake Bay*, p. 201-202.
7   *Eastern Shore News*, 13 April 1945. James C. Richardson, *7 Acres: The Story of the New Testament Church on Tangier Island* (Shippensburg, Pa.: Companion Press, 1997), pp. 19-23, 34, 38, 42.
8   Richardson, pp. 49-53, 61, 64. Mariner, *Revival's Children*, p. 222.
9   Richardson, pp. 64-65, 68-69, 79-81. Mariner, *Revival's Children*, p. 222.
10   "Trouble in Tangier," *Newsweek* 30 #74 (13 October 1947), pp. 74-75. Richardson, pp. 83-85. *Peninsula Enterprise*, 31 October 1947. *Eastern Shore News*, 31 October 1947. Many readers from the Eastern Shore of Virginia first learned of the religious troubles on Tangier from *Newsweek*, for the two "county papers" did not cover the story until after its appearance in that magazine.
11   Richardson, p. 86. Mariner, *Revival's Children*, pp. 222, 512. L. W. George, *This Is Tangier Island and Its Church* (Martinsville, Va.: The Radio Fellowship, 1965), p. 35.
12   *Town Records*, 2 April 1947, pp. 36*ff*. Larry S. Chowning, *Chesapeake Legacy: Tools and Traditions* (Centreville, Md.: Tidewater Publishers, 1995), p. 169. Chowning, *Barcat Skipper*, pp. 138*ff*. Horton, "Crab Wars," p. 30. Wennersten, pp. 112-113. *Peninsula Enterprise*, 25 October 1946, 15 August 1947, 2 September 1949. *Eastern Shore News*, 15 August 1947, 7 November 1947, 1 November 1951. Gentile, pp. 144-145. *Acts of Assembly*, 1948, p. 474. Jander, p. 113. *Records of Accomack County School Board*, 14 May 1947, p. 428. W. B. Alig, "Forgotten Island," *Americas* 8 (December 1956), p. 19. "Tangier: A World Apart," *Rural Virginia*, p. 9.
13   *Eastern Shore News*, 6 June 1957, 28 March 1968. *Accomack Deedbook #129*, p. 502. *Northampton Marriage Register #5*, p. 99. Pruitt, *Beacon of the Soul*, 37. "Tangiermen Again Call for a Doctor," *Rural Virginia* 19#4 (February 1965), p 10.
14   Pruitt, *Beacon of the Soul*, p. 37. Warner, *Beautiful Swimmers*, p. 244. "Tangiermen Again Call for a Doctor," *Rural Virginia* , p. 10. *Eastern Shore News*, 6 June 1957. James Birchfield, "It's 'Hi, Doc!' Now on Tangier," *Sunday, the Star Magazine* [Baltimore, Md.], 27 July 1958, pp. 8, 10. "Doctor Answers Distant Call," *Life* 42 #20 (20 May 1957), pp. 119*ff*. George, pp. 27-28.
15   Pruitt, *Beacon of the Soul*, 37. Dize, *Something Fishy from Tangier*, p. 28. *Eastern Shore News*, 2 November 1961. "Tangiermen Again Call for a Doctor," *Rural Virginia* , pp. 10-11. Warner, pp. 244-245. Georgia Harmon, "Tangier Island Welcomes a New Doctor," *Daily Press* [Newport News, Va.], 25 July 1965. Roger Treat, "Tangier Island in the Bay and in Time," *Maryland Living, The New American* [Baltimore, Md.], 3 October 1965, p. 9. Stephan Wilkinson, "Flying Visit," *Flying* 87 #4 (October 1970). Nathaniel T.

Kenney and Bates Littlehales, "Chesapeake Country," *National Geographic* 126 #3 (September 1964). Glen McCaskey, "Tangier," *Commonwealth* 32 #4 (April 1965). Sheldon van Auken, "Island and Creek in the Chesapeake," *Yachting* 100 #2 (August 1956), describes a voyage to Tangier made prior to the death of Henry Jander in 1951. *Chesapeake Doctor*, a "Candlelight Romance" by Adelaide Humphries (New York: Dell Publishing Co., 1966), is set on "Tranquillus Island," a conflation of Tangier and Smith Island, and contains several references to Tangier events.

16    Gentile, pp. 145-146. *Eastern Shore News*, 28 March 1947, 4 April 1947. *Virginian-Pilot* [Norfolk, Va.], 3 November 1967, 6 April 1970. *Accomack Deedbook #245*, p. 314. When the range was discontinued in 1982, the Town of Tangier acquired the remaining station near the airstrip. The remains of the two target ships were still visible in the early 1990s, but now rest completely under water.

17    deGast, *Lighthouses of the Chesapeake*, p. 168. Carolyn Pruitt, " Brief History of Tangier Lighthouse," *Eastern Shore News*, 7 August 1996.

18    "Traveler Counselor Makes Tangier Trip," *American Motorist* 33 #5 (September 1964), pp. 10, 15. Max Ailor, "Tangier Revisited: Tourism Is Taking Hold," *Richmond Times Dispatch*, 20 July 1967. Elaine Justice, "Tangier Island Blends Past with Present," *Daily Press*, 12 August 1973. *Accomack Charter Book #5*, p. 270. *Richmond Times-Dispatch*, 28 December 1969. The Thomas tour boat business, if measured from the beginning of the earlier mailboat franchise, shares with the Parks store at 16315 Main Ridge the distinction of being the oldest continuous business on the island still operated by the same family, both of them dating from at least the 1920s; see Mears, "The Shoreline," *Eastern Shore News*, 4 May 1967.

19    Frances Hallam Hurt, "There Lies Tangier," *Commonwealth* 42 #9 (October 1975), p. 16. Warner, pp. 243-247. George, p. 29. *Eastern Shore News*, 6 May 1976.

20    Wilkinson, "Flying Visit," p. 114. *Eastern Shore News*, 29 January 1970, 23 November 1976, 30 March 1980. *Virginian-Pilot*, 20 April 1971, 18 June 1974. Hurt, p. 20. Zack Taylor, "The Great Tangier Raid," *Virginian Pilot*, 24 July 1977. See also Jim Phillips, "How They Cracked Duck Hunting's Isle of Shame," *Outdoor Life* 161 (January 1978).

21    Harold G. Wheatley, "This Is My Island, Tangier," *National Geographic* 144 #5 (November 1973). Hurt, p. 17. Justice, p. B-2.

22    *Eastern Shore News*, 18 March 1995. *Washington Post*, 20 April 1995.

23    "Winter '77: Tangier Island, Va.," *Rural Living* 33 #5 (March 1977), pp. 34-37. Lehmann, p. 13. *Washington Post*, 14 April 1984.

24    *Washington Star*, 21 December 1975. *Washington Post*, 4 July 1976. *Eastern Shore News*, 26 April 1989, 14 February 1990, 14 September 1991, 27 August 1997. George Reiger, "It Can't Happen to Me," *Field and Stream* 92 #3 (July 1987), p. 37.

25    *Journal Messenger* [Manassas, Va.], 22 August 1975. *Accomack Plat Book #16*, p. 126; *#20*, pp. 34-35. Wheatley, pp. 700-701.

26    *Chesapeake Bay Foundation News*, 13 #2 (May 1988), p. 2; 13 #4 (November 1988), p. 3, 17 #3 (November 1992), p. 4. *Eastern Shore News*, 13 December 1962.

27    *Eastern Shore News*, 21 October 1954. Robert A. Hedeen, *The Oyster: The Life and Lore of the Celebrated Bivalve* (Centreville, Md.: Tidewater Publishers, 1986), pp. 132-133. William A. Pruitt and John Travelstead, Virginia Marine Resources Commission, interview 14 June 1999.

28    *The Island Crabber*, Summer 1994. Wheatley, p. 703. Warner, p. 239. "Tangier: A World Apart," p. 9. Chowning, *Chesapeake Legacy*, pp. 181-189.

29    *The Island Crabber*, Summer 1994. *Washington Post*, 28 April 1999. Travelstead, interview 14 June 1999.

30    Pruitt and Travelstead interview, 14 June 1999. *Chesapeake Bay Foundation News* 23#1 (Winter 1998), pp. 1, 4.

31    Treat, p. 10. *Eastern Shore News*, 7 November 1987, 12 November 1988. *Daily Times* [Salisbury, Md.], 11 May 1995. *Virginian-Pilot*, 13 June 1999.

32    Pruitt, pp. 3, 21-22. *Eastern Shore News*, 10 May 1989.

33    *Eastern Shore News*, 8 April 1995. *Maranatha Manna* [Princess Anne, Md.], October 1995.

34    Pruitt, *Beacon of the Soul*, pp. 30-31. Interviews with Rev. Edward Pruitt and Rev. Wade Creedle.

35    *Eastern Shore News*, 18 February 1998, 14 March 1998, 14 March 1998, 21 March 1998, 28 March 1998. *Washington Post*, 12 March 1998. *Virginian-Pilot*, 15 March 1998.

36    *Eastern Shore News*, 21 March 1998. *Washington Post*, 13 March 1998, 21 March 1998, 12 February 1999.

37    *Eastern Shore News*, 18 February 1998, 18 March 1998, 9 September 1998. *Virginian-Pilot*, 16 March 1998.

38    Travelstead interview, 14 June 1999. *Daily Press*, 19 July 1998.

# Bibliography

## Books

### I. Tangier and the Islands

Chowning, Larry S., *Barcat Skipper: Tales of a Tangier Island Waterman*. Centreville, Md.: Tidewater Publishers, 1983.

Crockett, Thomas, *Facts and Fun: Historical Outlines of Tangier Island*. [Norfolk, Va.?]: Berkley Daily News Print, 1890.

Dize, E. Frank, *Something Fishy from Tangier*. Privately published by the author, 1974.

Dize, Frances W., *Smith Island, Chesapeake Bay*. Centreville, Md.: Tidewater Publishers, 1990.

George, L. W., *This Is Tangier Island and Its Church*. Martinsville, Va.: The Radio Fellowship, 1965.

Hall, S. Warren III, *Tangier Island: A Study of an Isolated Group*. Philadelphia: University of Pennsylvania Press, 1939.

Jander, Anne Hughes, *Crab's Hole: A Family Story of Tangier Island*. Chestertown, Md: The Literary House Press, 1994.

Johnson, Paula J., *The Workboats of Smith Island*. Baltimore: Johns Hopkins University Press, 1997.

Lehmann, Stuart, *Visitor's Guide to Tangier Island*. Tangier, Va.: Printed privately by the author, 1974.

Mears, John Neely, *Tangier Island*. Onancock, Va.: The Eastern Shore News, 1937.

Parks, Rick, *Tangier Island*. Parsons, W. Va.: McClain Printing Co., 1997.

Pruitt, John, *Beacon of the Soul: A Centennial Remembrance of Swain Memorial United Methodist Church*. Tangier, Va.: Swain Memorial United Methodist Church, 1997.

Richardson, James C., *Seven Acres: The Story of the New Testament Church on Tangier Island*. Shippensburg, Pa.: Companion Press, 1997.

Shores, David, *Tangier Island: Place, People and Talk*. Newark: University of Delaware Press, 2001.

Swain, C. P., *A Brief History of Tangier Island, Va., with a Review of the Rise and Growth of the Methodist Episcopal Church*. [n.p.], 1899.

Walczyk, Gail, *The Ancestors of Thomas L. Crockett, "Sugar Tom."* Coram, N.Y.: Peter's Row, 1999

Walczyk, Gail and Rebecca Furniss Miller, *Four Generations of Evans on the Eastern Shore*. Coram, N.Y.: Peter's Row, 1997.

Walczyk, Gail, *Four Generations of Parks on the Eastern Shore*. Coram, N.Y.: Coram, N.Y.: Peter's Row, 1997.

Walczyk, Gail and Rebecca Furniss Miller, *A Primer on the Crocketts of the Eastern Shore*. Coram, N.Y.: Peter's Row, 1995.

Wallace, Adam, *The Parson of the Islands*. Published privately by the author, 1861.

Wilson, Woodrow T., *History of Tangier Island, Virginia*. [n.p.], [n.d.].

## II. Chesapeake Bay

Brewington, M. V., *Chesapeake Bay: A Pictorial Maritime History*. New York: Bonanza Books, 1956.

Burgess, Robert, *This Was Chesapeake Bay*. Cambridge, Md.: Cornell Maritime Press, 1963.

Burgess, Robert and H. Graham Wood, *Steamboats Out of Baltimore*. Cambridge, Md: Tidewater Publishers, 1968.

Byron, Gilbert, *Early Explorations of The Chesapeake Bay*. Baltimore: The Maryland Historical Society, 1960.

Byron, Gilbert, *The War of 1812 on the Chesapeake Bay*. Baltimore: Maryland Historical Society, 1964.

Chowning, Larry S., *Chesapeake Legacy: Tools and Traditions*. Centreville, Md.: Tidewater Publishers, 1995.

deGast, Robert, *Lighthouses of the Chesapeake*. Baltimore: Johns Hopkins Press, 1973.

deGast, Robert, *The Oystermen of the Chesapeake*. Camden, Me.: International Marine Publishing Company 1970.

Duke, Maurice (ed.), *Chesapeake Bay Voices: Narratives from Four Centuries*. Richmond: Dietz Press, 1993.

Footner, Geoffrey M., *Tidewater Triumph: The Development and Worldwide Success of the Chesapeake Bay Pilot Schooner*. Centreville, Md.: Tidewater Publishers, 1998.

Morrison, Russell and Robert Hansen, *Charting the Chesapeake*. Annapolis, Md.: Maryland State Archives, 1990.

Morrison, Russell *et al.*, *On the Map: Maryland and the Chesapeake Bay*. Chestertown, Md.: Washington College, 1983.

Plummer, Norman H., *Maryland's Oyster Navy: The First Fifty Years*. Chestertown, Md.: Literary House Press, for Chesapeake Bay Maritime Museum, 1993.

Shomette, Donald G., *Pirates on the Chesapeake*. Centreville, Md.: Tidewater Publishers, 1985.

Shomette, Donald G., *Shipwrecks on the Chesapeake: Maritime Disasters on Chesapeake Bay and Its Tributaries, 1608-1978*. Centreville, Md.: Tidewater Publishers, 1982.

Tawes, William I., *God, Man, Salt Water, and the Eastern Shore*. Cambridge, Md.: Tidewater Publishers, 1967.

Vojtech, Pat, *Lighting the Bay: Tales of Chesapeake Lighthouses*. Centreville, Md.: Tidewater Publishers, 1996.

Warner, William W., *Beautiful Swimmers: Watermen, Crabs, and the Chesapeake Bay*. Boston: Little, Brown and Company, 1976.

Wennersten, John R., *The Oyster Wars of Chesapeake Bay*. Centreville, Md.: Tidewater Publishers, 1981.

## III. Fiction with a Tangier Setting

Cornwell, Patricia, *Isle of Dogs*. New York: G. P. Putnam's Sons, 2001.

Cornwell, Patricia, *Unnatural Exposure*. New York: G. P. Putnam's Sons, 1997.

Humphries, Adelaide, *Chesapeake Doctor*. New York: Dell Publishing, 1966.

Nels, R. [Roland F. Nelson], *The Unpolished Diamond: A Romance*. Federalsburg, Md.: J. W. Stowell Printing Co., 1930.

Whitney, Phyllis A., *The Ebony Swan*. New York: Doubleday, 1992.

## IV. General

Ames, Susie M., *Studies of the Virginia Eastern Shore in the Seventeenth Century*. Richmond: Dietz Press, 1940.

Barbour, Philip L., *The Complete Works of Captain John Smith*. Chapel Hill: The University of North Carolina Press, 1986.

Barnes, A. Parker, *Local Government in Accomack County, 1634-1994*. Published privately by the author, 1994.

Barnes, A. Parker, *Pungoteague to Petersburg: Eastern Shore Militiamen before the Civil War, 1776-1858*. Onancock, Va.: Lee Howard Books, 1988.

Barnes, A. Parker, *Young No More: The Tragedy of 1918*. Published privately by the author, 1994.

Barnes, Brooks Miles and Barry R. Truitt, *Seashore Chronicles: Three Centuries of the Virginia Barrier Islands*. Charlottesville: University Press of Virginia 1997.

Clark, Charles B. (ed.), *The Eastern Shore of Maryland and Virginia*. New York: Lewis Historical Publishing Co. Inc., 1950.

Davis, Burke, *The Billy Mitchell Affair*. New York: Random House, 1967.

DiPaolo, Joseph F., *My Business Was to Fight the Devil: Recollections of Rev. Adam Wallace, Peninsula Circuit Rider, 1847-1865*. Acton, Mass.: Tapestry Press Ltd., 1998.

Emmerson, John C., Jr., *The Steamboat Comes to Norfolk Harbor*. Portsmouth, Va.: Published privately by the author, 1949.

Footner, Hulbert, *Rivers of the Eastern Shore*. New York: Farrar & Rinehart, 1944.

Frye, John, *The Men All Singing: The Story of Menhaden Fishing.* Norfolk, Va.: Donning Press, 1978.

Gentile, Gary, *Shipwrecks of Virginia*. Philadelphia: Gary Gentile Productions, 1992.

Gillespie, Richard, *The James Adams Floating Theatre*. Centreville, Md.: Tidewater Publishers, 1991.

Goode, G. Brown, *The History and Present Condition of the Fishery Industries*. Washington: Department of the Interior, 1881.

Hast, Adele, *Loyalism in Revolutionary Virginia: Norfolk and the Eastern Shore*. Ann Arbor, Mich.: UMI Research Press, 1979.

Hedeen, Robert A., *The Oyster: The Life and Lore of the Celebrated Bivalve*. Centreville, Md.: Tidewater Publishers, 1986.

Hayman, John C., *Rails Along the Chesapeake: A History of Railroading on the Delmarva Peninsula, 1827-1978*. Salisbury, Md.: Marvadel Publishers, 1979.

Johnson, Leonard W., *Ebb and Flow: A History of The Virginia Tip of The Delmarva Peninsula, 1561-1892*. Verona, Va.: McClure Press, 1982.

Lord, Walter, *The Dawn's Early Light*. New York: W. W. Norton & Co., 1972.

Marine, F. E., *Sketch of Rev. John Hersey, Minister of the Gospel of the M. E. Church*. Baltimore: Hoffman & Co., 1879.

Mariner, Kirk, *Off 13: The Eastern Shore of Virginia Guidebook*. New Church, Va.: Miona Publications, 1997.

Mariner, Kirk, *Revival's Children: A Religious History of Virginia's Eastern Shore*. Salisbury, Md.: Peninsula Press, 1979.

Mason, A. Hughlett, *History of Steam Navigation to the Eastern Shore of Virginia*. Richmond: Dietz Press, 1973.

Mears, James E., *The Eastern Shore of Virginia in the Civil War and Reconstruction Period*. Unpublished manuscript, 1957.

Mears, James E., *The Temperance Movement on the Eastern Shore of Virginia*. Onancock, Va.: Eastern Shore News, 1966.

Robinson, Calvin H., *Along the Shoreline*. Onancock, Va.: Published privately by the author, 1931.

Sanford, Samuel, *Underground Water Resources of the Coastal Plain Province of Virginia*. Charlottesville, Va.: University of Virginia, 1913.

Shreve, L. F., *Tench Tilghman: The Life and Times of Washington's Aide-de-Camp*. Centreville, Md.: Tidewater Publishers, 1982.

Tazewell, William L., *Norfolk's Waters: An Illustrated Maritime History of Hampton Roads*. Woodland Hills, Calif.: Windsor Publications Inc., 1982.

Truitt, Charles J., *Breadbasket of the Revolution: Delmarva in the War for Independence*. Salisbury, Md.: Historical Books Inc., 1975.

Turman, Nora Miller, *The Eastern Shore of Virginia, 1603-1964*. Onancock, Va.: The Eastern Shore News, 1964.

Gail M. Walczyk, *St. George's Parish Vestry Book, 1763-1787*. Coram, N.Y.: Peter's Row, 1998.

Watson, Eva M., *Glimpses of the Life and Work of George Douglas Watson*. Cincinnati, Ohio: God's Bible School and Revivalist, 1929.

Weaver, James C., "An Epitomized History of Education in Accomac County," in *Report of the State Superintendent of Education*. Richmond, 1885.

C. A. Weslager, *The Nanticoke Indians — Past and Present*. Newark, Del.: University of Delaware Press, 1983.

West, Elmer T., *Some Descendants of Anthony West of Accomack, Virginia*. Silver Spring, Md.: Published privately by the author, 1980.

Whealton, Louis N., *The Maryland-Virginia Boundary Controversy, 1668-1894*. Baltimore: Albert J. Leon, 1897.

Whitelaw, Ralph T., *Virginia's Eastern Shore*. Richmond: Virginia Historical Society, 1951.

Wilson, Edith Bolling, *My Memoir*. Indianapolis, Ind.: Bobbs-Merrill Company, 1938.

Wilson, Woodrow T., *History of Crisfield and Surrounding Areas on Maryland's Eastern Shore*. Baltimore: Gateway Press Inc., 1973.

Wise, Barton Haxall, *The Life of Henry A. Wise of Virginia*. New York: MacMillan Co., 1899.

Wise, Henry A., *Seven Decades of the Union*. Philadelphia: J. B. Lippincott & Co., 1872.

# Periodicals

Alig, W. B., "Forgotten Island," *Americas* 8 (December 1956).

Berdan, Marshall S., "The Pestilence that Walketh in Darkness: The Cholera Epidemic of 1832," *Virginia Cavalcade* 43 #1 (Summer 1993).

Birchfield, James, "It's 'Hi, Doc!' Now on Tangier," *Sunday, the Star Magazine*, 27 July 1958.

Cassell, "Slaves of the Chesapeake Bay Area and the War of 1812," *Journal of Negro History* 56 (April 1972).

Church, J. W., "Tangier Island," *Harper's Monthly Magazine* 128 (1913-14).

Cronin, William B., "Tangier Island," *Chesapeake Bay Magazine* 18 #5 (September 1988).

"Doctor Answers Distant Call," *Life* 42 #20 (20 May 1957).

Hamilton, J. Norwood, "Electricity Changes Life on Tangier," *Sunday Star Magazine*, 24 February 1952.

Horton, Tom, "The Chesapeake Crab Wars," *Mid-Atlantic Country* 13 #8 (August 1992).

Hurt, Frances Hallam, "There Lies Tangier," *Commonwealth* 42 #9 (October 1975).

Jones, Robert E., "Crab Island," *Saturday Evening Post* 216 #13 (15 September 1943).

Kenney, Nathaniel T. and Bates Littlehales, "Chesapeake Country," *National Geographic* 126 #3 (September 1964).

Mariner, Kirk, "The Hermit of Watts Island," *Chesapeake Bay Magazine* 12 #10 (February 1983).

McCaskey, Glen, "Tangier," *Commonwealth* 32 #4 (April 1965).

"Methodist Americana," *Together* (March 1960).

Nordlinger, Stephen E., "Keeping a Way of Life Nearly 300 Years Old," *Sunday Sun Magazine*, 11 October 1959.

Phillips, Jim, "How They Cracked Duck Hunting's Isle of Shame," *Outdoor Life* 161 (January 1978).

Reiger, George, "It Can't Happen to Me," *Field and Stream* 92 #3 (July 1987).

"Tangier: A World Apart," *Rural Virginia* 15 #9 (July 1960).

"Tangiermen Again Call for a Doctor," *Rural Virginia* 19 #4 (February 1965).

"Traveler Counselor Makes Tangier Trip," *American Motorist* 33 #5 (September 1964).

Treat, Roger, "Tangier Island in the Bay and in Time," *Maryland Living, The New American*, 3 October 1965.

"Trouble in Tangier," *Newsweek* 30 #74 (13 October 1947).

van Auken, Sheldon, "Island and Creek in the Chesapeake," *Yachting* 100 #2 (August 1956).

Walker, Henry Pickering, "Teacher to the Mohaves: The Experiences of George W. Nock, 1887-1889," *Arizona and the West* 9 #2 (Summer 1967).

Wheatley, Harold G., "This Is My Island, Tangier," *National Geographic* 144 #5 (November 1973).

Wilkinson, Stephan, "Flying Visit," *Flying* 87 #4 (October 1970).

"Winter '77: Tangier Island, Va.," *Rural Living* 33 #5 (March 1977).

Wise, Barton Haxall, "Memoir of General John Cropper," *Virginia Historical Collections* 11 (1892).

## Newspaper Articles

Ailor, Max, "Tangier Revisited: Tourism Is Taking Hold," *Richmond Times-Dispatch*, 20 July 1967.

Harmon, Georgia, "Tangier Island Welcomes a New Doctor," *Daily Press*, 25 July 1965.

Justice, Elaine, "Tangier Island Blends Past with Present," *Daily Press*, 12 August 1973.

Mariner, Kirk, "The Movies: Tangier," *Eastern Shore News*, 15 April 1992.

Mariner, Kirk, "The Rebel Raid that Never Was," *Eastern Shore News*, 12 February 1997.

Mears, James Egbert, "The Shoreline," *Eastern Shore News*, 1938, 1940, 1950, 1959.

Pruitt, Carolyn, "Brief History of Tangier Island Lighthouse," *Eastern Shore News*, 1996.

Taylor, Zack, "The Great Tangier Raid," *Virginian-Pilot*, 24 July 1977.

Turman, Nora Miller, "The Eastern Shore, 1775-1783," *Eastern Shore News*, 10 July 1975 - 1 July 1976.

Walczyk, Gail, "Smith Island, Crossroads of the Chesapeake Bay," *The Island Crabber*, October 1994.

Whealton, Connie, "Tangier Island," *Eastern Shore News*, 1 November 1951.

## Unpublished Articles

Barnes, B. Miles, *Readjusters, Funders, and Oysters: Economics and Politics on the Eastern Shore of Virginia During the Readjuster Movement.* Unpublished typescript, 1981.

*A Brief History of Education in Accomack County, 1632-1963.* Accomack County Historical Association, unpublished typescript, 1963.

Downs, Donald, "The Moors of Delaware." Unpublished typescript, 1960.

Mihalyka, Jean M., *Abstracts of Tangier.* Unpublished typescript, 1978.

Mihalyka, Jean M., *Tombstone Inscriptions, Tangier, Va.* Unpublished typescript, 1978.

Nock, George W., *Tangier.* Unpublished manuscript, c. 1895.

Turman, Nora Miller, *A Brief History of Saxis.* Unpublished manuscript, 1976.

## Newspapers and Newsletters

*Accomack News* [Onancock, Va.], 1905, 1907, 1909, 1912, 1915, 1916, 1921.

*Chesapeake Bay Foundation News* [Annapolis, Md.], 1988, 1992, 1998.

*Christian Advocate* [New York, N.Y.], 1840-1842, 1847, 1848, 1866.

*Daily Press* [Newport News, Va.], 1965, 1973.

*Daily Times* [Salisbury, Md.], 1995.

*Eastern Shore Herald* [Eastville, Va.], 1904.

*Eastern Shore News* [Onancock, Va.], 1928, 1931-1933, 1935-1938, 1945, 1947, 1951, 1957, 1961, 1962, 1967-1968, 1970, 1976, 1980, 1987-1991, 1995-1998.

*Island Crabber* [Tangier, Va.], 1994.

*Journal Messenger* [Manassas, Va.], 1975.

*Maranatha Manna* [Princess Anne, Md.], 1995.

*Peninsula Enterprise* [Accomac, Va.], 1883-1884, 1886-1891, 1893, 1896, 1900, 1903, 1907, 1914, 1919-1920, 1923, 1931-1933, 1936, 1938, 1946-1947, 1949, 1975-1976.

*Richmond Dispatch* [Richmond, Va.], 1889.

*Richmond Times-Dispatch* [Richmond, Va.], 1967, 1969.

*The Sun* [Baltimore, Md.], 1866, 1916, 1932.

*Virginian-Pilot* [Norfolk, Va.], 1967, 1970-1971, 1974, 1977, 1998.

*Washington Post* [Washington, D.C.], 1912, 1916, 1932, 1972, 1976, 1984, 1995, 1998-1999.

*Washington Star* [Washington, D.C.], 1975.

## Church Records

*Journal of the Accomack Circuit, Methodist Episcopal Church, 1805-1858.*
*Record of the Methodist Episcopal Church for Northampton Circuit, 1858-1903.*

# Public Records and Documents

Town of Tangier, Virginia:
*Tangier Book of Records* (Tangier School District)
*Minute Book #2* (Town Council)

Accomack County, Virginia:
*Charter Book #5.*
*Common Law Orders*, 1914-16, 1920-22, 1922-24, 1924-25, 1928-29.
*Deedbooks*, #3, #29, #44, #47, #59, #70, #72, #87, #96, #129, #132, #245.
*Plat Books*, #16, #20.
*Register of Deaths, 1853-1871.*
*School Board Records*, 1947.
*Surveyor's Records*, #1.
*Wills, Etc. 1692-1715.*
*Wills*, 1842.

Northampton County, Virginia:
*Register of Marriages*, #5.

Commonwealth of Virginia:
*Acts of Assembly*, 1906, 1910, 1948.
*Final Report of the Virginia Commissioners on the Maryland and Virginia Boundary to the Governor of Virginia.* Richmond: R. F. Walker, 1874.
*Report of the Commission of Fisheries*, 1916.
*Report of the State Superintendent of Education*, 1885.
*Virginia School Reports*, 1880.

United States of America:
*Official Records of the Union and Confederate Armies*, Series I, Volume 43.
*Official Records of the Union and Confederate Navies*, Series I, Volume 5.

# Interviews and Correspondence

Dr. B. Miles Barnes, Onancock, Va.
Mary Frances Carey, New Church, Va.
Ruth Wallace Clarke, Tangier, Va.
Rev. Robert E. Cooper, Norfolk, Va.
Rev. L. Wade Creedle, Jr., Tangier, Va.
Alva Crockett, Tangier, Va.
Dewey Crockett, Tangier, Va.
Lois S. Crockett, Tangier, Va.
Stanley Mulford, Williamsburg, Va.
Annie K. Parks, Tangier, Va.
Betty Deal Parks, Tangier, Va.
Lewis Parks, Richmond, Va.

Rick Parks, Newport News, Va.
Asbury Pruitt, Tangier, Va.
Rev. C. Edward Pruitt, Burke, Va.
Elizabeth B. Pruitt, Tangier, Va.
John Pruitt, Suffolk, Va.
Portia W. Pruitt, Burke, Va.
Wallace Pruitt, Tangier, Va.
William Pruitt, Newport News, Va.
Dr. David Shores, Virginia Beach, Va.
Rev. Robert J. Thorne, Stuart, Va.
John Travelstead, Newport News, Va.
Gail M. Walczyk, Coram, N.Y.
Sandra Wheatley, Tangier, Va.

# Photo Credits

*Arizona and the West* (Summer 1967): p. 74.

Carter, J. B. H. *et al.*, *An Economic and Social Survey of Accomac County* (Charlottesville: University of Virginia, 1929): p. 99.

Davis, Burke, *The Billy Mitchell Affair*: pp. 103, 104 (U.S. Navy photograph).

DiPaolo, Joseph F., *My Business Was to Fight the Devil*: p. 57.

*Eastern Shore News*, 2 September 1982: p. 117; 22 July 1977: p. 162(b).

Hall, S. Warren III, *Tangier Island: A Study of an Isolated Group*: p. 112.

*Harper's Monthly Magazine*, 1913-14: pp. 93, 94.

*Harper's Weekly*, 16 March 1872: p. 69; 1 March 1884: p. 79; 9 January 1885: p. 70; (unidentified date) 1892: p. 80.

Marine, F. E., *Sketch of Rev. John Hersey*: p. 58.

*Maryland Living (Baltimore News American)*, 3 October 1965: pp.125, 161(b).

Mason, A. Hughlett, *History of Steam Navigation to the Eastern Shore*: p. 71.

Mears, John Neely, *Tangier Island*: p. 142.

Morrison, Russell, *On the Map: Maryland and the Chesapeake Bay*: pp. 3, 11.

Nordlinger, Stephen E., "Keeping a Way of Life Nearly 300 Years Old," *Sunday Sun Magazine*, 11 October 1959: pp. 107, 115(b).

*Rural Virginia* (February 1965): p. 122.

Shreve, L. F., *Tench Tilghman: The Life & Times of Washington's Aide-de-Camp*: p. 18.

*Sunday Star Pictorial Magazine*, 24 February 1952: p. 159(b).

*Sunday: The Star Magazine*, 17 July 1958: p. 160(b).

Swain, C. P.: *Brief History of Tangier Island*: pp. 86, 87, 155(b-c).

*Together*, March 1960: p. 43.

Vallandigham, Edward N., *Delaware and the Eastern Shore of Maryland* (Philadelphia: J. B. Lippincott Co., 1922): p.101.

*The Virginian* (May-June 1987): p. 151.

Wallace, Adam, *The Parson of the Islands*: pp. 23, 41, 47, 55, 154.

*Washington Post Magazine*, 21 August 1994: p. 155(a).

## From Private Collections

Crockett, Alva: pp. 100, 145, 160(a).

Crockett, Lois S.: p. 157(a).

Marshall, Wanda: pp. 100, 157(b).

Parks, Lewis: pp. 8, 77, 162(b).

Pruitt, Elizabeth B.: pp. 24, 75, 78, 89, 113, 128, 130, 139, 149, 153, 155(d), 156, 157, 159(a).

Pruitt, Portia W.: p. 158(b).

Pruitt, Wallace: pp. 98, 158(a).

Thorne, Robert J.: pp. 147, 161.

Turman, Nora Miller: p. 109.

Wheatley, Sandra: pp. 76, 90, 121.

## The Gravestones

Page 1:   Lewis A. Charnock (1870-1904)

Page 12:  John B. Thomas (1882-1901)

Page 22:  Elmer S. Crockett (1888-1902)

Page 34:  Nellie Pruitt (1821-1891)

Page 46:  Robert H. Thomas (1890-1908)

Page 60:  Matilda J. Parks (1847-1906)

Page 68:  Charles B. Crockett (1860-1891)

Page 88:  Ellen E. Evans (1866-1903)

Page 114: Leroy F. Moore (1892-1908)

Page 138: Willie E. Crockett (1888-1909)

# Index